EDUCATIONAL TECHNOLOGY

EDUCATIONAL TECHNOLOGY

Editor

V. C. Pandey

ISHA BOOKS

DELHI-110 033

Educational Technology

ISBN: 81-8205-173-8

Reprinted in 2011 in India by
Isha Books
B-63, Ist Floor
New Gupta Colony
Near DDA Market
Delhi-110009

Printed at: G. Print Process. Delhi

Preface

Educational technology comprises a variety of electronic tools, media, and environments that can be used to enhance learning, foster creativity, stimulate communication, encourage collaboration, and engage in the continuous development and application of knowledge and skills. It has now evolved to a point where its power to transform schools is evident.

The field of technology is in a state of constant change. Development has been uneven. Leaders in the field see pockets of excellence but also areas of genuine need such as more universal individual classroom access to the internet and home computers for more students, particularly on the part of underserved populations. Many in the education community are aware of the need for more guidance and discourse on how to maximize any investment in technology. Many educators want to know how technology will make a difference to their students in the classroom. Trained to evaluate curricula and develop methods for teaching traditional disciplines, many educators feel unprepared to evaluate or use technology, yet they have an obligation to explain their technology expenditures to the tax-paying public by demonstrating how technology improves educational outcomes.

The use of technology cuts across all academic areas, and it is changing rapidly, gaining greater capabilities seemingly every day. Most institutions—from businesses supported by resource-rich technology departments dedicated to mastering these powerful, expensive, and evolving electronic tools, to schools and school districts—are hard-pressed to keep current. Few general, informative, and stable guidelines exist anywhere. Thus, concrete examples of successful technology use and thoughtful criteria can be an important source of practical expertise and information for others.

This book, focused on the potential of technology to affect student learning outcomes, is expected to advance the dynamic field of educational technology by helping practitioners make better informed curriculum and budget decisions; researchers design studies, assessments, and evaluations that are immediately relevant and meaningful to practitioners; and policy makers shape and support initiatives that are well thought out and that include evaluation as an essential element.

Editor

CONTENTS

1

Concepts of Educational Technology

Educational technology is a term widely used in the field of education, but it is often used with different meanings. The word technology is used by some to mean hardware—the devices that deliver information and serve as tools to accomplish a task—but those working in the field use technology to refer to a systematic process of solving problems by scientific means. Hence, educational technology properly refers to a particular approach to achieving the ends of education. Instructional technology refers to the use of such technological processes specifically for teaching and learning.

Other terms, such as instructional development or educational media, which refer to particular parts of the field, are also used by some to refer to the field as a whole. The most recent definition of the field has been published by the Association for Educational Communications and Technology (AECT): Instructional Technology is the theory and practice of design, development, utilization, management, and evaluation of processes and resources for learning.

The field is essentially a 20th century movement with the major developments occurring during and immediately after World War II. What began with an emphasis on audio-visual communications media gradually became focused on the systematic development of teaching and learning procedures which were based in behavioral psychology. Currently, major contributing fields are cognitive psychology, social psychology, psychometrics, perception psychology, and management.

Most educational technologists carry out one or a few of the functions performed in the field. For example, some design instruction, some produce instructional materials, and others manage instructional computing services or learning resources collections.

Until recently, most educational technologists were employed in schools and colleges as directors of resource centers and developers of curriculum materials. Many are still employed in such positions, but increasing numbers are being employed by training agencies in business, industry, government, the military, and the health professions. Colleges and universities employ individuals who are involved in instructional improvement programs that use a variety of technologies.

COMMUNICATIONS TECHNOLOGIES

Communications technologies (CT) are developing at rapid pace, carrying the potential to deliver education to more learners in more satisfactory ways. For adult educators, CT might overcome some of the barriers to student participation. Career educators and counselors could provide a higher level of career guidance to greater numbers. The need for currency in vocational preparation can be facilitated by CT. An earlier ERIC Digest by Miller described some of these technologies and how they will influence education and the role of the educator.

Types and Uses

CT delivery modes include video (low-power, closed-circuit, and cable television; videotapes; interactive videodisks), audio and audiographic (audiocassettes; radio; electronic blackboards; telefacsimile; freeze-frame, slow-scan, or compressed video), and computer (electronic mail networks, bulletin boards, teletext, videotex). Integrated systems can link videodisks, compact disks (CD-ROM), and microcomputers with telecommunications devices such as satellites to allow the exchange of large amounts of information and interactive communication. Examples of CT uses in adult, career, and vocational education include the following:

— The AgriData Network provides reports of news, markets, trends; collections of agriculture teaching plans; daily condensed listing of current agriculture news; and an electronic mail system. Developers plan to expand its use to adult evening classes.

— Instructional Television Fixed Service is used in the Silicon Valley to offer training to employees of computer companies. In the pilot project, stress management and chemical safety training were broadcast by Mission College in cooperation with the local Industry-Education Council. Off-campus sites committed $800 to the installation of receiving equipment.

— Ohio State University's Cooperative Extension Service uses microwave transmission to operate a TV classroom 15 hours per week. Average hourly cost for uplinking and satellite time is $846. Expenses are contained by sharing costs of equipment, facilities, and personnel with research and instructional programs.

— Electronic networks include AEDNET for adult educators, CAPS:HITECH for career counselors, and ADVOCNET for adult and vocational educators.

INSTRUCTIONAL EFFECTIVENSS

The variety of media and wide range of potential students prompt the questions: What is the best way to use a medium for a learning task? Is the way a medium is used more important than which medium is used?. As with other forms of instructional technology, more research is needed about the effectiveness of

CT. Norenberg and Lundblad offer matrices to aid in choosing technologies. One matrix examines learner, teacher, and instructional considerations for print, audio, audiographic, video, and computer technologies; the other compares costs. They suggest that the choice of medium be based on such factors as objectives, cost, personnel, users, anticipated use, level of interactivity, legal barriers, compatibility, and jurisdiction.

Some findings are summarized as follows: o At the University of Victoria, evaluation of continuing education telelectures found that instructors covered too much material, students were inhibited from interacting because of the broadcast format, and despite the potential of the medium, the presentation remained more verbal than visual.

The teleconferencing experience at the University of Georgia's Division of Vocational Education prompted the following recommendations:

(1) make instruction "high touch" and interactive, for example, demonstrations replicable by students at remote sites;

(2) prepare students in advance with materials and agenda; and

(3) remember that teleconferencing is different from face-to-face instruction and need not imitate it.

The Ontario Institute for Studies in Education's computer conferencing system enables students to access adult education courses through their personal computers at any time of the day. Assignments, discussion comments, and requests for library materials can be sent online. Problems were encountered in accessing the system, understanding the instruction sheets, and uploading or downloading materials. Participants expressed satisfaction with the convenience, the relationship of the course to the required readings, the quality of interaction with the instructor, and the sense of community among the students.

Issues of Communications Technologies

The examples given here illustrate some of the advantages and disadvantages of using CT. On the positive side, CT can increase access to learning opportunities, especially for learners in distant, isolated areas possibly lacking subject experts or for learners with limited physical mobility. It can increase access to more and better information resources, be individualized to meet student needs, and enhance the immediacy of inservice training while saving time and money. On the other hand, some argues that CT can isolate students, undercut local autonomy and instructor control, reduce diversity and pluralism, and make students passive recipients of overstructured packets of knowledge. The capacity for greater interactivity in today's technology may have the potential to overcome some of these problems.

The changing technological workplace, telecommuting, global competition, lifelong cycles of education, training, and work—these are some of the challenges facing adult, career, and vocational educators. Because today's youth tend to take technology for granted, living in ever-more high-tech electronic households, an enormous potential market exists for education delivered by means of communications technologies. Educators can take advantage of this opportunity by letting the machines do what machines do best and continuing to do what they do best: design instruction, manage learning, and motivate human beings to learn.

MULTICULTURAL EDUCATION AND TECHNOLOGY

In recent years multicultural education and technology have emerged as key issues in teaching and teacher education. But whether they represent pedagogy's perfect pair or its odd couple is still being determined as teachers at all levels seek ways to integrate the two.

Scholars specializing in multicultural education agree that at its most fundamental level, multicultural education represents an orientation to schooling and the teaching-learning process that is grounded in the democratic ideals of justice and equality. Some would argue that justice and equality have always been the focus of schools in America, but there is a substantial body of historical and contemporary evidence which demonstrates that the schooling experiences of most students of color, as well as many white students from economically poor and politically disempowered backgrounds, are inferior to those provided to white students from middle class, politically dominant backgrounds. Due to this disparity, proponents of multicultural education call for a studied restructuring of many of the long-standing policies and conventions of public schooling. There are five critical dimensions of multicultural education: content integration, knowledge construction, prejudice reduction, equity pedagogy, and empowering school culture and social structure.

Technology, Teaching and Content Integration

The goal of content integration is to expand the curriculum by incorporating contributions of diverse cultures into traditional disciplines of study. Arguably, this dimension is easily realized through technology. For instance, teachers at all levels have used the World Wide Web to extend the available learning resources. Electronic mail and multimedia technologies promote communication and interactions between diverse groups with the purpose of helping students learn more about content they study in subject areas as social studies, science, psychology, and even foreign language. Many educators who acknowledge potential benefits of a merger between technology and multicultural education call for updating the physical infrastructures of schools. In schools where such updates (i.e., re-wiring) have occurred, teachers are making widespread use of the internet and other computer-based technology. And the knowledge and skills students acquire in these schools typically are being reinforced by computer availability and internet access in their homes. This reality contrasts sharply with that of students from poor/working class backgrounds who attend schools where the notion of re-wiring for internet access may seem superfluous in light of the absence of basic resources. Nor are these students likely to have internet access at home. Citing a 1999 report of the National Telecommunications and Information Administration, Gorski notes that "African American and Latino households are only about one-third as likely to have access to the Internet from home as Asian, Asian American, and Pacific Islander households.

The same group is only two-fifths as likely to have access as White households". This situation is reflective of the "digital divide" phenomenon. Thus, while technology can facilitate the content integration in the teaching-learning process, educators must be aware that in some circumstances this dimension of multicultural education will need to be addressed by other means due to lack of access to technology.

The knowledge construction dimension promotes critical literacy by examining the manners in which scholars and scientists contribute to their respective fields of study. Knowledge construction builds upon content integration by making explicit the worldviews and perspectives that inform knowledge claims. Similarly, it expands the legitimate sources of knowledge by helping learners recognize that their own experiences both within and beyond school are viable foundations for acquiring knowledge and skills.

Teacher educators are being called upon to use technology to promote and reinforce the knowledge construction process. Part of acquiring facility in knowledge construction is understanding phenomenon from the perspectives of others. To this end, teacher educators are making use of Internet technology to promote more critical engagement with subject matter. For example, Merryfield discusses advantages of threaded discussions in an online graduate course. Student-generated threads facilitate a class learning community that allows those of diverse cultural and national origins to perspective-take while simultaneously examining their own ideas about cultural diversity.

Technology as a tool to reduce prejudice

Prejudice reduction is about eliminating all forms of bigotry. Also, it involves promoting healthy personal identity devoid of the tendency or need to denigrate those who differ from self. Multimedia presentations and distance learning technologies are being used to establish learning exchanges between students of diverse cultural backgrounds and thereby reduce prejudice and stereotyping.

Likewise, technology is being used to promote positive self-concept and foster positive relationships between students from diverse backgrounds in geographically diverse areas. Such efforts have included videoconferences, computer conferences, interactions on the Web, and e-pals. Technologies used with middle grade students have included interactive compressed video and use of two-way televised communication systems via telephone lines. Teacher education students are using distance learning technology, multimedia, and e-mail to engage in cross-cultural and diverse regional interactions with other prospective teachers.

Equity pedagogy is about equalizing opportunities to learn. It involves incorporating various strategies and techniques that attend to learning styles and intelligence types. Writers interested in the nascent relationship between technology and multicultural education are discussing the urgency of using technology to address the various ways in which learners from diverse backgrounds best acquire school knowledge and skills. Nevertheless, it is difficult to discern whether current efforts to merge technology and multicultural education are addressing this fourth dimension directly. Indeed, some writers are concerned that technology may inadvertently privilege certain ways of processing information while it devalues others.

An important issue for many contemporary educators, particularly in the university setting, is whether internet technology is in any way superior to face-to-face instruction. It would appear that one advantage internet technology holds over face-to-face classroom format is in its ability to provide educators and students wide access to a cross-cultural professional and learning community. This can be accommodated through e-mail, bulletin boards, and chatroom sites.

Multicultural education proponents contend that in order to provide high quality experiences for all students, many traditional aspects of schools will need to be reconfigured. This is referred to as empowering school culture and social structures. Its ultimate purpose is to change the taken-for-granted policies and practices of schools that, while useful to some students, have greatly diminished the schooling experience for many others. For example, some describes how the new California State University, Monterey Bay, is making extensive use of technology to provide access to higher education to the burgeoning population of Latinos and other people of color who historically have been excluded from such opportunities.

Throughout the U.S., access to university courses and degree programs are being made available to students by expanded distance education opportunities that now routinely include courses offered online in part or in their entirety.

Various efforts are underway to merge multicultural education and technology, yet it is too soon to crown the duo a perfect pair. Concerned observers cite the divergent ideological underpinnings of multicultural education versus technology as being perhaps predictive of a turbulent long-term relationship. For example, Roblyer et al. note that multicultural education emerged from the efforts of people of color and at its most fundamental level is concerned with justice and equity for all.

This contrasts with internet technology, which they report emerged from the efforts of a white male elite and remains fraught with problems of access and equity. But this perplexing outlook notwithstanding, increasing cultural diversity in schools demands that teachers seek alternative ways to address learner needs effectively. Teachers at all levels accept that technology has become integral to the teaching-learning process, and many enthusiastically albeit cautiously hope to make the best use of it to provide high quality schooling for all students.

Educational technologies are not single technologies but complex combinations of hardware and software. These technologies may employ some combination of audio channels, computer code, data, graphics, video, or text. Although technology applications are frequently characterized in terms of their most obvious hardware feature (e.g., a VCR or a computer), from the standpoint of education, it is the nature of the instruction delivered that is important rather than the equipment delivering it.

Tutorial uses are those in which the technology does the teaching, typically in a lecture-like or workbook-like format in which the system controls what material will be presented to the student. In our classification scheme, tutorial uses include (1) expository learning, in which the system provides information; (2) demonstration, in which the system displays a phenomenon; and (3) practice, in which the system requires the student to solve problems, answer questions, or engage in some other procedure.

Exploratory uses of technology are those in which the student is free to roam around the information displayed or presented in the medium. Exploratory applications may promote discovery or guided discovery approaches to helping students learn information, knowledge, facts, concepts, or procedures. We also include reference applications, such as CD-ROM encyclopedias, in this category. In contrast to tutorial uses in which the technology acts on the student, in exploratory uses the student controls the learning.

Application uses, such as word processors and spreadsheets, help students in the educational process by providing them with *tools* to facilitate writing tasks, analysis of data, and other uses. In addition to word processors and spreadsheets, applications include database management programs, graphing software, desktop publishing systems, and videotape recording and editing equipment.

Communication uses are those that allow students and teachers to send and receive messages and information to one another through networks or other technologies. Interactive distance learning via satellite, computer and modem, cable links, or other technologies constitutes another example of communication uses.

There are four uses of technology in education is discussed below. A brief history of the technology use is presented, along with specific examples. A variety of media (e.g., computers, videodisc, audio) may be involved in any of these educational uses, sometimes stand-alone, other times in hybrid technology systems. Under each use, we stress examples of technology applications that are well suited for teaching advanced thinking skills, especially with educationally disadvantaged students. Finally, this survey of technologies for education concludes with a review of the availability of these technologies in schools.

Historically, the dominant teaching-learning model has been one of transmission: teachers transmitting information to students. Not surprisingly, the first uses of educational technology supported this mode. Although other ways of using technology to support learning are now available, tutorial uses continue to be the most widespread, especially with disadvantaged students.

Computer-based technologies

Computer-Assisted Instruction—some of the first computer-assisted instruction (CAI), developed by Patrick Suppes at Stanford University during the 1960s, set standards for subsequent instructional software. After systematically analyzing courses in arithmetic and other subjects, Suppes designed highly structured computer systems featuring learner feedback, lesson branching, and student record keeping. During the 1970s, a particularly widespread and influential source of computer-assisted instruction was the University of Illinois PLATO system. This system included hundreds of tutorial and drill-and-practice programs. Like other systems of the time, PLATO's resources were available through timesharing on a mainframe computer.

Today, microcomputers are powerful enough to act as file servers, and CAI can be delivered either through an integrated learning system or as stand-alone software. Typical CAI software provides text and multiple-choice questions or problems to students, offers immediate feedback, notes incorrect responses, summarizes students' performance, and generates exercises for worksheets and tests. CAI typically presents tasks for which there is one (and only one) correct answer; it can evaluate simple numeric or very simple alphabetic responses, but it cannot evaluate complex student responses.

Integrated learning systems (ILSs) are networked CAI systems that manage individualized instruction in core curriculum areas (mathematics, science, language arts, reading, writing). ILSs differ from most stand-alone CAI in their use of a network (i.e., computer terminals are connected to a central computer) and in their more extensive student record-keeping capabilities. The systems are sold as packages, incorporating both the hardware and software for setting up a computer lab. ILSs are typically sold in sets of 30 workstations, with an average cost of about $125,000. Major producers include Josten's Learning Corporation, WICAT Systems, and CCC. About 10,000 ILSs are in use in U.S. schools, most of them purchased with funds from the ESEA Chapter 1 program for at-risk students.

The instructional software within ILSs is typically conventional CAI: instruction is organized into discrete content areas (mathematics, reading, etc.) and requires simple responses from students. ILS developers have also made a point of developing systems that tie into the major basal textbooks. Some notes that the systems "can correlate almost objective by objective to a district's K-8.... language arts, reading, math, and even science curricula". Users of ILSs enjoy the advantage of having one coordinated system, making it easy for students to use a large selection of software.

A new trend in integrated learning systems is represented by *ClassWorks*, developed by Computer Networking Specialists. ClassWorks offers the school access to whatever variety of third-party software the teachers select, along with all the instructional management features associated with an ILS.

CAI in general, and integrated learning systems in particular, have found a niche in America's schools by fitting into existing school structures. Cohen describes these structures as follows:

— Most instruction occurs in groups of 25 to 35 students in small segments from 45 to 50 minutes long.

— Instruction is usually either whole-class or completely individual.

— Instruction is teacher dominated, with teachers doing most of the talking and student talk confined largely to brief answers to teacher questions.

— When students work on their own, they complete handouts devised or selected by the teacher. Students have little responsibility for selecting goals or deadlines and little chance to explore issues in depth. Most responses are brief.

— Knowledge is represented as mastery of isolated bits of information and discrete skills.

Many features of tutorial CAI are consistent with the traditional classroom described by Cohen. Tutorial CAI provides a one-way transmission of knowledge; it presents information and the student is expected to learn the information presented. Much CAI software presents information in a single curriculum area and uses brief exercises that can easily be accommodated within the typical 50-minute academic period. CAI is designed for use by a single student and can be accommodated into a regular class schedule if computers are placed in a laboratory into which various whole classes are scheduled.

Basic skills lend themselves to drill- and-practice activities, and CAI, with its ability to generate exercises (e.g., mathematics problems or vocabulary words) is well suited to providing extensive drill and practice in basic skills. Students at risk of academic failure often seen as lacking in basic skills and therefore unable to acquire advanced thinking skills become logical candidates for CAI drill-and-practice instruction. Recent research and thinking on the needs of disadvantaged students stress a different need, however. Disadvantaged students need the opportunity to acquire advanced thinking skills and can acquire basic skills within the context of complex, meaningful problems. This latter approach to instruction, which is stressed in education reform, has not been well served by traditional CAI.

Intelligent Computer-Assisted Instruction

Intelligent computer-assisted instruction grew out of generative computer-assisted instruction. Programs that generated problems and tasks in arithmetic and vocabulary learning eventually were designed to select problems at a difficulty level appropriate for individual students. These adaptive systems (i.e., adapting problems to the student's learning level) were based on summaries of a student's performance on earlier tasks, however, rather than on representations of the student's knowledge of the subject matter.

The truly intelligent systems that followed were able to present problems based on models of the student's knowledge, to solve problems themselves, and to diagnose and explain student capabilities. Historically, ICAI systems have been developed in more mathematically oriented domains—arithmetic, algebra, programming—and have been more experimental in nature than has conventional CAI.

Although ICAI is an area of active research projects, ICAI programs in the schools are not widespread. ICAI tends to call for more meaningful interactions than traditional CAI and tends to deal with more complex subject matter. ICAI's focus on modeling student knowledge lends itself to applications in teaching advanced thinking skills. ICAI has not been used extensively with disadvantaged students.

One intelligent tutoring system, Geometry Tutor, provides students with instruction in planning and problem solving to prove theorems in geometry. Geometry Tutor comprises an expert system containing knowledge of how to construct geometry proofs, a tutor to teach students strategies and to identify their errors, and an interface to let students communicate with the computer.

Geometry Tutor monitors students as they try to prove theorems, instructing and guiding them throughout the problem-solving process. Some studied the implementation of Geometry Tutor in a public high school and found changes in the behavior of teachers and students using this system: teachers spent more time with students having problems, collaborated more with students, and based more of a student's grade on effort; students increased their level of effort and were more involved in the academic tasks. Thus, ICAI can be implemented in ways that support the kind of learning that education reformers advocate. Although most of these applications control instructional content, they can be used within a broader instructional framework that stresses joint work with the automated tutor.

Distance-Learning with One-Way Transmission

As with computer-based instruction, the first applications of distance- learning were tutorial in nature. The term *distance-learning* is used to describe the delivery of instruction from a single site to multiple remote sites. In the early part of this century, film and radio were the distance-learning methods used to instruct students. As technologies have become more sophisticated and diffuse, many other methods and delivery systems have been incorporated.

One- way video technology (broadcast, cable, and videotape) has been widely used as an instructional medium and as a vehicle for distance-learning in both homes and schools. Technology was used in the 1950s in part to help alleviate a lack of qualified teachers. In one well-known example, the school district in Hagerstown, Maryland, provided closed-circuit television programming in nearly all core curriculum areas to all of its schools. The courses were taught live from six studios and represented an attempt to change the way schooling took place in the district. Although the actual instruction tended to be traditional, a strength of those programs was that they brought qualified instructors to an audience of students who would not otherwise have had access to them.

In addition to bringing students instructional content they could not receive otherwise, distance-learning can provide teachers with models of new ways to teach. During the "new math" era of the 1960s, educators at the University of Wisconsin developed Patterns in Arithmetic, a program that included, in addition to workbooks, television lessons broadcast to elementary school classes. Use of the program was high initially but subsided as teachers learned the content and began to provide instruction in new math themselves.

This unintended outcome suggests that teachers can internalize content and teaching techniques displayed through distance-learning technology. Most early uses of instructional television featured conventional, lecture- based approaches to instruction, recreating the basic elements of the traditional classroom. In the 1970s, a new breed of instructional programming appeared. Following the widespread popularity and success of Children's Television Workshop's Sesame Street, a host of similar programs were produced for home and school viewing.

These programs made rich use of the visual and auditory capabilities of video, combining teaching with entertainment as a way to gain and maintain the attention of the learner, while getting the information across in interesting and innovative ways. Currently, educators and parents have a broad diversity of programs from which to choose. Instructional television programming is limited in being one-way communication, but the production values and creativity of these presentations can be very high, reflecting a level of resources that no single teacher could command.

In the past, incompatibility between broadcast schedules and school timetables was a major impediment to the use of instructional television, but current technology has overcome this difficulty: programming can be received and videotaped for use at any convenient time. Instructional programming can be communicated over cable television, broadcast television, or satellite. The Public Broadcasting Service (PBS) offers educational video programming in mathematics, reading, social science, and other content areas. Series such as Square One TV, Reading Rainbow, and Voyage of the Mimi have proved to be immensely popular with children. Cable television is another source of instructional programming, which is typically noninteractive and designed to fit specific academic content areas. Millions of homes receive educational broadcasts from The Learning Channel, The Discovery Channel, and other instructional sources.

A more recent trend in educational television is the transmission of educational news broadcasts. *CNN Newsroom* and Channel One offer news and current events information. *CNN Newsroom* is broadcast week nights without commercials on Cable News Network for use with students in grades 6-12; It contains news and current events and is meant to be videotaped during the night and used in the following day's classes. In contrast, Whittle Communications controversial *Channel One*, with an audience of over 6 million students, broadcasts not only news but also commercial advertising.

Educational video, used thoughtfully, can contribute to education reform goals, insofar as it integrates various subject matter areas e.g., history, archaeology, research methods, art, reading, literature, and mathematics and challenges students to understand the complex relationships that exist among various domains. Moreover, research on instructional television has demonstrated positive effects of viewing upon learning in a variety of domains, such as children's math problem solving and social attitudes.

A consistent finding within the research is that the potential benefits associated with instructional programming are most likely to be realized within settings where teachers (or parents) assist young viewers in making sense of what they see. Students get more out of watching instructional television when teachers set the stage for what they will watch and follow up with discussion, probing questions, and/or relevant activities.

Videodisc technology combines the features of video with the flexibility of a computer. Videodisc technology can be used in either a tutorial or an exploratory fashion (the latter type of video applications is discussed later). Used alone, a videodisc player enables the user to access and sequence visual images (still and motion) and accompanying audio tracks in a nonlinear and selective manner.

Used in combination with appropriate hardware and software, videodisc technology may be used as an individualized, interactive learning tool, integrating visual and auditory information with electronic text. In some states, notably Texas, videodiscs are being used for tutorial instruction by either supplementing or, in some cases, supplanting textbooks. Optical Data Corporation's *Windows on Science*videodisc and associated print materials have been adopted by at least 65 percent of the schools in Texas. Using videodisc images, teachers can demonstrate science information to their students. Additionally, individual students or groups of students can review material on the machine. Teachers can present lessons by picking video clips and still photographs from a set of videodiscs approved by the state as a textbook.

The merging of video and computer technology, and the flexibility this affords, make videodisc technology a potentially powerful vehicle for instruction, especially in areas where visual and auditory information are essential to understanding. Disadvantages cited for videodisc technology include the need for fairly expensive equipment, lack of teacher facility with the technology, and nonstandardized videodisc equipment. Because of the high cost and the high level of technical facility previously associated with the production and utilization of videodisc programs, most videodisc applications have been targeted for use within business and industry.

However, recent technological developments are making videodisc technology more cost effective, more compatible with standard computer systems, and much easier to use (e.g., barcode readers and symbols within a text can simplify access to relevant video). In addition, other technological innovations, such as CD-ROM, offer advantages similar to videodisc (e.g., random access to graphics, sounds, text) in a relatively inexpensive and easy-to-use format. These advances are likely to increase the use of videodisc and related technologies within the educational arena.

Technologies for tutorial learning typically use a transmission rather than constructivist model of instruction. For this reason, although they have found their place in education and have the greatest rate of adoption within schools thus far, they are unlikely to serve as a catalyst for restructuring education. The focus of drill-and-practice CAI on basic skills allows little room for the presentation of complex tasks, multistep problems, or collaborative learning. ICAI, on the other hand, has the potential to deal with complex domains, to provide models of higher- order thinking, and to probe students understanding, but has seldom been well integrated into a school's mainstream curriculum. One-way video technologies can be very motivating but are nearly always viewed as enrichment and have not instigated fundamental changes within schools.

TECHNOLOGIES FOR EXPLORATORY LEARNING

Exploratory uses of instructional technology allow students to direct their own learning. Through the process of discovery, or guided discovery, the student learns facts, concepts, and procedures. In this section, three broad types of technology used for exploratory learning: computer-based information retrieval systems (e.g., electronic databases), microworlds (including microcomputer-based labs and simulations), and interactive video.

Although different in form and application, each of these uses of instructional technology provides a context in which the student may access, discover, and construct knowledge through a self-directed learning process. Exploratory uses of technology tend to deal with complex learning activities. Such uses of technology are very congruent with the goals of education reform.

Electronic Databases

Electronic reference works provide students with a way to access large bodies of information quickly and in a self-selected manner. In addition to serving as information retrieval systems, electronic databases can provide students with capabilities for organizing and manipulating data that they have accessed or entered. Within the physical and social sciences, databases can be used to explore and test the relationships between variables within complex systems.

Some electronic reference works and databases incorporate graphics and/or sound, providing students with additional sources of information. Electronic databases and references are developing at a dizzying speed. Some of these, such as Sony's *Data Discman* or Franklin's *World Almanac*, are at an elementary level beginning to fulfill Alan Kay's vision of a dynabook a powerful, hand-held computer that will allow students to access a wide array of information.

The *Data Discman* is a hand-held compact disc player that can read books published on compact disc. Each compact disc can hold up to 100,000 pages of text—enough for encyclopedias of all types. Currently available is an abridged *Encyclopaedia Britannica*, a health encyclopedia, and a comprehensive language translator. Although not yet widely in use, the Data Discman could become a compact, economical machine for knowledge retrieval. In a similar vein, Franklin Electronic Publishers is planning to introduce a hand-held, electronic version of *The World Almanac* and *Book of Facts*.

All of this hand-held power does have a potential disadvantage: it is easy to imagine students getting lost in the myriad of facts available to them at the touch of a button. It should be remembered that access to information is great, but true intellectual capability comes from having a conceptual framework within which to assimilate that information. Teachers need to take an active role to make sure that students have the conceptual structures needed to profit from the reference information.

Computer-based exploratory applications

Microcomputer-based labs and microworlds have proven to be effective contexts for learning in mathematics and the physical and social sciences. Microcomputer-based labs put the tools of the scientist at the students disposal, enabling them to engage in scientific inquiry with real-life phenomena. Simulations create self-enclosed microworlds that mimic real-life phenomena, allowing students to explore and manipulate complex systems.

Simulations are available for a wide variety of subject areas, including biology, genetics, geology, chemistry, physics, environmentalism, social studies, economics, and mathematics. Some simulations are multidisciplinary, allowing students to develop and apply their knowledge in a variety of subject areas. The examples that follow provide an exemplary, but by no means exhaustive, overview of the range of software supporting inquiry-based learning through interaction with microworlds.

Microcomputer-based laboratories (MBLs) allow students to explore real- life, real-time phenomena. Typically, MBLs consist of measurement equipment or sensors connecting a computer and the environment. The equipment measures physical phenomena, such as sound, light, or temperature, and records data that can be displayed as it is being recorded, or saved and analyzed at a later date. This real-time measurement with real-time display capabilities offers students an opportunity to better understand the connection between a phenomenon and its graphic or mathematical representations.

Rather than fostering the rote memorization of unconnected facts, MBLs facilitate the direct observation of, and inquiry into, scientific phenomena. Students utilize the tools of the scientist to engage in the processes of hypothesis testing, data collection, and data analyses. One of the earliest and best known examples of computer-based exploratory learning is the use of LOGO, a computer language developed in the 1970s by Seymour Papert and his colleagues at the MIT Artificial Intelligence Laboratory.

LOGO was specifically designed as a programming language to facilitate the acquisition of critical thinking and mathematical problem-solving skills in learners of all ages. In many schools across the country and around the world, LOGO, in its various incarnations, has been used by students to create microworlds in which mathematical and physical principles are tested and explored.

In one of its simplest forms, LOGO can be used by young children to create designs through programming the movements of a "turtle" on the computer screen. In the process of building upon simple commands to get the turtle to "draw" a variety of shapes, children discover and construct knowledge regarding geometrical concepts. In another, more advanced application, students learn the laws of physics through programming the movement of objects (such as dynaturtles) that simulate Newton's laws of motion. Concepts needed to understand these laws (velocity, acceleration, and position) are discovered, explored, and tested as students use simple commands to manipulate the objects within this microworld. LOGOWriter provides students with the word-processing, graphics, and animation capabilities to create their own animated games and stories.

With LegoLOGO, students use construction materials (Lego building blocks, pulleys, gears, motors), sensors (temperature, light, and sound), and the LOGO programming language to design, produce, and control real objects in the physical world. Taking on the roles of inventors and engineers, students have used LegoLOGO to build and operate mechanical devices (such as robots, cars, and moving sculptures), as well as whole environments (such as model cities).

LOGO can serve as a project-based vehicle for multidisciplinary learning, as when students use LegoLOGO to create their own version of Willy Wonka's Chocolate Factory, or use LOGOWriter to create animated narratives on historical events. In providing students with the tools for creating their own microworlds, LOGO offers a meaningful context for learning about the design process as well as discovering complex scientific and mathematical concepts.

Although much of the exploratory computer software available concerns science phenomena, there is also a growing body of social science software that allows students to explore decision-making and complex relationships in sociopolitical spheres. Two rather new and popular software programs, *SimCity* and *SimEarth*, allow users to act as civic or world leaders, manipulating variables to maintain the system. In the course of building and managing simulated cities or planets, students encounter a range of problems and issues (political, economic, environmental) that lead to learning and problem solving across interrelated domains.

The immensely popular *Where in the World Is Carmen Sandiego?* and related programs in the series require students to track a fugitive by looking for clues and gathering information not only from the software but from outside reference sources, to make predictions, and to confirm hypotheses. In addition to teaching geography, by requiring students to explore, experiment, evaluate, and revise, these self-contained worlds facilitate student collaboration in the higher-order thinking skills of deduction, inference, synthesis, and evaluation.

Stanley Pogrow of the University of Arizona designed the *Higher Order Thinking Skills* (HOTS) program to teach disadvantaged students advanced thinking skills. This program uses a combination of teacher activities and computer software to promote the development of metacognition, inference, generalizing, and synthesis. In a typical unit, students spend one period using a computer simulation to study the dynamics of a balloon in flight. The next day, the teacher asks students to describe the effects of fuel, wind direction, terrain, and the balloon's capabilities on its movement. Students are asked to describe the strategies they used in controlling the balloon. Those whose balloons crashed are asked to describe their strategies and what happened.

Video exploratory applications

Video exploratory applications support higher-order thinking by presenting complex, authentic tasks that transcend the boundaries of academic disciplines. Students engaged in video exploration may learn how to solve novel problems requiring several steps and involving several disciplines (e.g., arithmetic, geography, and reading). Recent theory and research suggest that children who learn with difficulty may particularly benefit from this kind of instruction with its focus on conceptual understanding and solving novel problems.

The Cognition and Technology Group at Vanderbilt University has designed a series of video adventures, known as the *Adventures of Jasper Woodbury*, requiring mathematical reasoning to solve complex problems in trip planning, probability and statistics, and geometry. Videos 17 to 20 minutes in length provide natural contexts for learning mathematics as well as geography, history, and science. Each video ends with a challenge, rather than a resolution. The information to solve the problem is embedded within the video, which can be reviewed and studied to pick out relevant facts.

The Cognition and Technology Group has based its design of these episodes on a set of principles drawn from research on cognition and instruction. These researchers argue that by being video based, the learning experience is more motivating and allows for more complex problems than could be presented in a written or audio-only medium. Motivation and comprehension are further heightened through use of a narrative format, that is, a story providing a realistic context and a familiar structure for the problems presented.

The narrative format provides for the introduction of other subject matter topics; for example, the skill of map reading is used in an episode dealing with trip planning, thus providing links to geography and navigation. The learning format is generative; the stories in the *Jasper* series must be completed with a resolution provided by the students. Generating this resolution requires solving a complex mathematics problem. This is motivating and allows students to participate actively in the learning process. Data needed to solve the problem are embedded in the story itself, just as in other good mystery stories. The videos are created in pairs of related adventures so that students can transfer any mathematics or reasoning concepts learned in one video context to new contexts.

The *Jasper* videos are being designed to be available through a variety of media: videotape, videodisc, and in conjunction with hypermedia. In the hypermedia version, students can engage in basic skills practice, change parameters of the original problem to generate an analogous problem (new locations, goals, etc.), and explore related mini-adventures.

The materials are being tried out and evaluated in 52 classrooms in nine states. An earlier major exploratory video project, *Palenque*, consists of a videodisc and software that allow students to explore a Mayan ruin in southern Mexico. Begun at the Bank Street College of Education in 1985, *Palenque* was developed as a prototype demonstration of digital video interactive (DVI) technology. Slides, film, video, graphics, text, sound effects, and audio narration are all integrated on an optical videodisc.

Students use a joystick to take user- directed simulated journeys through a rain forest or a museum database of the ancient Mayan site at Palenque. The Palenque materials are designed to be student directed rather than dependent on a teacher's instructional sequence and objectives the materials foster browsing that will be both informative and enjoyable. Students are given simulated travel tools, such as a camera, photo album, and compass. When they want to know more about something they are seeing, they can click on a button and get commentary from a simulated 8-year-old Mayan specialist.

Other examples of exploratory video include *GTV*, a multimedia, video- based geography program produced by LucasFilms and National Geographic; *Animal Pathfinders*, an exploratory program focusing on animal migration; and *Civil War Interactive*, a multimedia work based on the popular public television series by Ken Burns.

These exploratory applications can support the kind of student learning that is the goal of education reform. They can present complex, authentic tasks, engage students in active problem solving, require utilization and synthesis of knowledge from a variety of domains, and provide a context for collaborative learning activities.

There are, however, significant practical limitations, to many of these applications. First, there is the issue of scarcity—complex simulations and exploratory videos are expensive to develop, hence they are few. The problem is made worse by the fragmentation of the American education market, with its decentralized buying decisions and wide variation in curricula. Technology application developers have little hope of being able to match the curriculum of enough schools well enough to have a broad market base.

Without such a broad base, they see little hope of recapturing a major investment. From the teacher's standpoint, these exciting and imaginative applications are fine for enrichment but don t match the core curriculum. Hence, they may find a home in the margins of education but don t really transform the core. Finally, exploratory applications have a relatively short "shelf life'. Once students learn how to solve, complete, or engage in the complex tasks required by the simulation or video, they are ready to move on to something else.

One factor that may change the economics of producing multimedia educational materials is the potential for a much larger home-use market. These materials are sufficiently entertaining that the home market is a feasible primary or secondary target. *Palenque*, in fact, was designed for home use by families with children 8 to 14 years old. Another multimedia technology being developed for home use is Commodore Dynamic Total Vision (CDTV), a hybrid television, personal computer, compact disc technology system, which combines an optical disc player with a computer. Priced at under $1,000, CDTV hooks up to a standard television and allows control of sound, animation, text, graphics, and quarter-screen full-motion video. The fast pace of multimedia technology development for home use with the expected drop in technology prices may prove to be a catalyst for major investments in materials that have both educational and entertainment value.

TECHNOLOGY AS APPLICATIONS

One of the most significant shifts in the way that technology is being used in education today is toward greater use of computers and other devices as *tools* in the learning process rather than as instructional delivery devices. Such uses mirror the ways in which technology is used in the workplace and at home. Word processing, desktop publishing, database and spreadsheet applications, and drawing, painting, and graphing programs are examples of technology tools. Whenever students compose using a word processor, spell check their composition, use an on-screen calculator or graphing program, manipulate data in a spreadsheet, look up information in a database, or publish a classroom newspaper, they are using computers as tools. Video and audiotaping and editing equipment are other tools finding their way into schools.

Using technology as tools solves a major problem that frequently arises in the use of technology for tutorial or exploratory uses—that of the technology's curriculum not being consistent with the teacher's curriculum. Often, tutorial or exploratory products that are interesting in their own right do not have a place in a given school s course of study. In contrast, when technology is used as a tool, the teacher can still control the curriculum and the instructional strategy.

The technology merely provides students with aids for studying that content or practicing those skills. Tool products can be applied in a variety of curricular—activities word processors for writing and revising assignments, graphing programs for mathematics instruction, desktop publishing systems for producing newspapers, and hypermedia systems for development of one's own study materials.

Technology tools are designed to facilitate educational and work-related tasks. They are flexible, lending themselves to a wide variety of activities across the grade levels and throughout the curriculum. From an education reform perspective, this flexibility is both a strength and a weakness. Whether technology tools are applied in ways that promote traditional instruction or education reform is dependent on the perspective, skills, and practices of the classroom teacher.

Word processing and related applications

The most frequently used computer-based tool in U.S. education today is word processing software. When the first personal computers began to appear in the early 1970s, they were quickly followed by word processing software modeled after the early text editing programs. During the 1980s there was an explosion of microcomputers, and word processing applications became easier to learn and use.

Both because facility with this software will assist students in higher education and work and because its support for revisions was expected to encourage students to edit their own work, teachers soon began experimenting with having students use word processing software for their compositions. Over the past decade, a broad range of word-processing software has become available for educational use, covering virtually every grade level.

Word processors may support higher-order thinking by allowing students to attend to the composing process, focusing more on ideas and ways to communicate them than on the mechanics of spelling and punctuation. With word processing software, students can easily review and revise their compositions, highlight key ideas, rearrange sentences or paragraphs to flow more logically, and try out alternative sentences or words to communicate their ideas better. The mechanics of spelling can be dealt with separately, assisted by a spell checker.

The authenticity of writing tasks is enhanced when students are given the opportunity to produce professional-looking documents, which can readily be shared with others. Standard word-processing software, when used in conjunction with printers, provides students with a flexible tool for creating polished documents. Desktop publishing tools further enhance this capability. Many teachers have found this aspect of computer-supported writing to be tremendously motivating for students. In addition to taking personal pride in the look of their products, students are eager to share their work with others. Their writing skills develop within the context of meaningful activities, as they become increasingly aware of audience concerns and learn to plan and revise their texts more carefully.

More recent technology developments add to the tools that students can use to support writing and editing processes. For example, word processors incorporating speech synthesis 'read back" what the student has written, allowing beginning writers to explore the relationship between sounds and written symbols. Instructionally enhanced word processors offer cognitive support, in the form of questions, prompts, and/or suggestions, for compositional tasks that are particularly difficult for many students, such as the planning and revision of text.

Grammar analysis programs, electronic thesauri, integrated software packages, and desktop publishing software are additional examples of tools that may serve to support and extend students developing capabilities as writers. Pea and Kurland see the next step in writing technologies as software that acts as critic, writing expert, teacher, audience, or collaborator. However, it is the teacher, not the technology, who designs the context within which students will learn and practice their writing skills. Word processing software in and of itself does not facilitate higher-order thinking, revision, or collaboration unless the teacher creates a structure for doing so.

Hypermedia tools

In addition to the new electronic databases and references discussed in the section on exploratory technologies, classrooms are starting to develop their own electronic reference and learning tools using *hypermedia*. Hypermedia consists of a database of information structured as nodes or frames, specified links between these nodes that allow for rapid movement through the information, and a user interface.

Hypermedia can be used for (1) exploring a large database of information, (2) accessing elaborations on core information, or (3) building a database. Although hypermedia can provide didactic instruction (by containing instructive text and graphics and tutorials) and exploratory learning (through simulations), in this discussion we stress its uses as a tool, either as a reference source for knowledge and information or as a tool for storing and structuring information to be accessed by others.

The most widely available hypermedia system is *HyperCard*, which has been distributed free by Apple Computer with its Macintosh computer systems. *HyperCard* stacks can contain still and animated graphics, text, and sound; they have been used for database management, demonstrations, and instruction. Given the ease of use of *HyperCard*, students and educators can create personal database stacks, educational simulation stacks, and tutorial stacks. With *QuickTime*, a multimedia integration package for the Macintosh, students and teachers can add video footage to their products.

In the Computer-Supported Intentional Learning Environments (CSILE) project in Canada, students use hypermedia to write, illustrate, read, and comment on material as they study science, history, and social studies. The system is used collaboratively, with students able to access each other's work and comment on it. Commenters may provide additional information, questions, or commendations. The author of the node being commented on is notified by the system, setting the stage for an electronic interchange concerning the content. In another project involving hypermedia, Discover Rochester, disadvantaged middle school students created a hypermedia exhibit, incorporating text, audio, graphics, maps, and music, describing their city for the Rochester Museum and Science Center. To gather material for the exhibit, the students conducted research on the city's weather, industry, culture, and economics. They worked in libraries and archives, performed observations in the field, interviewed people by telephone and face-to-face, and conducted experiments.

Students learned to use a variety of computer software in order to best present their findings, and carefully crafted and revised their presentation. Teachers in the Rochester project integrated computer tools, such as *MacPaint, MacWrite, CricketGraph, and HyperCard,* into the software environment to create a natural work environment, where tools for exploring real-world topics were an invisible part of the work space. Multiple experiences in using these tools in their research are designed to help students learn to select the appropriate tool for any stage of an investigation, without teacher guidance.

Hypermedia, insofar as it allows the creation of personal education applications, has the potential to circumvent the problems of "hard-wired" information retrieval systems (such as CD-ROM). If students themselves create or manipulate data in hypermedia (i.e., control the creation and linking of nodes or cards in hyperstacks), they should have better conceptual maps of the information. Some finds that students using hypermedia develop and retain more elaborated concepts, chiefly for those areas in which they themselves developed materials (personal communication). Hypermedia may be less useful for the person accessing information compiled by others. Students will not learn much from hypermedia if they get lost in a myriad of facts and information, lose track of where they are within the hypermedia, and do not understand the links created by another hypermedia author. Developers are working on tools to assist users in navigating through hypermedia stacks.

Video production

With the increasing affordability and popularity of video cassette recorders and hand- held video cameras, this technology is finding its way into more and more schools. Many of the high-level planning and communication issues that enter into the process of composing written text have their analogs in designing video reports. Teachers are finding video equipment to be highly motivating and educationally valuable when used within a context that promotes study and analysis of socially important themes.

With more sophisticated technology, students can produce compositions combining computer text, video, and audio media. The *MultiMedia Works* Club is an example of an application that promotes an innovative and restructured conception of education, taking learning beyond the school walls. The technology used in the club, *MultiMedia Works*, is based on a film-making metaphor and allows students to combine text, video, computer graphics, and sound to compose, in effect, multimedia movies. The *MultiMedia Works* Club was held after school for students and teachers from a high-poverty area. The students selected topics, collected video and audio information in the field, assembled relevant media clips for their compositions, collaboratively produced their compositions, allowed their work to be critiqued, revised their work, and presented their compositions to others noted that "students learned to employ critical thinking skills while conducting their own discussions to analyze the media they had collected, focus on their chosen topic, and then select and logically organize the media to communicate their ideas".

Used well, technology applications can support higher-order thinking by engaging students in authentic, complex tasks within collaborative learning contexts. Moreover, the projects described above have made it clear that projects using technology applications to support advanced skills can be successful with disadvantaged students.

Word processors facilitate the process of writing as a complex task. Both by facilitating the revision process and by handling mechanical aspects of writing, this technology can help focus attention on higher-level issues of content and organization. Use of this technology within a collaborative learning format appears particularly promising for providing students with modeling of the metacognitive skills involved in writing and editing.

Proponents of hypermedia argue that its nonlinear format, allowing students access to vast amounts of information with complex links to other information, promotes "rich" learning. Although intriguing, these claims are still speculative. The clear advantage to hypermedia systems is their invitation to students to enter and manipulate information—copy it, modify or analyze it, or link it to other nodes. Thus, the technology invites active processing on the part of users. Additionally, hypermedia databases can be developed collaboratively by groups of students interested in particular information, subjects, or topics. Used in this way, hypermedia encourages students to act as researchers and to figure out how to organize the fruits of their research in a way that will be easy to use and interesting for others to explore.

Multimedia application systems redefine the teaching learning process and model the kind of education reform possible with new technologies. The tasks in which the students engage—library research, scanning media, talking to experts, recording information, writing or otherwise producing compositions—reflect the kinds of tasks in which they will continue to engage throughout their careers. The tasks are authentic and multidisciplinary. Additionally, students who use multimedia tools are active learners: choosing composition topics, doing fieldwork, and, at times, teaching the teachers. Students work collaboratively, not only with each other, but with researchers and teachers. Finally, given the complex nature of producing multimedia compositions, heterogeneous student groups function well; students with skills in different areas (e.g., videography, script writing, editing) complement each other and teach and learn from one another.

TECHNOLOGIES FOR COMMUNICATION

By communication applications we mean those educational uses that allow students or teachers at different sites to send and receive written, vocal, or visual information. These communications may come over telephone lines, through computers and modems, via voice or audiographic communication, or through satellite or other technologies. One-way transmission of information was discussed earlier, as a tutorial use of technology. Here we focus on technology uses that are interactive, with both parties providing information and shaping the nature of the exchange. Interactive communication technologies in common use today include two-way text-based (e.g., computer networks), two-way audio (e.g., telephone, cellular telephone), two-way video/two-way audio (e.g., fiber optic), and one-way video/two-way audio (hybrid) systems. Two-way video/two-way audio systems are still rare, but on the increase.

Computer networks

A relatively inexpensive technology, computer networking increasingly is being used in classrooms across the nation. These networks allow computers to send and receive information to and from other geographic sites. Harasim identifies a number of advantages shared by these on-line systems. Networks allow many students/teachers to communicate with many other students/teachers, hence encouraging collaboration and active participation on the part of learners.

Freeing learning from the constraint of geographic location, networks let learners and teachers participate in the education experience without regard to their physical location. Likewise, networks free learning from the constraints of time; students and teachers can log on to networks at times that are most convenient for them. Participants need not be confined to traditional school-day hours and can take time in reviewing information presented on the network before responding, thus allowing for more thoughtful responses. Given the text-based nature of networks, many believe that they encourage verbal communication, writing skills, and the articulation of ideas. Finally, networks are computer-based, hence they tap into record-keeping and management functions that might be costly in non-technology-based communication.

Various networks for children or for education have been established. Networks are being used for "learning circles" or for innovative writing applications. Benefits of networks include collaborative learning and greater exposure to national or global perspectives. The National Geographic Society in association with the National Science Foundation sponsors the Kids Network (developed by the Technical Education Research Center, or TERC), on which students can electronically send data they have collected to other schools around the United States. Scientists produce a national report utilizing the students data, and they make themselves available, via electronic mail, to answer students questions. Along similar lines, NASA's SpaceLink program connects students with astronauts and scientists.

Another model of collaborative learning uses networks to allow students at diverse sites to share activities and ideas and learn from each other. AT&T's Long Distance Learning Network has been used to promote "learning circles", electronic communities composed of about eight classrooms each whose students and teachers collaborate on relevant educational projects. These projects come from within the classrooms curricula and allow students actively to research, locate, and share knowledge with students and teachers at the other sites. Some noted that the "learning circle" requires collaborative work among the students, with students taking on the role of teacher and participating actively in the learning process. Similar network-based educational experiences have been reported for the FrEdMail network. Electronic communication can start when someone proposes an idea on the network. Others respond favorably to the idea, or the idea dies away. If there is favorable response, the interested individuals exchange electronic mail, and the idea's proponent sets up a conference. Some found that successful networks exhibited at least four of the following five features:

— Students and teachers, even though they were not in the same location, shared an interest in the educational projects;

— Educational projects were well specified;

— Sites had easy access to a reliable computer network;

— Students and teachers had a sense of responsibility to the project or the network community; and

— Strong leadership and a final evaluation of the project were provided.

Students can use networks merely to communicate with other students or with adults, and these simpler communications may hold educational benefits. Griffin and Cole described innovative applications of communications technology in their research with minority students. An international exchange in real time between students in San Diego, California, and students in Pistoia, Italy, resulted in the American students identifying some similarities between the Italian and Spanish languages (some of the students were bilingual) and learning concretely about the notion of time zones. Another group of students used the network to write rap to university researchers in real time. Thinking and composition skills that were not apparent in much of their school work became evident when students were engaged in a task that was meaningful to them. Barriers created by differences in age and cultural group were lessened when communicating over a network.

Videotapes

Not all communication technologies involve a computer and modem. Alternative communication technologies may be quite economical, small scale, and under considerable student and teacher control. VideoPals, a program founded in 1990, promotes video pen pals. Classes join the service and are matched with an appropriate class in another part of the world. The U.S. class makes a videotape, sends it to VideoPals for conversion to the foreign video standard (if different from the U.S. standard), and mails the converted tape to the videopal class. After viewing the video, the foreign class creates a video and sends it to the U.S. class. Richard Ray, the founder of the program, reports that interest is maintained when the videos point out differences between the two classes/communities, have visual or emotional impact, and require student research and script writing.

Interactive learning at a distance

Distance-learning systems supporting one-way transmission as a technology for tutorial instruction. The more interactive forms of distance-learning made possible when audio and visual signals can travel in both directions.

Two-way video/two-way audio— Systems that provide both visual and auditory communication allow the maximum amount of interactivity between teachers and students. These two-way video/two-way audio systems provide monitors, cameras, and microphones at the teacher's and multiple students sites.

The teacher can see and hear the students; students can see and hear the teacher and can see and hear each other. Communication between teacher and students takes place in real time. A variety of technologies can provide this type of communication. These include fiber-optic lines (thin glass rods that transmit laser light impulses and are laid underground), microwave technology (where data are transmitted by a series of towers established across the terrain), and satellite.

Historically, two-way video/two-way audio has been stymied by the high cost of the broad bandwidth needed to transmit full-motion video. Past attempts to compress video resulted in poor-quality images. However, video compression techniques have improved dramatically. Video signals, when transmitted through fiber-optic lines, show virtually no loss of image quality. Currently, video images transmitted via microwave are not compressed. The compression of video images for delivery via satellite still presents some problems (e.g., "jerkiness' in the picture). However, a great deal of development work is being done in this area, and improvements and breakthroughs are measured by months rather than years.

At present, these systems are expensive by school standards. For example, the codecs (encoders/decoders) to convert the sender's analog signals to digital signals and the digital signals back to analog currently cost about $20,000 to $30,000. Cameras and monitors, too, are expensive. There is a strong interest in making this technology more affordable, however. The Communications Competitiveness and Infrastructure Modernization Act, originally sponsored by Senators Al Gore and Conrad Burns, would set as a national goal the establishment of an "advanced, interactive. . .broad band communications system" to serve homes, schools, and other users, and to provide a "broad range of new educational opportunities for students of all ages". Many states are also investing a considerable amount of money in planning and establishing networks capable of providing two-way video/two-way audio. In Oregon, for example, Network 2 of the state's EdNet has been used by higher education institutions and became available to K-12 users in the fall of 1992.

One-way video/two-way audio— Satellite technology can deliver relatively affordable instruction. Direct broadcast satellite (DBS) technology consists of high-powered satellite transmissions received by small, low-power receivers. These receivers are low in cost ($300 to $400) and easy to operate and install, making them good choices for the needs of individual schools. In an attempt to reduce the costs of satellite communication (and thereby increase utilization), the EDSAT Institute, a not-for-profit organization, is actively working to bring to fruition a satellite dedicated to education.

Audio/video signals can be broadcast via satellite to an unlimited number of sites and over large geographic areas. It should be noted, however, that limits must be placed on the number of receive sites to enable the teacher to handle effectively the load of students in multiple classrooms. The Los Angeles County School District recently launched a satellite education project beaming mathematics and science lessons (in English and in Spanish) to at-risk students. In this program, classroom teachers team up with the on-camera teachers in a new kind of team-teaching approach. When coupled with a telephone, satellite systems can provide live, one- way, full-motion video with two-way audio interactivity. This hybridizing of discrete technologies is a significant development in communication and can provide economical, customized systems to meet the needs of individuals, classrooms, schools, and districts. Live-broadcast teachers can communicate in real time with the students in their audience, fine- tuning their instruction to meet student needs. Students may regard these one- way video/two-way audio, satellite-based systems as being similar to television; accordingly, production values must be high, and the teacher must be able to "perform" during the broadcast.

Other, newer hybrid systems are exemplified by the network emanating from Spokane, Washington's Educational School District (ESD). This satellite-based network uses one video channel, one audio channel, and one data channel. The teacher interacts with students through the audio channel as he/she delivers instruction through video. At the same time, information (text and graphics) can be delivered from the teacher's site to the students site, where it is captured on a computer. Students also use the channel to respond to the teacher after class hours, deliver homework assignments, and so on. A scanner is available at each school site, so students can input text and other data.

Telephone and voicemail— Telephone companies are exploring a variety of educationally relevant services that they may begin offering over regular telephone lines. These include linking school or home computers to database services, voicemail services to keep parents informed of homework assignments and school activities, cellular telephones, and audiographic communication, including today's slow-scan visual images and future, faster imaging.

Star schools program—The Star Schools program provides U.S. Department of Education funds for telecommunications projects offering instruction to students and training for teachers. Star Schools programs bring together colleges, universities, and businesses to help schools acquire equipment (usually satellite or microwave, but also computers, modems, monitors, etc.) and instructional programming to improve science, mathematics, foreign language, and other subject instruction especially for students in Chapter 1 schools or students who lack access to instruction in those fields.

In 1988, the first year of the program, four demonstration projects were funded: three of the projects used video satellite broadcasts in conjunction with telephones and modems to achieve one-way video/two-way audio communication; one program used an electronic mail (e-mail) system. Four additional projects were funded in 1990. The Department of Education estimates that 6,000 schools are now participating with over 20,000 elementary and 20,000 high school students enrolled in Star Schools courses. New courses are being offered in advanced placement as well as those emphasizing higher-order thinking skills.

State and regional distance learning initiatives— The past decade has brought a dramatic increase in distance-learning in K-12 education, reflecting the rapid development of cost-effective, powerful communications technologies. Given the nature of the technology, systems are usually developed at the state or regional, rather than the local, level. Virtually all states are interested in using distance-learning technologies for K-12 education. States vary in the level at which they are currently implementing distance education projects: some have projects in place while others are in planning stages; some have postsecondary programs only but are looking to expand into elementary/secondary education.

Most state distance-learning projects involve hybrid systems (e.g., some combination of satellite, cable, computer network, and fiber-optic technologies). Many states are very active in distance-learning, including Alaska, Texas, Utah, Kansas, Kentucky, Washington, Oregon, and Iowa. The Alaskan Teleconferencing Network and the University of Alaska Computer Network are used by school districts not only for electronic mail and teleconferencing, but also for the delivery of some instructional resources. Video programming is used extensively in Alaska, where, often in small villages in isolated communities, many of the students fall into at-risk categories of one type or another. Video can be used to reduce the mental distance between communities there, provide more global views of the world, and increase students' motivation and involvement in education.

The Texas Education Network (TENET), started in 1991, provides electronic mail, bulletin board, conferencing, and database capabilities to more than 4,300 public school users statewide. A commercial program started in Texas, TI- IN, provides live instructional broadcasts to more than 700 sites in 32 states. Utah has a microwave communication system, EDNET, which is used for two-way audio and video presentation of high school instruction around the state. Other projects in Utah include using audiographic communications to deliver advanced placement courses and a distance-learning project using two-way cable/microwave technologies to link an elementary, a junior, and two senior high schools with the College of Eastern Utah.

Southwestern Bell Telephone Company is installing 168 miles of fiber optic cable for an interactive video network that will enable schools throughout Kansas to share teachers, with students at remote sites participating in class discussions via two-way video. Kentucky is developing a statewide instructional satellite network, transmitting centrally to downlinks for each of the state's 1,300 elementary and secondary schools. Kentucky's plan calls for programming to be live and interactive. Washington has a variety of distance-learning systems in place, including the one emanating from Spokane described above and the Washington Higher Education Telecommunications System (WHETS). WHETS is a microwave-based, two-way video/two-way audio system that connects multiple campuses.

In Oregon, EdNet provides one-way video, two-way audio capability to more than 100 schools and school districts and has also established a two-way video/two-way audio system network currently used by 40 institutions of higher education, state government agencies, and industry. In Iowa a one-way video/two-way audio network has been initiated and is in the process of deployment.

The cooperative network projects described above illustrate how distance-learning can give students and teachers access to a broader range of resources and support collaborative projects involving complex themes. Collection and sharing of acid-rain data over the Kids Network or interaction with complex data sets and with astronauts and scientists over NASA's SpaceLink illustrate the interesting issues and access to experts that can be supported with a network. Involvement in such projects brings students into the realm of "real science" and involves them in more complex, abstract tasks than they generally encounter within individual classrooms. Outside scientific domains, the prospects of "publishing" and sending work to other students at a distance provide authenticity and importance to tasks that are often viewed as mundane when undertaken for the benefit of a classroom teacher.

Two-way video/two-way audio and one-way video/two-way audio are providing larger groups of students with access to instruction in advanced courses and to exemplary teachers. If used merely to present lectures to groups of students, however, these technologies do not fulfill their potential to support active student-centered learning. States have exerted leadership in developing the infrastructure for interactive distance-learning. What we need now are models for effective instruction using the full capabilities of the technology in ways that support collaborative learning with complex, authentic tasks. Just as it took some time for educators to develop effective ways to use computer networks, it will probably be some time before the best practices with interactive video technologies are discovered and disseminated.

2

Educational Technology and Systems Approach

More than three decades ago, computers and related information technologies were introduced to educators as educational tools. Today, there are computers of various descriptions in nearly all schools in the United States. Teachers, school administrators, government officials, and others faced with the costs involved in technology implementation must constantly evaluate the educational benefits of technology.

The Johns Hopkins University's Center for Social Organization of Schools has conducted three extensive surveys of U.S. school computer use over the last decade: in 1983, in 1985, and, as part of the 1989 International Association for the Evaluation of Educational Achievement (IEA) Computers in Education Survey, in the spring of 1989. More recent estimates place the number of computers installed in U.S. schools (public and nonpublic) at 3.5 million. In percentage terms, in 1981 only about 18 percent of U.S. public schools had one or more computers for instruction; by 1987 that percentage had grown to 95 percent and in 1990 it reached 97 percent. Current estimates put the percentage of public schools with at least one computer at 98 percent. In other words, nearly every school has at least one computer. The more pertinent question becomes the number of computers per school and per student.

The median number of computers in computer-using K-6 elementary schools rose from about 3 in 1985 to about 18 in 1989. In high schools the median number of computers rose from about 16 in 1985 to about 39 in 1989. The average number of computers per 30 students nearly tripled between 1984 and 1990, rising from 0.60 to 1.53.

Although the numbers of computers per school and per student have increased dramatically from the mid-1980s to the early 1990s, student access to computers must still be considered limited. In 1987, students averaged only 1 hour each week on a computer. Even the recent computer:student ratio of 1.53:30 conjures up images of classes of students jockeying for time on a limited number of machines. The most common arrangement is a computer lab of 20 to 30 machines into which whole classes are scheduled for small amounts of time. Most schools do not have enough computers for them to be used frequently by all or most students.

In 1983, computers were used primarily for three tasks: to teach students about computers (i.e., computer literacy classes), to teach programming, and for rote learning through drill-and- practice programs. In 1985, teachers reported using computers primarily for enrichment and variety, or for teaching students about computers, and rarely to provide students with instruction in core academic subjects.

A more recent trend is increasing use of computers as tools and less emphasis on teaching about computers per se than in 1985. At the same time, use of computers to teach basic skills continues to be the dominant practice in elementary schools and is increasing in high schools. Integrated learning systems (ILSs) represent an increasingly common application of computers to basic skills instruction. Approximately 10,000 ILSs are currently in use, funded primarily with Chapter 1 monies. QED survey results indicate that, as of 1990 1.4 percent of public schools had integrated learning systems. ILSs, then, represent a small niche in the educational applications of computers, but given their funding from programs for disadvantaged students, they represent a significant use of technology for this group.

MODEMS AND NETWORKS

Networks are systems that connect two or more computers to each other. These computers can be at distant sites, allowing students or teachers to communicate with peers or with each other districtwide, statewide, nationally, or even internationally. Networks can also be local. Locally networked computers have numerous advantages: they do not require software programs on multiple copies of floppy disks; they give students access to databases; they allow several computers to share a single printer; and they promote collaborative writing. In spite of these advantages, only 24 percent of high schools and only 7 percent of elementary schools had networked computers in 1989. Networks represent an area ripe for rapid growth.

Modems allow for communication between computers at remote sites. In the 1988-1989 school year, approximately 25 percent of schools had modems; during the 1991-1992 school year, this percentage was expected to double to 50 percent. Modems can be used to connect schools to network services, such as Prodigy or CompuServe, or to access other institutions participating in a wide area network (WAN). Many teachers use Internet, a system developed by the National Science Foundation to connect universities, government, and research centers. Some notes that most local area networks (LANs) within schools are used to deliver tutorial instruction as part of an integrated learning system. In 1990 only a small minority of schools had both LANs and access to wide area networks. Even when they did, the computers on the LAN were seldom connected to the WAN, and hence the networks were not being used to provide large numbers of students with data and communication from the outside world.

Despite lots of talk about telecommunications tearing down the school walls, neither the basic technology infrastructure nor the understanding of how best to capitalize on it is common at present. The potential is there, however. Plans are being developed for a National Research and Education Network (NREN), which would connect schools to major research and information centers, providing students and their teachers with access to information, databases, and special instruments, such as supercomputers, telescopes, or particle accelerators.

VCRs and educational video

Chen has noted that the best national data on instructional television use are the 7-year-old estimates from the School Utilization Study funded by the Corporation for Public Broadcasting. According to this study, 54 percent of the nation's teachers used instructional television, one-third of them using at least two television series. QED data indicate that between 1982 and 1989 the number of schools using videotapes more than tripled, from 31 percent to 99—percent near total saturation. During these same years, the number of VCRs increased threefold from 26,000 to 81,000. Around 91 percent to 96 percent of schools own at least one VCR. VCRs have taken their place in schools as a basic technology for education.

CD-ROM and videodiscs

A recent QED survey found that, of approximately 15,000 school districts in the United States, 1,377 had CD-ROM drives, representing an increase of 70 percent over the previous year. Videodisc players were in use in 1,273 districts, a figure up 38 percent from the previous year. CD-ROM players, then, were in use in about 9 percent of the school districts and videodisc players in about 8.5 percent of the districts. QED predicted that both CD-ROM and videodisc use in schools would more than double during the 1991- 1992 school year. Thus, although CD-ROM and videodisc technologies are available in only a small percentage of schools and school districts currently, with expected decreases in cost, they will become increasingly common.

Satellite technologies

Distance-learning programs are currently supported in nearly every state. Many of these programs focus on using satellite technologies to instruct children in isolated communities. An estimated one-third of all rural schools have telecommunications links; about one-third of these receive funding through the U.S. Department of Education's Star Schools program. Data suggest that 15 percent to 16 percent of public schools have satellite dishes.

After 1981, the number of public schools with computers increased around 11 percent annually. Approximately 300,000 to 400,000 computers have been added each year to U.S. schools. Given the current number of computers in U.S. schools (about 2.6 million), if the number of computers added annually remains constant, we can anticipate about 4.2 million computers in public schools by 1995 and 6 million by the turn of the century. This projection is only slightly more conservative than the projection of 4.8 million computers in 1994 for public and private schools combined offered by LINK Resources. If current trends continue, the median number of computers per school will rise from today's 33 to about 51 in 1995 and 74 in the year 2000. These average figures will mask large differences among schools, however, with some schools, districts, and states providing near universal access to computers, while others offer very little.

Even with an anticipated major increase in computers and other technologies overall, there is concern that subgroups of students may have unequal access to these resources. Schools serving high socioeconomic status students report higher computer-to-student ratios than do schools with low socioeconomic status students. The National Assessment of Educational Progress (NAEP) 1985-1986 survey found that white students were more likely to have used a computer than were African- American or Hispanic students, although this difference diminished at the high school level.

The problem is exacerbated by large differences in access to computers in the home. The NAEP survey found that nearly one-third of white high school students owned computers, compared with a little over one-fifth of African- American and Hispanic students. In 1985, African-American students were less likely to attend elementary schools with computers and, at both the elementary and secondary levels, tended to attend schools with fewer computer-using teachers than did white students. Higher socioeconomic status and white students, then, are more likely to have access to computers for education than are lower socioeconomic status and minority students. Although smaller than socioeconomic and ethnicity differences, there is also a gender difference in access to computers in the schools, with boys having more access than girls. In addition, families of male students are more likely to own computers than are families of female students, and boys are more likely than girls to attend summer computer camps. Finally, academically more able students tend to use computers more than less able students.

Even when access to computers is equivalent, there may be important differences among groups in the way computers are used. Students in low-ability classes tend to use computers for drill and practice, while higher-ability students tend to use them more broadly, in ways that are more congruent with education reform goals.

In summary, research indicates that higher socioeconomic status students, white students, male students, and higher-ability students tend to use computers more than lower socioeconomic status students, minority students, female students, and lower-ability students. Comparable data are not available on other technologies, but similar patterns are likely to be common to many of them.

If we consider access to the kind of collaborative, student-centered learning of advanced skills we have described above, inequalities are almost certainly even greater. Convincing those who develop instructional programs for disadvantaged students and those who purchase equipment and software, technology-based projects for their students is one step in confronting the inequality. Even so, policymakers will need to address the issue of the proper state and federal roles in addressing the fundamental problem of large differences in the funds available for technology purchase and implementation.

SHIFTING PERSPECTIVES IN EDUCATIONAL TECHNOLOGY

When we begin to seriously discuss what it means to learn, some interesting things happen. Although we begin by feeling that we share some understanding of what learning means, it rapidly becomes clear that there is a broad range of perspectives, each passionately articulated and defended. Our differing constructs of learning have profound implications for how we approach each educational moment, whether we are acting as faculty member, student, or administrator. As institutions seek to incorporate educational technology into a coherent and sustainable extension of their teaching and learning practices, some effort should be spent in a discourse that considers pedagogical frameworks and perspectives, their validity, and their application.

There has, over the last 20 years or so, been a shift in pedagogical perspectives from a "transmission" model (the idea that learning is essentially the assimilation of information) to the adoption of a more "constructivist" framework (the idea that learning is an active process of constructing meaning on the part of each individual learner). This shift is essentially driven by two theoretical forces:

— cognitive science research, from which human knowledge is understood to be highly complex, idiosyncratic, and, in the case of expertise, often tacit, and

— social educational theory espoused by groups such as feminist and radical educators, from which knowledge is understood to be personally, socially, culturally, and politically indexed.

Educational technology has also shifted as these perspectives have emerged. Three additional theoretical frameworks have significantly impacted upon the discourse concerning educational practice and technology: constructivism, situated cognition, and cognitive apprenticeship.

Constructivism

A very important theoretical perspective, developed and influenced largely by science teaching, is constructivism. This perspective asserts that knowledge is constructed by the learner, not passively received or assimilated. Meaningful knowledge is the result of active reflection and integration on the part of the learner, and is best accomplished by means of tasks that bear some relationship to real-world experiences. Effective instruction, therefore, aims at asking the learner to model the world, predict outcomes, and attempt to reconcile actual outcomes with predictions based on the student's own cognitive model. Consequently, learners must actively engage in meta-cognition—"thinking about their own thinking." This means fostering chances for the articulation of, and reflection on, their own conceptual models.

Situated cognition and cognitive apprenticeship

Two other theoretical pedagogical perspectives—arguably sharing constructivist theory—have recently emerged: situated cognition and cognitive apprenticeship. Situated cognition states that usable knowledge is indexed by real-world experience; most real-world problems do not have clearly delineated solutions, but rather blurry or "gray" edges that can only be effectively solved in situations. Solving real-world problems often depends on the best compromise between competing demands. Therefore, learning should be accomplished in a real-world context. Cognitive apprenticeship is the recognition that learning an intellectual task should be supported in the same way apprentices learn trades: through a process of expert modeling and appropriately scaled support.

Extending the paradigm

These theoretical frameworks are presented not as dictates for instructional design, but rather as ways in which the concepts of instructional design might be extended to help instructors design better online teaching materials. Both university and corporate educational technology arenas we have encountered some common practices that can be problematic in terms of student engagement and learning. These include:

- A lack of multiple and repeated contexts for the representation of content, and consequently support for longer-term retention of the material; content is likely to be viewed once and not revisited. Good design should focus on ensuring that the learner is given the opportunity to revisit and apply core concepts throughout each learning experience.
- The implicit assumption that all material should be viewed by the student before the assessment component is engaged in. Most approaches to online learning use the formula: access a module, read/view/listen to the material, complete the assessment. There are usually a complete distinction and separation made between content and assessment. It may be far more effective to embed some forms of assessment directly into the learning material in a way that engages learners to apply new and previously learned concepts, especially within "real world" contexts.
- The infrequent use of assessment as an instructional strategy.
- The infrequent use of pre- and post-assessment analyses as the basis for determining instructional need.

A lack of focus on the interrelationships between concepts. A learning system offers the ability to link to—and integrate—content elements between modules or courses that cannot easily be accommodated within a paper-based delivery system, but this advantage is seldom exploited.

IMPLICATIONS FOR EDUCATIONAL TECHNOLOGY

Structuring content for an online environment is deceptively complex. Many instructional designers see the process of structuring content as simply one of successively "atomizing" what needs to learned into a categorical/hierarchical order of discrete elements. This order can be a useful, productive, and legitimate way of representing information, but a greater challenge lies on the opposite side of the coin: making sure that content is integrated into a meaningful conceptual whole.

Meaningful learning, even in a purely training context, is not about absorbing isolated curricular components, but about struggling to understand, at a conceptual level, the underlying context and principles that relate that information to a larger picture. The instructional needs of a target population center on context, communication, support for practice, and clear and unambiguous feedback in terms of learning outcomes. Context is the authenticity of the learning experience; in other words, matching the working experience of the learners with the matrix in which the instructional objectives are embedded. This determines how well the tasks in the learning environment reflect the real world.

Communication is the interface through which the instructional materials are accessed and presented. It thus includes both interface design and imagery and the instructional media used. The critical factor in communication is ensuring that learners know where they are at all times regarding the instructional content and instructional intent. A well-designed learning system can provide dynamic support for both navigation and presentation of content.

Support for practice is a key determinant in the retention of information. The focus should be on the authentic representation of real tasks relating to appropriately delimited segments of content. There should also be support for both elemental and integrated learning. Games, simulations, predictive reasoning, and traditional assessment can all play a role in this process.

Learning outcome representation is critical for ensuring that learners retain a clear conceptual picture of their progress through the instructional material. Multimedia technology can support this in a variety of methods and formats. In addition, the essence of self-paced learning is ensuring that a review of recently-learned material is always easily accessible.

Teaching should focus on ensuring that content is meaningfully integrated into a solid and sustained conceptual framework. Understanding and adopting several principles may assist in achieving that goal.

What is perceived and attended to is idiosyncratically determined by a learner's prior knowledge, experiences, and frameworks; ultimately, the meaningfulness of new information is determined by the degree to which it can be linked to existing knowledge frameworks.

"Activating" prior knowledge is an important part of teaching new material; learners must be actively coached or mentored to understand how to articulate existing cognitive models, and how to integrate new information into extending and reshaping these models.

Learners need a high-level view of the material to be learned in order to provide a conceptual framework into which new material can be integrated. The "cognitive load" that learners can carry is based on their level of expertise. Novice learners cannot attend to more than a very small amount of material at any one time. This amount increases with expertise.

The axiom "less is more" is an important consideration in terms of the trade-off between learning outcomes and the amount of presented material, especially in the case of novice learners. The amount of supported practice is a critical determinant of learning, especially during the early stages of learning.

Lower-level cognition and psychomotor skills must achieve some degree of automaticity before higher-order skills can be successfully learned and utilized. This does not, however, negate or deny the importance of higher-level conceptual frameworks.

Ultimately, online learning development should focus on supporting and fostering the active participation of the student in constructing personally meaningful representations of the material. It is not simply a matter of breaking down the content into constituent components, but about asking the student to think about what he or she already knows and the extent to which these existing models make sense, reconciling differences between the predictive accuracy of these and alternative models, determining and refining first principles, and integrating new information into coherent frameworks. When these processes are supported, then online learning moves beyond the function of a reference source to become a true semblance of teaching.

TRENDS IN EDUCATIONAL TECHNOLOGY

A large portion of the educational technology literature is about the design, development, and evaluation of instructional materials. Issues in design include the application of cognitive psychology, such as in helping learners to conceptualize unfamiliar content; semiotics and the effects of message configuration characteristics, such as text design, text density, visual design, and use of symbol systems; and the effects of media use on motivation, including learner interest, achievement, and attitude development.

Development includes such activities as needs assessment, course development, and product development. Finally, evaluation is concerned with measures and procedures for determining program effectiveness. Related to this is a call for better procedures for evaluating computer-assisted instruction software and software evaluation databases that are accessible to individuals.

Professional education for teachers in the use of educational technology

Literature in this area is directed both at professional specialists within the field of educational technology and at individuals who teach. Currently, the emphasis appears to be on the teacher/instructor. The basic question is, "What competencies do teachers/instructors need to use technology effectively with their learners?" The assumption is that all classroom presenters should be using media and technology but are not, or that they are using it in less than optimal ways. Much of the literature discusses the use of computers and microcomputers by classroom teachers, and it emphasizes the need for teacher training in the area of information technology rather than educational technology or library instruction. This subtle difference is indicative of the gradual blending of educational media and technology with library and information science in the elementary and secondary schools.

Interest in distance education is stimulated in part by concerns over equity of access in the face of shortages of qualified elementary and secondary school teachers. Distance learning protocols have developed in direct response to real teaching/learning problems. Distance education offers practicable solutions to shortages of resources and teaching personnel. To prepare material for delivery requires a systematic approach to instructional design and a concern for the individual student rather than for group teaching. Much of the literature about distance education refers to the use of various telecommunications systems to provide optimum participation by the learners.

The computer is the dominant medium in the field of educational technology

Elementary schools use their micros primarily to supplement lessons with basic skills exercises and opportunities for drill and practice. In secondary schools, the micros are used primarily for teaching formal computer literacy. Teachers express interest in having publishers develop software that teaches problem-solving skills and higher order thinking skills. While the literature reflects the growing enthusiasm for school computer use, it also shows continuing criticism of software quality.

The apparent preoccupation of educators with computers often overshadows the increasing interest in telecommunications and video. While schools continue to use the traditional audiovisual equipment such as films, filmstrips, slides, audiotape recordings, and overhead transparencies in a more-or-less routine fashion, new development seems to be with video in the classroom for large group instruction, and telecommunications for individuals and small groups within the school and in distance education programs. The Quality Education Data study notes that over 90% of the schools in the U.S. are using videocassette recorders, while in 1983 only 30% of the schools used VCRs.

The role of the educational technologist is unclear and varies from location to location

There are very few professionals who actually hold the title of "educational technologist." They are usually represented by such titles as: media specialist, media coordinator, or library media specialist; sometimes they are the director, supervisor, or coordinator of educational media, instructional media, or communications. Newer and more specific titles are emerging, including microcomputer coordinator, instructional computer teacher, or specialist in educational computing. Although it is now likely that most large schools and school districts have one or more persons who are responsible for the administrative, logistic, and instructional aspects of instructional media (or, in some cases, just computers), these professionals are assuming such roles from a variety of previous positions and with varying types of education and experience.

People who study the adoption of educational innovations know that one of the most powerful factors affecting adoption is evidence that an innovation has worked in a situation similar to the one where it is being considered. Although they do not carry much information in the way of theory, research, or development, case studies serve as "lighthouses" or "pilots" for other institutions or organizations.

Much of the journal literature is about educational technology as a profession, discussing such issues as status, ethics, legal aspects, history, and future developments of the field. It is obvious that practitioners of educational technology are concerned about their professional development and identity. They are attempting to understand who they are, what they should be doing, and how others view them. Such concerns are typical among individuals who feel that they are in an emerging profession without the tradition of an established discipline. It is a generally healthy trend which will probably be evident for many years to come.

Educational technology, principles, products, and practices

The history of media in education is one of enrichment or enhancement. Not surprisingly, some of the literature examines the ways in which educational technology and media specialists provide support to teachers/instructors to improve their effectiveness. There is, however, increasing interest in media specialists as curriculum consultants. Some argues that schools must take the initiative and begin designing curricula that will provide teachers and students with a variety of options and strategies for achieving curriculum goals.

To this end, he describes the Integrated Instructional Information Resource, a group of broadly accessible, electronically searchable, and interrelatable databases that are designed to assist educators in developing "opened-out" curricula. Information power states that the library media specialist must develop a new, multi-faceted role as information specialist, teacher, and instructional consultant, and offers guidance for assuming these roles.

The recent flood of studies decrying the lack of quality in public education is causing individuals in the field of educational media and technology to once again beat the drums for technology as a solution to the problems of public education.

Current application of educational technology

Those who are familiar with current applications of media and technology do not require further evidence of the potential benefits from using media to teach. The ability of media to transmit instruction has been widely demonstrated:

— A few years ago, when blizzards and the energy crisis closed the schools in Columbus, Ohio, the mass media, working with teams of local educators, were able to maintain student progress by means of televised instruction coordinated with study guides published in local newpapers

— Radio and television, via satellite distribution, are used to deliver instruction in developing countries and remote parts of the United States

— Students from a number of engineering schools are currently attending classes in factories and offices by means of videotape cassettes

Systems for individualised instruction

Progress in microelectronics and interactive videodisc systems has allowed the development of prototype instructional systems in which students work through learning tasks. The tasks are built around individual abilities and interests and are designed to move the student toward established goals and objectives. Student responses are examined for errors and misunderstanding. Next, problems are diagnosed, and specific remedial instruction or elaboration is provided to correct the problems.

Working through a series of successful, individually planned, interactive experiences, the "ideal" of education, in which each student is stretched to individual limits of achievement, is achieved. However, before such an ideal can be achieved in the typical classroom certain factors must be taken into consideration.

The potential effectiveness of media is not found in any variables that are inherent in the devices (assuming they are capable of delivering the necessary stimulus), but in how the devices are used. This implies that technology is a technique for designing instruction rather than the more common perception of technology as machine.

This broad definition of technology implies the interaction of individuals, materials, and machines in a variety of instructional settings and employing a variety of instuctional strategies—each item of the mix being called upon to do what it does most effectively.

Patterns of media utilisation

Three basic patterns of media use, each with different potential effects on the cost and effectiveness of education, currently exist: additive, integrated, and independent.

The Additive Approach

In the additive approach, materials are added to regular instruction as supplementary or enrichment activities and are not necessary for the achievement of basic instructional outcomes. The use of media is dependent on the classroom teacher, does not have a significant impact on student achievement, and represents an added expense for the educational system. Such an approach is not cost-effective.

The Integrated Approach

In the integrated approach, carefully selected or produced materials are integrated into regular instruction and provide an essential element leading to the achievement of basic instructional outcomes. Media and the teacher are mutually dependent. This approach represents an additional cost for the school system and requires extensive planning and preparation by the teacher, but has the potential to create a significant increase in student achievment.

The Independent Approach

In the independent approach, instruction is redesigned so that basic instructional outcomes are achieved though the active interaction of students and instructional materials without the direct intervention of the classroom teacher. Although this approach represents a major initial cost to the school system, it has the greatest potential for increasing the cost-effectiveness of education.

Enhanced use of learning time

The effectiveness of time spent in learning should be increased. A major cause of ineffective time use is the "batch processing" approach to instruction. Although education is one of the most labor-intensive "industries" in existence, it provides little opportunity for individual work with students. Faced with a class of 25 to 35 students, the teacher is forced to direct attention to groups of students rather than individuals. A possible solution to this problem would be to significantly reduce class size. However, the increased number of teachers required for such a solution, along with the necessity of increasing salaries to a level sufficient to attract more qualified teachers, would increase the costs of education beyond any hope of taxpayer approval.

One less expensive alternative would be to redeploy teachers through using media. Such an approach is based on the demonstrated effectiveness of media to transmit conventional instruction and employ a combination of integrated and independent use of media. Using this approach, students spend a major portion of their time either receiving basic information in a large-group setting by means of television or working on individual activities by means of microcomputers. In both cases, direct supervision is provided by paraprofessionals.

Different instructional approaches and levels of materials are developed for, and presented to, different groups of students. Teachers, thus freed from basic presentation of instruction and supervision, devote their time to small-group activities and to individual interaction with students. Under this strategy, students would spend less actual time in the presence of the teacher but the quality and effectiveness of the time would be greatly enhanced. Using media and technology to redeploy teachers requires a reorganization of the school and redefinition of the teacher's role.

Teachers must shift from dispensing knowledge to managing learning. Although no fully developed examples of such systems exist in the United States, such programs have been organized in underdeveloped nations where a shortage of trained personnel has made traditional patterns of instruction impossible, and in the extension programs of many higher education institutions. What is necessary, in order to achive excellence through the use of media, is the capital investment in tools to make possible the application of the "techniques" of educationl technology, a reorganization of the structure of teaching and learning, and the will to make these changes.

TECHNOLOGY AND EQUITY

Books and news stories regularly focus popular attention on

inequities within our educational system. In about one-third of our states, lawsuits have sought or are seeking to remedy funding disparities correlated with lower achievement for students from poor communities. Concerns about our changing school population, the plight of our cities, and the perceived failures of public education have all fueled cries for educational reform that meets the needs of all our children. Technology is routinely touted as a potentially powerful agent of that reform.

For years, the microcomputer was cited as the vehicle for overcoming a wide array of inequities. Today, distance education approaches like teleconferencing, interactive television, electronic mail, and expanded telecommunications networks are promoted as avenues to improved resources for underserved students. But despite the promise of emerging technology, it is important to remember that technology and equity are not inevitable partners.

Computers and equuty

The literature on computer equity reveals that many students—not only minority, disadvantaged, and inner-city but also female, handicapped, and rural—have been hampered by inequitable access to computers and by widespread patterns of inequitable distribution and use of computers within and across schools.

Problems begin at the "counting" level, with wealthy districts having a 54:1 student-computer ratio and poor ones having a ratio of 73:1. Limited hardware and software can in turn lead to scheduling patterns that limit the numbers and types of students who have access to computers. Some reported that "better" students use computers more than either average or slower students in elementary, middle, and, especially, high schools. Further the most exciting computer opportunities are disproportionately available to students with the highest abilities; low achieving, high risk students, particularly in high school, are less likely to be in classes in which these opportunities occur. While these conclusions stem from data collected in 1985, preliminary analysis of data collected in 1989 shows only modest changes in schools' overall patterns of hardware and software use.

Factors other than sheer numbers can also limit computer access to selected groups. Locating hardware in labs and classrooms restricted to advanced students and setting unnecessarily difficult prerequisites for computer courses can easily deprive average and slower students of computer opportunities. Handicapped students can be withheld from computer opportunities by lack of adaptive devices, special software, or information about how to adapt regular software.

Finally, software that incorporates stereotypes and uses of technology that reflect subtle biases can create the most pernicious inequities of all. "Drill and kill" programs heighten the "masculinity" of both math and computers, thus reinforcing girls' frequently negative attitudes towards both.

Economically disadvantaged students, who often use the computer for remediation and basic skills, learn to do what the computer tells them, while more affluent students, who use it to learn programming and tool applications, learn to tell the computer what to do. Within the literature on computers and equity, authorities often concentrate on problems and solutions for individual categories of students. Gender equity has been the focus of considerable research.

The nature of computer, a resource guide and teaching manual for fostering increased computer competence by female students and adults, is one of the many programs and publications directed at this audience. The Council for Exceptional Children sponsors the Center for Special Education Technology, which focuses on technological equity for students with physical, sensory, and learning handicaps. Both Apple Computer and IBM support units about adaptive technology and special software for students with physical and other disabilities.

While each category of students embodies equity problems that merit specific attention, many of the concerns and techniques cited within individual segments of the literature apply across categories. The central recommendations—gaining awareness of the scope and complexity of the issues and taking active steps to promote equity for the group in question—are found in the literature for all groups.

Creating positive attitudes toward technology so that underserved students understand its relevance to them is a basic theme that runs throughout the literature. Finally, the need for active, committed involvement by equity advocates concerned about the needs of underserved groups is also necessary to ensure equity with and through technology. Inequity often results from oversight rather than intent, and sensitivity to the danger of excluding some students from technology's opportunities can prevent. As CD-ROM and online searching enter the curriculum, vigilance will be especially necessary to provide all student groups with the benefits of electronic information resources.

Technological equity is a complex issue that encompasses disparities in access to and uses of powerful learning tools because of differences in socioeconomic status, gender, ability level, racial and ethnic identification, geographic location, and handicapping condition. Each of these areas has its own problems, research community, and suggested solutions. What the areas share is a need for unremitting attention. Only when all students are routinely granted access to hardware and to appropriate software, and only when technology is used to help each student achieve his or her own personal best, can we speak of technology and equity as partners.

TECHNOLOGY TO IMPROVE THE CURRICULUM OF SMALL RURAL SCHOOLS

Developments in two types of technology have important implications for curriculum and instruction in small rural schools. While both of these technologies are rich in promise for those interested in improving the curriculum in small rural schools, there are drawbacks as well.

The two technologies involve microcomputers and distance education technologies. On the one hand, microcomputers are becoming a more familiar part of the educational landscape, and teachers are using programmed instructional materials more and more frequently. On the other hand, improvements in telecommunications make it increasingly easy to transmit instructionally useful images and sound over geographically forbidding distances.

Computerised learning programmes

A critical feature of programmed learning packages, computerized or otherwise, can be their "stand-alone" feature. Stand-alone programs are completely self-contained in the sense that they do not require the presence or involvement of an on-site teacher. To the extent that effective stand-alone programs become available, it will be relatively easy to enlarge curricular offerings in small rural as well as in other kinds of schools. Important questions concern whether or not stand-alone programs really are possible, desirable, cost-effective, or feasible.

In fact, it is not yet clear if the market for the kinds of stand-alone programs desired by small schools will be sufficiently large, even under the most favorable circumstances, to prompt their development. Students may learn more, thanks to the innovation, but unless the programs have a stand-alone quality they will not enhance the ability of small rural schools to enlarge and broaden their curricular offerings. Indeed, microcomputers would actually add to, rather than reduce, the costs of education.

If programmed instruction merely supplements on-site teaching resources, their potential for making small rural schools more viable will be minimal. New course offerings will require additional teachers with subject matter expertise, just as is currently the case. And no teaching resources will be freed for other uses thanks to the arrival of programmed materials.

On the other hand, a simplistic view of what is required will not serve development well. The requirement for an on-site teacher is not an all-or-nothing matter. It is not so much a question of whether programmed instruction can succeed without any involvement of an on-site teacher as it is a question about the kind of skills and experience the on-site teacher will need to have. If learning programs can be developed which reduce, but do not eliminate the level of subject matter expertise required of on-site teachers, then there can still be considerable potential for improved curriculum and instruction in small rural schools. The possibilities for such improvement are enhanced if the use of programmed materials with some stand-alone qualities are coupled with use of the evolving distance technologies discussed in the next section.

Telecommunicaiton technologies

Educators in the United States are currently showing great interest in two-way interactive instructional television and its potential for expanding the curriculum of small rural schools. Moreover, the range of technological options has been steadily increasing. It seems reasonable to expect this trend to continue. Numerous technologies, not just two-way interactive instructional television, make it possible to join geographically separated students and teachers, short of levels. Schools and classes can—and have increasingly—been linked together through the use of telephone lines, cables, and radio and television waves of various kinds.

Even if distance technologies do become more sophisticated, more reliable, and less costly, important additional barriers must still be overcome. Schools using distance technologies to share programs must solve numerous problems. These problems range from the trivial to the more substantive.

These are organizational or, in a sense, "political" problems, but they are at least as important as the technological problems. The most important of the substantive problems, however, may be teacher training. That problem will be examined after an examination of what a productive combination of stand-alone programmed materials and distance technology might look like.

Distance technologies, when they are coupled with the programmed materials described above, seem to offer considerable potential for small rural schools that are interested in improving their curriculum. To help readers imagine this potential more clearly, the discussion that follows develops an idealised example of how these two technologies might be fruitfully combined. Without some such vision, however, the research and development necessary to help move educational practice toward this potential is not likely to occur.

It seems clear that the greatest promise attends combinations of technologies in nontraditional forms of instruction. And yet, there are a disquieting number of unanswered questions. For example, it is largely unknown how successful the new conception of a generalist teacher might be. It is also unclear how possible it will be to develop instructional programs that can substitute to some degree for on-site teacher subject matter expertise. Although the seriousness of these questions highlights the dangers of viewing technology as an easy and readily available means of solving small rural schools' curriculum problems, the potential is self-evident, and the direction for future research and development efforts seems clear.

3

Educational Technology for Skill Development and Behaviour Modification

Technology can facilitate learning by providing real world contexts that engage learners in solving complex problems. Computer simulations and computer-based micro worlds also offer appropriate contexts for learners to explore and come to understand complex phenomena in a variety of subject areas. "Tell me, I forget. Show me, I remember. Involve me, I understand." This Chinese proverb illustrates well the importance of getting learners mentally involved in learning activities, generating connections between what they already know and what they are being asked to learn and constructing meaning from their experiences.

When students become active participants in the knowledge construction process, the focus of learning shifts from covering the curriculum to working with ideas. And using technology tools "to think with" facilitates working with ideas and learning from that process. Technology tools provide "the means through which individuals engage and manipulate both resources and their own ideas". Some kinds of technology tools can extend memory and make thinking visible. Good examples include brainstorming and concept mapping software such as Inspiration(r). Others help to represent knowledge and facilitate communication. For instance, the Collaborative Visualization or CoVis Project provides visualization software designed to help students collect and analyze climatological data and visualize effects due to greenhouse gases and other phenomena.

Finally, some tools, like simulations mentioned above, enable learners to experiment with modeling complex ideas. NetLogo provides a programmable modeling environment for simulating natural and social phenomena, such as how segregated neighborhoods can arise, not from any specific bias, but from the simple desire of people to live near others who are like themselves.

LEARNING IS SOCIAL

Teachers have long recognized the value of having students work together in a group to accomplish some types of learning tasks. Students benefit from hearing perspectives other than their own, and they may bring different strengths to a complex and lengthy activity. However, a social theory of learning reflects a fundamentally different view, where knowledge "is a matter of competence with respect to valued enterprises" and knowing "is a matter of participating in the pursuit of such enterprises".

Learning, then, amounts to increasing participation in and contribution to the practices of a social community. Concepts such as knowledge building, apprenticeship, and mentoring become paramount, as learners are conceived to be under the tutelage of more experienced peers or instructors. A social view of learning focuses attention on making connections among students within a school and between students in the school and the broader community. How can modern technologies support and enhance these connections?

Computer-Supported Intentional Learning Environment (CSILE) is one example of software that supports a networked, multimedia environment in which students collaborate on learning activities. They do this by creating 'notes' to express their ideas or integrate outside information about a topic. Then they read and respond to the notes of others, all of which builds a communal database producing shared knowledge about the topic or problem.

The effects of CSILE have been notably positive, with students performing better on standardized tests than their non-CSILE counterparts. CSILE students also demonstrate greater depth in their explanations. At a conference reporting some of the CSILE findings, Marlene Scardamalia read a few notes posted in one class's database and challenged the audience to determine who wrote them - a fourth grader, a college student, or a scientist.

With migration to the Internet, CSILE, now known as Knowledge Forum, facilitates connections between schools and the scientific community, allowing practicing scientists to serve as mentors to students. Other projects, such as Kids as Global Scientists, also bring students and various experts together in virtual communities through Internet links. Such "a dialogue-based approach to learning creates a rich intellectual context, with ample opportunities for participants to improve their understanding and become more personally involved in explaining scientific phenomena".

A few parting thoughts

Technology by itself does not guarantee learning. Rather, it is in how teachers and students use available technologies that determines whether transformative learning happens. Educators can respond to the challenge like the principal who banned PDAs from his school. Or they can explore the power of technology to help learners achieve important outcomes. Understanding principles of learning is a good way to begin.

STUDENT LEARNING ACTIVITIES

Capabilities provided by technology

Technology offers powerful support for learning skills through inquiry and problem solving. In this chapter, the specific ways in which technology enables the kind of challenging instruction. Technology can promote student exploration through collaborative involvement in authentic, challenging multidisciplinary tasks by providing realistic complex environments for student inquiry, furnishing information and tools to support investigation, linking classroóms for joint investigations, and presenting data in ways that support mathematical thinking and problem-solving.

Realistic complex environments for inquiry

Teachers can draw on technology applications to simulate real-world environments and create actual environments for experimentation, so that students can carry out authentic tasks as real workers would, explore new terrains, meet people of different cultures, and use a variety of tools to gather information and solve problems. Working on "authentic tasks", which Brown, Collins, and Duguid define simply as the ordinary practices of the culture, engages students in sustained exploration and provides multiple opportunities to reflect on the decisions made in trying to address the problem.

Authentic tasks are highly motivating for students, leading them to acquire advanced skills and knowledge because they become engrossed in the problems that, for example, navigators, anthropologists, or historians face. Just as important, simulations address the problem of "inert knowledge". Many typical school tasks are stripped of the meanings and the context that they hold for real practitioners. In learning tasks in this stripped-down form, students are unable to extract anything that they can apply in richer, more complex situations outside of school. "Case-based instruction", as it was termed by earlier writers, presents students with the same problems that expert practitioners attempt and provides a motivating environment for cooperative learning and teacher- directed mediation Computer-Supported Intentional Learning

EnvironmentComputer-Supported Intentional Learning Environment. Simulated environments allow students to get involved with the problem, often through visual media, which provide integrated context and help students comprehend new ideas more easily.

Simulations are student centered, since students make decisions and see the results of their actions. The teacher is present, but in the role of coach, using discussion to prompt students to explore different aspects of the problem space, answering students' questions, and encouraging students to elaborate their thinking and listen to other points of view. Because the problem space is always accessible, students can revisit and revise their conceptual understanding.

The nature of the teacher student relationship is altered as both become co-learners; knowledge is constructed in collaboration rather than transmitted from teacher to student. Students help each other learn, working together in a generative and cooperative environment. The examples below are provided as illustrations of how technology can support student involvement in authentic tasks.

Voyage of the Mimi— Since 1985, when it first became available for commercial use, teachers have been using *The Voyage of the Mimi I*, developed by Bank Street College, to create environments for exploration. The centerpiece of the first voyage is a 13-part television drama that portrays the adventures of a group of young scientists, including several adolescents, who are studying whales off the coast of New England. Viewers observe the crew conducting scientific experiments and solving technical problems. A separate documentary accompanies each television show, portraying scientists engaged in their work. Four computer modules engage students in using navigation concepts and instruments, for example, to free a trapped whale in the Atlantic. The modules also include a microworld ecosystem, a tool for measuring and graphing physical events, and a programming environment. A book version of the TV show, classroom activities, and additional resources are also available for teachers.

Not all of the *Voyage of the Mimi* environments are simulated. One video shows young scientists studying the sound frequencies of whales. In their classroom labs, students can then carry out careful studies of their own voices and of musical instruments and create real-time audio frequency spectra.

The Second Voyage of the Mimi exposes students to archaeology and to the culture of the ancient Maya in Mexico's Yucatan peninsula. The goal of the curriculum is to motivate children's interest in science as a real- world activity, and to make various scientific concepts understandable to a wide range of children. The multimedia package includes a 12-episode television series as well as two software programs *Maya Math* and *Sun Lab*.

The latest development effort by the Bank Street researchers/developers of the Mimi materials is the Palenque project, a digital video interactive (DVI) prototype. The locations and several of the characters from *The Second Voyage of the Mimi* have been used again in the Palenque project. Palenque embodies the same instructional strategy as its Mimi predecessors in a DVI system that provides for electronic as well as thematic integration.

Immigrant 1850—Developed by Project Zero at Harvard University, *Immigrant 1850* encourages students to identify with the Irish immigrant experience of the mid 1800s by taking on the role of one who leaves Ireland to face the difficulties of establishing a new life in Boston. Students have access to a core set of computer-based activities in which they can adopt an immigrant family and "live through" the complex decisions the family may have made in finding housing and a job, calculating finances, and shopping within their earnings.

Students can use a database, spreadsheet, and word processor to calculate expenses and keep diaries. In multiple rounds of field testing *Immigrant 1850* with more than 100 classrooms, researchers found that both regular and special-needs students could sustain involvement with this learning environment for periods ranging from several weeks to an entire school year.

Many teachers involved with the *Immigrant 1850* unit used the existing materials as a starting point to create additional innovative learning environments for their particular students, drawing on additional technology applications and corollary activities. Researchers also found that some teachers used *Immigrant 1850* as a model to create their own engaging computer-based curriculum units.

In all of these programs, the technology both draws groups of students into a richly complex setting a whaling vessel, muddy streets of an earlier Boston, a Mayan city that stimulates their questions and provides them with the resources to gather and integrate information themselves. Thus, these technology applications support student exploration, engagement with complex, multidisciplinary tasks, and collaborative work. The benefits of these authentic, challenging environments for students increase as both teachers and students get comfortable with the materials and the various learning pathways within them.

Information and tools to support investigation

The applications just described provide the content, the materials, and the varied pathways students can follow in learning through interaction with a simulation. Alternatively, technology can be used to enable students to investigate questions within curriculum units that individual teachers or teams of teachers have designed. Teachers make accessible to students technology applications that allow students to gather information; and to represent and convey to others what they have learned.

The essence of the innovation lies in the development of an instructional framework within which these tools are used. The overarching themes and "big questions" investigated in these projects are usually interdisciplinary, and they need to be carefully selected to respond to students developmental needs and interests and to reflect issues of social and scientific consequence. Students work individually or in collaboration with others in these inquiry-oriented units, and work over extended periods of time on projects culminating in presentations or "exhibitions" that provide the basis for assessing their learning.

Two examples of projects using technology to provide information and tools for student inquiry are provided below.

Make it Happen—In four middle schools in New York, Massachusetts, and New Hampshire, teachers used a rich variety of technology applications within an interdisciplinary, I-Search unit. An I-Search unit has four instructional phases:

— *Phase 1:* Teachers immerse students in a theme or topic, eliciting students prior knowledge, helping students build background knowledge, and motivating students to choose a personally meaningful question to explore.

— *Phase 2:* Students develop a search plan for gathering information and building knowledge.

— *Phase 3:* Students gather and integrate information.

— *Phase 4:* Students develop an I-Search Report and disseminate to others what they have learned.

The teachers implementing this approach were field testing *Make it Happen*!, a manual developed by Education Development Center based on 5 years of research and development. *Make it Happen*! guides interdisciplinary teams of teachers in designing and implementing an I-Search Unit. Each of the four field test sites carried out a different inquiry-based, thematic unit that integrated various technology applications.

In a suburb of New York City, the unit was on the human body. Teachers and students used simulations, a CD-ROM magazine index, videos, and word processing. The suburban

Boston school in this study implemented a unit focused on Africa. Teachers and students used videos, word processing, *MacPaint*, and *Inspiration*. In a rural community in New Hampshire, the unit focused on the history of the town. The technology that became part of the unit included *TimeLiner*, *meccGraph*, a teacher-made video, a database program, and word processing. In a small urban area in Massachusetts, the unit was on Race and Culture. Besides using videos and filmstrips, the students used *The New Grolier Electronic Encyclopedia* and word processing.

Across all four schools, every student identified a question that he or she felt motivated to investigate. Students commented that they felt like explorers, learned information that would affect their lives, and found new ways of gathering, organizing, and conveying information.

Software evaluation project—Middle school social studies students participating in the Software Evaluation Project at the State University of New York at Buffalo used technology to navigate their own paths through a vast body of data. By using a series of multimedia resources, including *Point of View, The New Grolier Electronic Encyclopedia*, and the CD-ROM interactive videodisc *The War in the Persian Gulf*, teachers created a research environment that both motivated and guided the students in searching for and presenting information. Within the classwide theme of the Persian Gulf War, small teams of students worked cooperatively to research particular aspects of the war that interested them and then created a culminating multimedia presentation. Using the software program *Point of View* as an authoring tool for the presentation, students were able to articulate their insights about complex issues.

Students take the initiating role in these classroom-designed curriculum units, with the teachers in a support and facilitating role. Rather than transmitting a body of facts and information about the subject to the students, teachers used technology applications such as *Point of View* to stimulate and then help structure the students' individual or small-group investigations. One teacher introduced that program using a projection system, then asked students to suggest various paths for exploration of the different lists. Even during the class demonstration, students could take the initiative to move around in the system, looking at maps, charts, documents, and text, and suggesting keywords for searching for information.

Once students were working on individual or small-group projects, the teacher provided guidance when students needed it as they searched for information and pictures and wrote brief essays to include in their presentations. Encouraged to carry out their investigations with partners, students got help from teachers when they needed it to work effectively in cooperative small groups.

Peggy Healy Stearns, like others researching computer-supported inquiry programs, finds that students sustain a high level of interest and curiosity when they are using a database to explore their own questions. According to Stearns, "The information that students retrieved in their investigations took on special significance because the questions were their own and the answers were viewed as personal discoveries. Students had a sense of ownership that is absent when they are spoon fed".

Programs such as *make it happen*!, the Software Evaluation project, but they are critically dependent on the teacher to set the context, model appropriate research strategies, and, until students become more expert computer users, cue students to the ways that technology can help them over the course of their projects. It is the selection of complex, interdisciplinary topics to explore, organization of learning into long-term inquiry-based units, and setting up of collaborative work teams that constitute the heart of the innovation.

Technology supports this kind of work and adds to students sense of excitement and belief that they are doing something important. An additional benefit of technology is the resulting products, which are motivating because they look much more professional than more conventional student work and provide products that can form the basis for meaningful assessment.

Link classrooms for joint investigations

Computer networks enable students and teachers to move the learning process beyond the boundaries of the classroom and into the world outside school. By bringing telecommunications applications into their classrooms, teachers create environments where students can communicate via electronic mail with other students, participate in collaborative projects, and gather and pool information in a joint endeavor to understand issues.

Learning circles—The AT&T Learning Network links classes from geographically diverse locations into "learning circles" to accomplish shared educational goals. The network matches teachers and their students with seven to nine other classrooms that share academic interests but represent different geographic or cultural perspectives. Each classroom within a learning circle has the opportunity to design projects and request information from the other circle partners for these projects. Examples of student-conducted research projects include how weather and seasonal patterns affect the daily lives of people in different locations, the influence of mass media on children's lives, and a survey of cities in transition.

Students in New York, Australia, and Canada, as well as other distant locations, researched and then traded stories about the history of their own communities. After collecting the information from their distant partners via the telecommunications network, the students worked with the information they received—analyzing, evaluating, synthesizing, and eventually publishing the project in a cooperative learning circle publication. A learning circle network fosters authentic inquiry-based learning by providing real purpose, motivation, and audience for students to conduct research and write to one another. Students are not working on arbitrary assignments but on novel tasks that were designed by their learning circle partners.

The telecommunications environment provides students with opportunities to develop new awareness and appreciation of individual differences that teachers could not provide within the boundaries of their own classrooms. Research suggests that students are better able to function as an intellectual critic for distant peers than for themselves or classmates and that they learn to write better when physical distance makes clear the need to provide explicit content for the reader.

An additional advantage is that physical and sensory limitations become "invisible" in this medium, since the recipients of messages in one classroom do not know what special efforts the senders may have made in order to communicate. In one learning circle, a classroom sent around an introductory packet about themselves to the other classes, including an audiotape of stories from the class. Another class in the circle was made up of hearing-impaired students who wrote back a cogent and personal statement about what it is like to be deaf and how they are often treated as stupid.

Some finds that relationships between students and their teachers change in learning circle projects. The teacher becomes a learner alongside students as each classroom designs activities for the learning circle and participates in other circle partners' investigations. Unlike a typical self-contained lesson in which the classroom teacher plans and implements an activity, individual classroom teachers do not have total control over the direction of a learning circle project. They do not know what students and teachers in other locations will contribute to the process and cannot predict the exact course the project will take. Instead, the students see the teachers in the role of a participant in the learning process. In this role, the teacher serves as a model of active learning setting a powerful example for students.

Technical Educational Research Centers (TERC)

Network Science Programs—Over the past decade, TERC has been linking groups of classrooms to each other and to professional scientists who can help students explore pressing global questions. TERC's network science programs are based on the premise that students can carry out scientific investigations with real scientists and that computers can enhance this enterprise. Students conduct experiments, analyze data, and share results with their colleagues using a simple computer-based telecommunications network. This collecting and making sense of data gives the students an opportunity "to experience the excitement of science that scientists feel".

Kids network. One of the TERC network projects, the National Geographic Kids Network, involves students and teachers across the United States and in a number of foreign countries working collaboratively on science projects. The project is funded by the National Science Foundation (NSF) and the National Geographic Society (NGS) and is now published by NGS. The initial unit of the Kids Network involved teachers and students in fourth through sixth grade from 200 schools in a study of acid rain.

Students collected data on the pH of their local water, then shared this data with the other schools on the telecommunications network. Using a word processor, data/record-keeping software, graphing utility, map software with data overlay, and telecommunications package, students were able to display their own data and the combined data from other schools in tables, graphs, and maps and then compare and analyze the data. The scientist who was involved in the project communicated with the students over the network, answering questions, commenting on their data, and suggesting ways they might analyze their data.

Since that initial unit, TERC has developed five other units for fourth- through sixth-grade students. Each unit involves students examining the topic in their local community and then guides them in expanding the inquiry by sharing data with other students in distant locations. The themes of the curriculum units are "Too Much Trash", "What's in Our Water?", "Weather in Action", "What are We Eating?", and "Solar Energy." Whenever possible, a professional scientist is involved in the unit, communicating with students over the network. Currently, TERC is developing nine Kids Network units for sixth- through ninth-grade classrooms, beginning with a unit on the human body.

TERC star Schools: TERC developed another network project, the Star Schools project, involving secondary students and teachers from across the country and recognized resource centers. These groups collaborated to create a new learning environment in which students work together to tackle compelling problems, such as measuring radon levels in their schools, designing solar houses, collecting weather data, and exploring mathematical chaos. Teachers feel that this environment allows students to realize that important problems are complex and may have more than one solution.

Earth Lab—The initial and primary goal of the Earth Lab project, directed by Denis Newman of Bolt, Beranek and Newman, Inc., was to create classroom environments in which students used collaborative workspaces to learn elementary earth science in much the same way as scientists do. All of the computers in the school were connected via a local area network (LAN) to a hard-disk drive, which allowed for central storage of data, text, and programs. A network interface such as this makes it very easy for individuals or groups to store and retrieve data that pertains to their projects. Students and teachers can be assigned to any number of independent or collaborative workspaces.

Although the most obvious effect of these computer-supported, global laboratories is that they open the boundaries of the classroom to global investigations. Newman's work shows that they are also affecting boundaries between classrooms and subject areas within the school. When teachers had access to the Earth Lab network, they created environments for teaching and learning that were decompartmentalized. Students in the network were more likely to carry their work from one context to another. They continued to work on assignments, both individually and cooperatively, even after class periods ended, on whatever computer they found available. Since their workspaces were always accessible from any computer, students had greater autonomy to choose when to continue work on their projects. As a result, the computer lab was increasingly used in a heterogeneous manner with groups of students from several classes working on different projects simultaneously.

Ironically, in opening up boundaries between the school and other parts of the globe, communication boundaries also appeared to shift between teachers and students in local schools. As part of the Earth Lab project, the electronic mail system was made available for both student and teacher use. Researchers found that students and teachers carried on individual conversations, something that rarely occurred in the regular classroom.

Supporting mathematical and scientific thinking

Computers, with their calculation, database, and graphic capabilities, support the work of practicing scientists and mathematicians. It is highly appropriate that they be used also to support student learning in these areas. Software specifically designed for this purpose is starting to gain acceptance in schools, as illustrated by the examples that follow.

Geometric supposer—Geometric supposer is a set of microcomputer software tools developed by Judah Schwartz and Michal Yerushalmy to teach high school geometry through a guided-inquiry approach. The Supposers allow the user to make geometric constructions of the sort created with a compass and straightedge. The software includes a facility to measure angles, areas, and line segments and to perform arithmetic operations on these numerical data. The software remembers a construction as a procedure and allows the user to repeat the construction on another geometric figure of the same sort. Students engage in inductive thinking and have a chance to reinvent definitions and theorems and to explore new and interesting and complex geometric ideas.

In a year-long research project on the implementation of a guided inquiry approach using *Geometric Supposer* in three Boston area suburbs during the 1985-86 school year, project staff assessed student learning and examined implementation issues. Interviews with a sample of "best" and "worst" students found that students had no technical difficulties with the software. However, nearly all students found the guided-inquiry approach more difficult than traditional, textbook mathematics and experienced some frustration. Many found conjecture-making difficult, and in general students voiced a need for direction and guidance. Some students became adept at stepping back to observe the teacher role and think about the kind of support that they needed.

The researchers found that in general students understood the power of the guided-inquiry approach and enjoyed learning that way, particularly when they were successful. They liked working with the computer, using the tools to make conjectures, and felt that they grasped the content more deeply as a result. At times, they had a real experience of discovery.

The research found that teachers using *Geometric Supposer* through a guided-inquiry approach need to strike a productive balance between providing thoughtful guidance and freedom for students to investigate their own ideas, falling neither into intellectual tyranny nor into abdication of responsibility. Teachers need to be "active learners in the classroom, modeling the activities of wondering, conjecturing, being mistaken or stymied, and proceeding without knowing whether they were on the right track".

Microcomputer-based laboratories—Microcomputer-based laboratories (MBLs) are tools teachers can bring into the classroom to expand the range of students learning in science. These tools can include a dozen sensors, a lab interface, and a low-cost microcomputer, allowing students to have measurement and computational power that can support projects where they do actual measurements.

Some point out that MBL is a realization of an earlier dream of science educators: a flexible instrument that speeds up computations related to force, light, pressure, temperature, heart rate, speed, etc. Equally important, the instrument leaves students the choice about what computations to use. Although the MBL equipment can facilitate open-ended exploration, the laboratory lessons used by teachers typically direct students to gather and analyze specific data as they perform particular experiments.

The MBL lessons are based on the belief that students today hold many of the misconceptions about heat and temperature once held by scientists. Simple instruction will not change deeply held misconceptions; rather, experiments need to stimulate students to fundamentally reorganize their understanding. This view echoes a constructionist perspective that students learn best through active engagement in their own studies in an environment that encourages them to construct and communicate their own knowledge and understandings.

Consistent with this perspective, some of the experiments that helped earlier scientists begin to question their concepts of thermal physics are incorporated into these materials, so that students can actively examine and reconstruct their own understanding.

Use of MBLs in schools with teachers and students indicates that real and accurate measurements motivate students, especially if student work mirrors scientific research. However, field testing has also revealed that teachers need to structure the environment to make learning efficient. Teachers have noted how important it is for students to communicate findings through class discussion, writing in lab guides, or informal student conversation in small groups.

Challenges for students using technology

Many adults have feared that students, especially so-called "at-risk students", would become frustrated by the technical demands of the kinds of technologies described above. Experience suggests to the contrary that learning the technical aspects of working with technology is not a major problem for most students. Students face several other kinds of challenges when they use technology to support them in active, inquiry learning, however. These include:

— understanding their responsibilities as active learners;

— getting help with individual learning needs; and

— integrating their technology-supported inquiry learning with their larger school experience.

Understanding their responsibilities as active learners

Authentic inquiry tasks provide exciting new challenges for students and can also require a host of advanced intellectual and social learning skills, involving new levels of independence. Some noted that for many of the students participating in the Software Evaluation Project and using *Point of View* to create multimedia presentations, working in cooperative groups was an innovation in its own right. The social studies teacher needed to help students develop productive working relationships, so that they could cooperatively research the topics and create a presentation to share with their classmates.

Teachers in that project and others we have discussed find that they need to explain to students explicitly that their responsibilities in these programs are different from the usual role of "listening, remembering, and repeating what the teacher told them". Developing their own questions is the reverse of the role that many students have honed anticipating answers to factual and narrowly focused teacher questions. Students' difficulties with conjecturing with *Geometric Supposer* were more acute when teachers did not provide clear models and facilitation, and they didn t grasp the kind of thinking they were to do.

More important, the kinds of inquiry learning teachers are trying to catalyze with *Voyage of the Mimi, Geometric Supposer*, and technology-supported inquiry learning in the *Make it happen*! program may challenge students fundamental view of what teaching and learning are all about. With these innovations, learning is no longer a process in which a teacher who knows all passes on knowledge and students passively take it in. Grasping how different her work with *Geometric Supposer* was from her other classes.

Some students need step-by-step guidance when becoming familiar with a new procedure for generating questions, gathering information, or carrying out a cooperative task; others, and most students over time, need a reminder of the "big picture". They need considerable discussion in the early stages of a new activity, less when their investigation is well under way.

Getting help with individual learning needs

Although the kinds of inquiry learning these programs foster is appropriate for all students, many students need special support to manage the social and intellectual challenges of posing and exploring their own questions and in sustaining attention and involvement in long-term projects. EDC's Problem Solving in Science project found that students with even mild learning problems may need considerable coaching in computer-based cooperative learning activities.

This issue was highlighted in observations of a fifth-grade class using *Voyage of the Mimi*, taught by a highly experienced science specialist who had introduced the program to many teachers in his district. EDC observers followed a bright boy, Max, who had a high interest in science but some learning difficulties, through the several-week unit. Max easily learned the navigation skills and software procedures but was unable to sustain the level of cooperation required by the course.

Rigidly critical of the ways members of his group used their navigation tools, Max disrupted their work and wandered in the room a good deal. More than once, he would seize a tool from another student's hands as he was plotting coordinates, with You can t do it that way! Despite good ideas and skills, he was gradually excluded from the cooperative activities by his exasperated peers.

In that same classroom, the research team followed another boy with learning difficulties. Aaron managed to mask his lack of understanding of basic navigation concepts with an amiable and attentive manner. However, he let the others in his group make most of the navigation decisions while he looked on.'When Aaron finally had to take a turn at the keyboard in a computer simulation requiring that students apply navigation skills to locating and saving a whale, the other students usually directed him through his confusion. In one competition, a girl in his group placed her fingers over his on the keyboard to help him select the correct commands, so that their group would not fall behind the others.

In a hands-on performance assessment by EDC staff at the end of the unit, Max showed that he knew the navigation games perfectly although the other students would no longer play with him. Aaron was totally unable to manage the computer procedures and did not know the underlying navigation concepts. Viewing videotapes of the performance assessments, the teacher was astonished at Max'ssocial difficulties and at Aaron'stotal lack of grasp of the navigation material. The challenges for the teacher were sobering, knowing what students are actually learning in this kind of complex learning environment and providing the different kinds of support required, particularly with several groups engaged in cooperative learning activities.

These cases and other research reports point up the subtle variation in the learning strengths and needs students bring to computer-supported inquiry learning. They point to the challenge for teachers of assessing students' learning in a complex, simulated learning environment. In all of these programs, there are multiple student learning outcomes at stake: acquiring new information, posing "researchable" questions, linking visual and print information, developing specialized computer skills for working with databases or computer games, cooperative abilities, reasoning and problem-solving abilities. Clearly, teachers need multiple assessment techniques and associated intervention strategies to meet varied student needs. Within the classroom, close monitoring of students learning can enable all students to benefit from reform-oriented learning activities. Beyond the classroom, particularly in middle and high schools that are in transition from traditional approaches to more inquiry-oriented approaches, students may need help in making sense of the differences in their experiences and their teachers' expectations across their learning settings.

Integrating technology-supported inquiry learning with the larger school experience

Many students' first experience with technology-supported inquiry learning is an isolated one—as part of a pilot project, a new program, or an individual teacher's experimentation. Until school reform makes this a more pervasive learning environment for students, they may experience a discrepancy between their inquiry learning experiences and the emphasis on factual memorization in other classrooms. When discrepancies in philosophy and approach across classrooms are made explicit, particularly at the middle and high school levels, students are more able to adapt to these discrepancies. Their resulting awareness of the ways they are learning can help them to generalize new inquiry skills to new, appropriate situations.

Technology supports teacher functions that are fundamental if teachers are to provide authentic, active learning experiences as envisioned by education reform goals. These functions include developing and tailoring instructional materials, conducting ongoing assessment of student learning, expanding teachers content and instructional knowledge, and communicating with parents.

In inquiry-based environments, students pursue different questions, work at different speeds, use a variety of materials, engage in different activities, and work in flexible groupings. Teachers are increasingly able to draw on technology resources to develop and tailor instructional materials to better meet individual student needs. Two different ways in which teachers can work with technology to provide appropriately tailored instruction are described below.

Creating technology-based instructional materials— Technology that enables teachers to invent their own materials can be immensely attractive. Teachers in the Saddleback Valley Unified School District in California participated in a hypermedia project whose original intent was to train them to incorporate existing hypermedia stacks into their curriculum.

Once the teachers recognized the limited availability of appropriate hypermedia stacks, however, they asked for training on how to write their own interactive stacks. By the end of the first year of the project, the teachers had received 36 hours of paid training and 4 days of release time. They were able to create 65 original hypermedia stacks along with corresponding lesson plans. This significant support for teacher training—30 percent of the project budget was an important factor in the teachers confidence and success with this new technology application.

During the second year of the project, each teacher developed another new hypermedia stack and lesson plan and served as the mentor for another teacher in using existing hypermedia lessons. Given support and time, many teachers would enjoy the challenge of developing their own curriculum materials. Not all teachers would welcome the activity, however, and certainly teachers and administrators want to avoid expending time and money to needlessly "reinvent the wheel". An alternative way of involving teachers in developing technology-based instructional materials is described below.

Modifying existing materials—When Judy Jones, a biology teacher in Chapel Hill, North Carolina, began using *Catlab*, a simulation of trait inheritance in cats, for her unit on heredity she found that the activity suggestions that accompanied the software were too open-ended for her students. Because she valued the software's simulation environment, she decided to keep using the software but to modify the procedures for her students, developing four levels of activities that would allow them to acquire the concepts and skills more gradually.

The first activity level began with a very structured simulation in which the students "mated" cats who differed in only one trait. The next two activity levels involved cats who differed in two and three traits. Jones also developed "hint cards" for students who were having difficulty. The final activity level involved looking at statistics on a variety of cat traits and determining how this inheritance pattern could have happened. These activities moved along a spectrum from very structured to open-ended, with the final activity requiring the most independent and creative problem solving.

Hearing of the teacher's invention, the author of the *Catlab* program obtained her permission to incorporate those activities in the software package. As a result, Judy Jones activities are now distributed with every copy of *Catlab*. Ideally, teachers and students would be involved in the development and field testing of educational software, but this is not always the case. Moreover, software that has been carefully tested and adapted to one group of students may not work well with students who are younger, have less background knowledge or less familiarity with computers, or have certain learning difficulties. Teachers would like to be able to adapt instructional materials to meet the needs of their particular students. Few teachers have programming skills, however, so the provision of tools to make it easy to extend and modify instructional software is very desirable. Although very feasible technically, this kind of capability is rarely built into commercial materials.

The discussion of individual student learning needs above points up the need for ongoing teacher assessment of students inquiry learning process. Technology can support the assessment of student work in ways that are useful for guiding instruction. Specifically, technology facilitates (1) obtaining a trace of student thinking processes, (2) collecting real-time feedback from multiple students, (3) storing and retrieving student work and associated comments, and (4) setting individual goals and managing instruction.

Create trace of student learning processes—Collins, Hawkins, and Frederiksen assert that appropriate technologies have a strong role to play in tracking the process of learning and thinking by

— Recording how students learn with feedback in novel situations.

— Recording students thinking and strategic processes by tracing the process by which students maneuver through a problem or task.

— Recording students abilities to deal with realistic situations.

Earlier technology (the *Mimi* is an example) did not have built-in ways to monitor or track students progress, making it difficult for teachers to follow the actual learning process, especially for students with learning difficulties. To assess student learning of navigation skills for the *Mimi* cases, Education Development Corporation designed a hands-on "performance assessment"—placing students individually at the computer with a researcher who took on the role of clinical interviewer as the student played the navigation game individually that is usually played collaboratively with other students.

This approach is one model for teacher assessment of individual student learning in a computer-based environment.

An alternative approach is made possible by recent *HyperCard* environments that have the capability to gather a "dribble file" of all of the students' activity in the environment. This file can be placed in a student's portfolio along with the student's visual and writing products. The teacher can examine the file in order to discern the blind alleys, alternative designs, and way of proceeding that characterized the student's efforts. Thus, more powerful technologies provide the capability of obtaining a "trace" of each student's thinking as he or she tackles problems.

In addition to supporting post hoc analyses of student performance, the increased visibility of work on a computer screen, as opposed to the more private nature of paper-and-pencil work, increases the likelihood that teachers will engage in informal, ongoing assessment as students are working. As the teacher circulates in the computer lab or in the classroom, it is easy to stop, observe, and intervene while the student is working on an assignment or project. Hawkins and Sheingold found that teachers noticed more about the way their students were learning as they circulated among students working at computers.

Video technologies provide another means for recording and tracking student learning processes. For example, teachers at Skyline Elementary, a Model Technology School in California, have used video equipment as a tool for observing and analyzing the strategies used by young children engaged in mathematical problem solving with manipulatives. While videocameras lack the diagnostic and summarizing capabilities of intelligent computer systems, they provide a rich source of data for examining learning processes in action.

Provide contexts for authentic assessment—Technology can be used to present authentic tasks in a standardized manner, thus providing a context for assessing advanced skills. An ongoing SRI project, for example, is using videotaped problem contexts as a vehicle for assessing students' understanding of mathematical problem solving. Each video episode in this *Becoming a Problem Solver* series presents two child actors engaged in an extended effort to solve an interesting, real-life problem. Accompanying the episodes are paper-and-pencil instruments and open-ended questions to help teachers get at students beliefs about problems. The teacher's guide provides similar problems for classroom use and suggestions for classroom discussions regarding the strengths and weaknesses of the problem-solving approaches illustrated in the videos.

Real-time feedback from multiple students—A well-known problem in many conventional classrooms is the mismatch between the level of presentation and the understanding of many students. As teachers describe concepts and procedures, they depend on student feedback to indicate any comprehension problems. Unfortunately, the students who understand the material best are most likely to contribute to class discussion. Students who don't understand simply remain silent, and the instructor continues with an explanation that some students find incomprehensible.

Technology can help ameliorate this problem by providing an instructor with real-time feedback from all the students in a class. At the Saturn School in Minneapolis, teachers use an application for networked computers called the *Discourse System* to facilitate interactive group-based instruction. All the computers in a room are networked to the teacher's computer so that a teacher or a student can present information to the class and then request a response from each student.

Every student's response appears in small text windows on the presenter's screen. By using the *Discourse System*, the teacher or presenter can get frequent feedback from all students at one time, as opposed to calling on one student at a time. As a result, the teacher can adjust his or her instruction on the basis of students responses and can see which students are having difficulty.

Store and retrieve student work and associated comments—The issue of assessing and meeting individual student needs in a simulated environment, where students are constructing knowledge over time through a variety of experiences, was a critical one in the immigration project described earlier. In a revised version of *Immigrant* 1850, researchers included an extensive chapter on how to assess student writing by providing guidelines for assessment along with samples of student work to exemplify those guidelines. Some teachers, particularly language arts teachers, found these to be extremely helpful, while others found them cumbersome. After further analysis, the research and development team determined that the development of separate assessments of writing, speaking, and drawing was counterproductive and that what was needed was a way to evaluate the student's whole learning experience This has led to their developing guidelines for developing and assessing portfolios, which are collections of student work produced over a period of time. Portfolios include drafts and plans, as well as final products, commentary, and reflection.

Until recently, no technology provided a comprehensive system for inputting, storing, retrieving, analyzing, and representing performance data. There has been a dearth of support for the teacher to create a systematic database on children's progress over time. In the area of writing, for example, where multiple thinking, language, and composing abilities are developing over time, teachers spend large amounts of time reviewing and commenting on student compositions, but these comments are generally lost from the system once the student has taken them home.

The teacher has had no way of storing a history of changing comments on the student's work, or of easily rounding up pointed examples of writing strengths and problems to use for teaching material in the classroom. Technology currently under development at Education Development Center by Midian Kurland will substantially enhance the teacher's ability to respond to, store, retrieve, assess, and manipulate student work. This tool, *TextBrowser*, provides an electronic analogue to teachers traditional methods for keeping track of assignments, marking student papers, providing feedback, and recording and monitoring student performance, but uses the power of the technology to vastly increase the extent and flexibility with which the teacher can accomplish those tasks. *TextBrowser* enables teachers to access anything a student writes on a computer, review the text, and mark and comment on the text.

The tool maintains a database archive of every text linked with the teacher's annotations and comments, so that portfolios of student work can be created and analyzed. Comments and annotations are automatically entered into an electronic grade book. The teacher can use the stored information to further analyze student work or create tables, graphs, or summaries of patterns and trends for each student. For example, the teacher could access all examples of a student's work that were marked "needs reorganization". In addition, the teacher can create custom writing exercises from the student's own work. *TextBrowser* can extract text units that meet specified criteria, such as a list of all words the student misspelled during the past week.

This tool supports and enhances the teacher's ability to use electronic writing tools in the classroom, giving the teacher the capability to store and manipulate an assignment so that it can be systematically reviewed, compared against previous work, or used for custom-designed writing exercises. Although *TextBrowser* originated as a system for writing assessment, it can be adapted to assessment in any content area.

The critical issues in the effective use of this tool are teacher knowledge about the process approach to teaching writing, children's development of writing abilities, and the particular abilities and needs of individual children. Presumably, comparable requirements will hold as the tool is extended into other content areas.

Set goals and manage instruction —Teaching involves a great deal of management of student instructional goals and performance records, especially when instruction is individualized. One of the biggest draws for integrated learning systems has been their inclusion of software to automate this process. Each student's learning objectives, units attempted and completed, and performance on end-of-module assessments are recorded. Many systems are able to generate reports of both individual and whole- class performance. It is possible to obtain these same instructional management features apart from an integrated learning system for instructional delivery.

Technology is supporting a particularly sophisticated system for instructional management at the Saturn School. Teachers are using technology to respond to, store, and manipulate complex student performance data. Each student has a Personal Growth Plan (PGP), consisting of goals negotiated with staff and parents but written in the student's own words. This plan is stored on both teacher- and student-accessible networks, where students and teachers can set goals and track student accomplishments.

The student or teacher can query the system for learning activities relevant to a particular goal. The system uses a keyword search strategy coupled with a data bank to provide this information. Students can insert changes and revise their goals, and the system supports reflection on their growth and development relative to their goals. Each student in the school has a portfolio of proficiencies, which is compiled throughout the student's years in the school. There are pop-up windows for teacher comments and notes regarding the student's activities and goals. The student's portfolio includes both hard copy and items that are stored electronically on the network, including text files, *HyperCard stacks*, and videos. As a result, both students and teachers are able to easily retrieve and review work from the current or previous year. Taken altogether, the various components of the system developed and used at Saturn school provide an interesting example of how technology can support a comprehensive, integrated approach to instructional management. A key feature of the system is the opportunity it provides for students to take an active role in managing and negotiating their own learning experiences.

Share and expand teacher knowledge

Telecommunication systems are helping teachers break out of their traditional isolation to connect with colleagues and professionals in distant locations. These interactions can help teachers develop a clearer image of effective teaching and learning environments, understand how technology enables them to create these environments, learn about effective instructional strategies, share information about students, and gain emotional support for change. Telecommunications enables the teacher to be in frequent communication with people outside of the classroom with no disruption of class activities. The teacher is not interrupted by a phone call; rather, the message waits until the teacher is ready to receive it. Participation in a telecommunications network can help a teacher develop new instructional strategies that promote inquiry learning.

Interaction with colleagues—One of the most frustrating features of the teacher's job is the paucity of opportunities to interact with colleagues in working on the central problems of curriculum and instruction. The opportunity for teachers to work cooperatively with other teachers is considered a crucial program ingredient in the AT&T Learning Network described previously. If teachers are engaged in cooperation and collaboration with their professional peers, it will be more natural for them to provide the same sort of environment for their students. Beyond providing an avenue for communication about cooperative projects, the AT&T Learning Network provides a forum for this more in- depth and reflective communication between professionals.

The learning circle projects have provided teachers with an opening through which they can communicate with each other. Some found that teachers who were part of the AT&T learning circles asked each other for suggestions and advice and thus gained new ideas about classroom organization and teaching practices. They also learned from one another by reading descriptions of events taking place in other classrooms. As teachers share descriptions of things happening in their own classrooms, other teachers may adopt some of those ideas.

The way in which technology can support this collegial process is illustrated by the extended electronic conversation conducted among teachers in one learning circle in response to a teacher's query about portfolio assessment. When the teachers participating in the AT&T Learning Network were asked about the benefits of educational electronic networking, most rated *their own learning*, not the learning of their students, as the most important benefit of the program. The network changed and improved the working conditions for teachers, enabling them to communicate and share ideas with other professionals. Research on the AT&T Learning Network suggests that participation in the learning circles increased teachers self-esteem as well as their knowledge. Network interaction can open a small window on classroom activities so that teachers receive recognition and praise from their peers.

Transcripts from the network show how teachers who were already using portfolio assessment received special praise and recognition from other teachers who were struggling to begin what seemed like an overwhelming task. When teachers select projects for the Learning Network, they are often showcasing some of their best lessons and receive much positive feedback from their circle partners. There is also a recognition among teachers that skilled performances by students usually mark skilled performances by their teachers, and the teachers receive a great deal of positive feedback in that respect. Also, when teachers see their ideas being adapted or evolving in other classrooms in distant locations, it is extremely exciting and rewarding. All of these opportunities for feedback and praise from peers in distant locations increase teachers excitement about the learning project. And when teachers get excited about learning, their students share their teachers enthusiasm and the quality of the students work increases.

Access to subject matter experts—In addition to providing links to colleagues, technology can give teachers access to experts in the subject matter they are trying to teach. Even the best-prepared teacher cannot know everything in a given field, and knowledge about new developments is by definition vested in just a few individuals. With technology comes the power to have increasing access to subject matter experts, giving teachers the opportunity to strengthen their knowledge of the content areas they teach. An example of this trend is the Urban Math Collaborative (UMC), which links teachers and university mathematicians in order to deepen teachers knowledge of mathematics and to help them respond to emerging new standards in the mathematics education community. Discussions on the electronic network of the UMC have deepened teachers content knowledge and have also touched on teaching issues that do not get dealt with as openly and meaningfully in other forums. Discussions are often more in-depth and reflective, since comments and opinions that are shared on the network are addressed to a potentially wide audience and tend to be more carefully thought through than those offered in more casual, face-to- face settings.

Support communication with parents

Voice Link services, provided to over two dozen Connecticut towns by the Southern New England Telecommunications Corporation, allow teachers to inform parents about homework, report cards, and field trips. Something as simple as having a telephone in the classroom can free the teacher from security concerns and can be a readily available channel between teachers and parents. Voicemail to update parents on material covered in class and on homework and voice bulletin boards to post school activities can keep students, parents, and the community informed about the activities of the school.

Using current telephone technologies, several communities have already established "Homework Hotline" or "Dial a Teacher" programs. Such programs have only begun to explore the ways in which technology could help parents become more involved in their students' learning, however. Parents could use this information as a starting point for engaging their children in related learning activities. They would also have a medium for ongoing discussions of their children's progress and learning needs.

When teachers use technology as a critical part of an inquiry-oriented learning-teaching process, they face a set of challenges, including :

— Learning how to use a variety of technology applications;

— Using, adapting, and designing technology-enhanced curricula to meet students needs;

— Expanding content knowledge;

— Taking on new roles; and

— Responding to individual students.

None of these challenges stand alone; they are tightly interrelated. We discuss each challenge below.

Learning how to use a variety of technology options

When we think of teachers learning to use a variety of technology applications, we tend to focus primarily on their need to learn how to operate hardware and software. Although this is a critical component, teachers also need to develop a method of keeping abreast of new technologies and finding out about the potential power each technology application has with respect to inquiry-based teaching and learning. Each new application brings new benefits and new problems to be solved. For example, although electronic networks are opening the classroom to new learning for both teachers and students, this medium brings new challenges for teachers. Some found that it is very difficult for teachers to sustain regular, substantive discussions on a network. The discontinuity in conversation can be a big disadvantage because if some questions go unanswered, a request is ignored, or interesting lines of discussion are not pursued, the conversation may falter and users may drop out. Riel has found that the use of bulletin boards is very time-consuming and that it is sometimes inefficient for teachers to negotiate their way through these bulletin boards in search of applicable and appropriate ideas or conversations.

In response to this problem, one junior high school in Maine hired a part- time computer network coordinator who monitors 11 different conferences on the PSINET network. The coordinator prints out the mail, reads through it, and sends copies to the teachers or administrators in the district for whom the information is useful. Occasionally, teachers will request particular information, and the network coordinator will send that request to the appropriate conference on the network. As teachers become more knowledgeable about the technology applications that are available, they need to develop criteria for selecting the applications that would be most valuable and effective, given the context of their class and student needs. They also need information that allows them to make wise decisions about allocating resources among students and managing instruction within the classroom. These decisions are closely tied to curriculum issues.

Using, adapting and designing technology-enhanced curricula

When teachers integrate technology applications into the curriculum, they knowingly or unknowingly are curriculum developers. In one model, teachers may find a particularly exciting technology application to integrate into existing instruction (e.g., *Catlab*). Room is made within the curriculum to accommodate this application. In another model, the teacher accesses a complete and comprehensive multimedia curriculum (e.g., *Voyage of the Mimi*). From the rich array of available resources, the teacher must select and sequence those she or he wants to use. In a third model, teachers construct a curriculum unit around a theme or topic, using a variety of technology applications. Regardless of how extensively technology is used or how state of the art the technology applications being used might be (word processing, laser disc, CD-ROM), any technology integration requires that teachers engage in rethinking, reshifting, and reshaping their curriculum.

Taking on new roles

Although teacher-designed inquiry environments can have enormous motivating power for students, they require advanced skills—in curriculum and instruction, in team building and interdisciplinary curriculum design, as well as in technology—on the part of the teacher. Field-test results of *MAKE IT HAPPEN!* reveal that teachers need to know a good deal about the I-Search process to design and implement these units. Morocco compared the case studies of the New Hampshire and Massachusetts design teams in the *MAKE IT HAPPEN!* field test to describe the importance of having a facilitator who acts as coach to a new teacher design team as they learn new curriculum design and teaching roles.

These computer-supported inquiry programs also require advanced teacher skills in integrating technology into inquiry learning. Beyond "procedural knowledge" of the software, teachers need "conditional knowledge" of the contexts and situations in which the tools are appropriate and the ability to recognize those situations as they arise. When students are beginning to generate related ideas for their topic, for example, the teacher needs to recognize *at that moment* the contribution a software mapping tool like *Inspiration* might make to students organizing of ideas.

Teachers using *Geometric Supposer* not only need to learn how to use the software but also must be able to apply it to a variety of teaching learning situations. When teachers use and develop inquiry-based curricula that integrate technology, their role in the classroom becomes more that of a coach or facilitator of student learning. In inquiry-based learning, teachers set the context, help students pose questions to explore, stimulate problem solving, and give students tools and resources to use so that they—the students—can construct knowledge.

The knowledge construction process takes place within an individual student: it is highly individualistic because of the knowledge maker's prior knowledge, experience, skills, and talent. Knowledge making can follow routes unanticipated by the teacher. For teachers and students to follow these new routes, a curriculum needs to be flexible.

Teachers cannot and should not expect to—have a total grasp of the content related to every topic. What they do need to know is how to help guide students through the meaning-making process: how to ask probing questions, how to connect students to relevant resources, how to organize students into cooperative learning groups, and how to give them tools to store, manipulate, and analyze information.

Although teachers may see the desirability of this type of teaching role, they often feel vulnerable as they take the risk of shifting from a more comfortable knowledge transmission mode of teaching to inquiry-based teaching. One reason for this discomfort is their appreciation of the difficulty of managing meaning- making across a class and within individuals.

Many technology applications (e.g., *TextBrowser*, word processing, databases) offer teachers a window into the student's thinking, inquiry, and problem-solving processes. When the work students are doing is visible on a monitor or printout, teachers have access to students misconceptions, the ways in which they sort and categorize information, the relationships they form among ideas, and the conjectures they make. In a teacher's view, a student's response may not be the most logical, appropriate, or even "correct" response.

However, trial and error is part of problem solving. Teachers are often tempted to intervene too early or too often, being motivated by their genuine desire to set a student "on the right track" and to avoid floundering. This tendency can be exacerbated by the public character of the computer monitor, which makes the students' work more visible and accessible to intervention by the teacher at all stages compared with the more private medium of paper and pencil.

Intervention in students' work at an early stage can be helpful, but it also can thwart students, short-circuiting their own construction of knowledge. Michael Hopkins, the lead teacher at the Saturn School, has had students use technology, such as *HyperCard* presentations, *LEGO Logo* projects, and other multimedia programs to produce projects.

Teachers need to know a great deal about cognitive processes and processing in general and the learning styles and strengths of individual students in particular. When students work collaboratively on a technology-based assignment, teachers face a thorny issue. In the Earth Lab project, for example, teachers can review both individual and group workspaces. Although teachers need to assess group performance on a project, they also need to tease out evidence of individual performance to help students who may become lost in the dynamics of a group situation.

ASSISTIVE TECHNOLOGY FOR STUDENTS WITH MILD DISABILITIES

Technology has become ubiquitous as a tool for teachers and students. P.L. 100-407, The Technology-Related Assistance for Individuals with Disabilities Act of 1988 (Tech Act) was designed to enhance the availability and quality of assistive technology (AT) devices and services to all individuals and their families throughout the United States. Public Law 105-17, the Individuals with Disabilities Education Act (IDEA), uses the same definitions for assistive technology as the Tech Act and mandates that assistive technology be considered in developing Individualized Education Programs (IEPs) for students with disabilities. IDEA also emphasizes access to the general education curriculum for all students with disabilities.

The Tech Act and the IDEA define an AT device as any item, piece of equipment, or product system that is used to increase, maintain, or improve the functional capabilities of a child with a disability. AT devices may be categorized as no technology, low technology, or high technology.

"No-technology" or "no-tech" refers to any assistive device that is not electronic. No-tech items range from a piece of foam glued onto the corners of book pages to make turning easier to a study carrel to reduce distraction. "Low-technology" or "low-tech" devices are electronic but do not include highly sophisticated computer components, such as an electronic voice-recording device or a "talking watch". "High-technology" or "high-tech" devices utilize complex, multifunction technology and usually include a computer and associated software. Lahm and Morissette identified areas of instruction in which AT can assist students. Six of these are described here: (1) organization, (2) note taking, (3) writing, (4) academic productivity, (5) access to reference and general educational materials, and (6) cognitive assistance.

Organisation: Low-tech solutions include teaching students to organize their thoughts or work using flow-charting, task analysis, webbing, and outlining. These strategies can also be accomplished using high-tech, graphic, software-based organizers to assist students in developing and structuring ideas. Such graphic organizers allow students to manipulate and reconfigure brainstormed ideas and color code and group those ideas in ways that visually represent their thoughts. Another high-tech solution might be the outline function of word processing software, which lets students set out major ideas or topics and then add subcategories of information. Using the Internet, local area networks, or LCD projection systems enables students and their teachers to collaborate, give feedback, and modify these applications either as a group or individually at different times.

Note taking: A simple, no-tech approach to note taking is for the teacher to provide copies of structured outlines in which students fill in information. Low- and high-tech methods include:

— Videotaping class sessions for visual learners or those who are unable to attend class for extended periods of time.

— Sending web-cam photography across the Internet to allow students to see and hear what is happening in class.

— Sending class notes or presentations to students via e-mail.

— Translating print-based notes to voice by using optical character recognition (OCR) software with a voice synthesizer.

— Using notebook computers, personal digital assistants (PDAs), or portable word processing keyboards to help students with the mechanics of note taking.

Writing: Word processing may be the most important application of assistive technology for students with mild disabilities. Writing barriers for students with mild disabilities include:

— *Mechanics:* spelling, grammar, and punctuation errors.

— *Process:* generating ideas, organizing, drafting, editing, revising, and producing a neat, clear final copy.

— *Motivation:* interest in writing.

Grammar and spell-checkers, dictionaries, and thesaurus programs assist in the mechanics of writing. Macros are available that will insert an entire phrase with the touch of a single key. Word prediction software helps students recall or spell words. During the writing process, word processors allow teachers to make suggestions on the student's disk. If computers are networked, students can read each other's work and make recommendations for revision. Computer editing also reduces or eliminates problems such as multiple erasures, torn papers, and poor handwriting. The final copy is neat and legible.

Motivation is often increased through the desktop publishing and multimedia capabilities of computers. A variety of fonts and styles allow students to customize their writing and highlight important features. Graphic images, drawings, video, and audio can provide interest or highlight ideas.

Multimedia gives the student the means and the motivation to generate new and more complex ideas. For early writers, there are programs that allow students to write with pictures or symbols as well as text. In some of these programs, the student selects a series of pictures to represent an idea, then the pictures are transformed to words that can be read by a synthesizer and then edited.

Academic productivity: Tools that assist productivity can be hardware-based, software-based, or both. Calculators, for example, can be separate, multifunction devices or part of a computer's software. Spreadsheets, databases, and graphics software enhance productivity in calculating, categorizing, grouping, and predicting events. The Internet, computers, and PDAs can also aid productivity in note taking, obtaining assignments, accessing reference material and help from experts, and communicating with peers. Instead of relying on the telephone, students are increasingly sharing documents, using instant messaging, and transferring documents to each other as e-mail attachments.

Access to reference and general educational materials: Access to the general education curriculum is emphasized by IDEA and includes the ability to obtain materials as well as the ability to understand and use them. Many students with mild disabilities have difficulty gathering and synthesizing information for their academic work. In this arena, Internet communications, multimedia, and universal design are providing new learning tools. Internet communications can transport students beyond their physical environments, allowing them to interact with people far away and engage in interactive learning experiences. This is particularly appropriate for individuals who are easily distracted when going to new and busy environments such as the library, who are poorly motivated, or who have difficulty with reading or writing.

Students can establish "CompuPals" via e-mail or instant messaging with other students, which often motivates them to generate more text and thus gain more experience in writing. Students can also access electronic multimedia encyclopedias, library references, and online publications. However, these experiences should be structured, because it is easy to get distracted or lost as opportunities are explored.

Multimedia tools are another way in which information can be made accessible to students. Multimedia use of text, speech, graphics, pictures, audio, and video in reference- based software is especially effective in meeting the heterogeneous learning needs of students with mild disabilities. While a picture can be worth a thousand words to one student, audio or text-based descriptive video or graphic supports may help another student focus on the most important features of the materials.

Used in conjunction with assistive technology, e-books can use the power of multimedia to motivate students to read. They include high-interest stories: the computer reads each page of the story aloud, highlighting the words as they are read. Fonts and colors can be changed to reduce distraction. Additional clicks of the mouse result in pronunciation of syllables and a definition of the word. When the student clicks on a picture, a label appears. A verbal pronunciation of the label is offered when the student clicks the mouse again. Word definitions can be added by electronic dictionaries and thesaurus. These books are available in multiple languages, including English and Spanish, so students can read in their native language while being exposed to a second language.

The Center for Applied Special Technology (CAST) promotes the concept of universal design, which asserts that alternatives integrated in the general curriculum can provide access to all students, including a range of backgrounds, learning styles, or abilities. Providing material in digital form, which can easily be translated, modified, or presented in different ways, can often attain the goal of universal design.

Cognitive Assistance: A vast array of application program software is available for instructing students through tutorials, drill and practice, problem solving, and simulations. Many of the assistive technologies described previously can be combined with instructional programs to develop and improve cognitive, reading, and problem-solving skills. Prompting and scheduling through PDAs, pagers, and Internet software also can assist students in remembering assignments or important tasks. They can help students to follow directions or a sequence of events, establish to-do lists, take and retrieve notes, check spelling or look up words in a dictionary.

Special educators are familiar with the need to create or customize instructional materials to meet the varied needs of students with disabilities. Today, assistive technology can be more specifically targeted to address an individual's needs through the emergent power and flexibility of electronic tools and the ways in which they are combined and used. These innovations affect teaching and learning as well as individual capabilities. For students with mild disabilities, assistive technology can help to balance weak areas of learning with strong areas.

4

INFORMATION AND COMMUNICATION TECHNOLOGIES

Communications technologies have the potential to transform the educational process. They also have the power to change the roles of faculty in community colleges, even to the point of reducing the number and status of teachers. Although the transformation is not occurring overnight, the likelihood of it strikes fear in the hearts of some faculty. On the other hand, some faculty approach communications technologies openly, expectantly and impatiently, wishing that progress in the direction of their ideals for improving education could occur more rapidly. In addition, many faculty see in communications technologies an opportunity for greater role differentiation and specialization.

Some teachers might become actively involved as instructional designers while others might develop specializations in assessment, small group facilitation, computer programming, media development, cross-cultural education, or distance learning. Since new technologies have the potential for spreading learning more pervasively throughout our culture, there is the likely possibility of a greater need for faculty as educational specialists.

TEACHER-LEARNER RELATIONSHIPS

The introduction of new technologies into the teaching and learning process initiates a change in power relationships. These technologies give students more control over their own learning. In fact, some technologies give students total control over their learning. For example, a freshman level mathematics course on an interactive videodisc can present the material to be learned, drill and test the student, record responses, and compute the grade without the assistance of a teacher. Such a course can be made available to students without an instructor's supervision in learning resource centers, public libraries, or the learner's own home.

Thus, technologies have the potential of upsetting traditional power relationships in the learning process, a process in which teachers have traditionally held authority and control. On the other hand, the technologies have the potential for freeing faculty from many roles that they often describe as dreary or unprofessional, such as drill, repetition, and other learning situations that require systematic responses. Moreover, computers already play a variety of roles in recordkeeping, and thus aid faculty in course management.

Communications technologies in education allow for much greater individualization of learning. Students are able to progress at their own speed: to start learning when they are motivated and stop when they are saturated. Since community college faculty have long sought to individualize instruction, communications technologies are a real asset toward that objective. Moreover, these technologies allow the instructor to individualize instruction without having to make individual prescriptions for each student in each class during each term. Material presented on well-designed software which is branching rather than linear can free the instructor of repetitious analysis and prescription and produce opportunities for more creative tasks. Such tasks could include assisting students as they are following their learning prescriptions, defining and measuring the outcomes of education, or structuring learning environments. Should teachers fear communications technologies in education? The answer may be "Yes" for some, but it should be "No" for most community college faculty.

Because computers more than other communications technologies are being incorporated into education, and because they are often being used for drill, practice and providing information, some teachers express concern that computer-based education stresses the functions of the left brain: the rote response. This is true in the drill and practice functions. However, those functions are being used less and less as educators realize the potential of computers for innovation in education.

Used with applications programs such as spreadsheets, data bases, and word processing, the computer can create realistic models and involve students in real-world computer applications. With this focus on applications programs, computer technologies are being used to support learning across the curriculum rather than confining it to data processing and engineering technology. Students throughout the college are using the computer as a tool to analyze data, draft and revise sketches or reports, and perform laboratory experiments. With this potential for enhancing student learning, faculty should feel less threatened by the computer in education.

The development of communications technologies and their application to learning has brought about the diffusion of higher education's monopoly on formal learning beyond high school. Long ago, a learner had to enroll in a course in order to learn how to write better business letters, compute more accurately, or read more rapidly. Now, however, with individualized instruction available in colleges, in public libraries, and in video outlets, the learning environment is changing. Nudging that change is the development of many forms of distance learning, including electronic universities. All of these allow students to learn within the settings of their own choosing and to acquire credentials for their achievements, if they so desire. The outcome for formal postsecondary education could seriously constrict on current providers. On the other hand, community colleges, and other components of the formal learning system, can benefit because, as research has repeatedly shown, the more education people have, the more likely they are to participate in further education.

Faculty may feel less threatened by technologies once they see their potential for furthering professional development. If colleges are going to expect productivity gains as a result of the incorporation of communications technologies into the learning process, administrators and policy makers must help faculty develop new skills. It is important for administrators and faculty to remember that the biggest expense involved in incorporating new technologies into any process is the expense for staff training. It is not uncommon for 75 percent of the cost of such a conversion, if it is successful, to be related to staff development. People who are trained merely to apply a new technology to their specific jobs do not learn enough about it to go beyond the current application. And it is in the potential for future applications that productivity gains can be the highest.

Thus if faculty and communications technologies are to become true partners in community college learning endeavors, administrators and policy makers must be fully committed to staff development. This means planning and allocating adequate resources for courseware development and review, plus the development of the new skills required to incorporate the technologies into the course and to transform the learning environment into one in which technology enhances learning. Leadership is required to change faculty from conveyors of information to directors of learning environments or to any of the specialized functions.

To the question, "Should faculty fear the use of communications technologies in education?" the answer is most likely "no" when faculty see technology's potential for stimulating the focus on essentials: What should students learn? How can learning be assessed? What must the curriculum contain? These are the questions central to education. The process of incorporating technology into education should encourage teachers to ask these questions again and again. Technologies offer opportunities for new strategies to implement the answers. Technologies, however, will not take the place of professionals asking the critical questions, nor will anything developed for technologies be really successful unless core questions are confronted first. Perhaps technology's primary gift to community college faculty is the demand that faculty look again at the essentials of teaching and learning.

EDUCATIONAL SOFTWARE PACKAGES

Thousands of packages of educational software, or courseware, exist on today's market, and the number is growing steadily. Unfortunately, a large percentage of the packages produced are found to be of poor quality in terms of instructional and/or technical design. Since a microcomputer in the classroom is only as effective as the software used with it, it is wise to investigate courseware thoroughly before purchasing it.

Once the need for educational software has been clarified, a list of potential software packages should be compiled. There are a variety of resources that will help educators sift through the great number of available titles. These include education journals, producer catalogs, indexes, databases, and guidebooks which make titles accessible by subject matter, grade level, hardware requirements, reviewers' score, and other criteria. In addition, software can often be seen in use at conference exhibits and at educators' resource centers. Word-of-mouth information supplied by colleagues having experience with specific courseware titles can also be valuable.

Regardless of one's source of information, there are two important points to remember regarding software evaluation: (1) to date, very little empirical research exists that identifies specific factors making educational software effective or not effective, and (2) what is judged to be effective in one situation may not be as useful when used in a different place, with different students, or in a different manner.

Therefore, a computer-using educator must not rely solely on existing reviews, but develop a set of criteria by which to evaluate software according to his or her own setting and goals. The best evaluative information comes from a firsthand examination of the software under consideration. Many software dealers have established 30-day preview policies. While others are reluctant to loan software, some educators are able to obtain preview copies by writing on school letterhead, explaining that the school policy requires software to be previewed before purchase, and guaranteeing that no duplicate will be made. When software cannot be obtained either way, it may be possible to borrow it from a library or to examine it at a nearby school where it is in use.

Alternate sources for preview copies include software preview centers, sometimes located at universities or affiliated with state departments of education. One such center is the Technology Center for Demonstration and Training of the Northwest Regional Educational Laboratory (NWREL). Educators trying to locate preview centers should call their state department of education.

EVALUATE

Once preview copies of software have been obtained, educators should thoroughly test them to assess the quality of their content and instructional and technical design. If possible, software that has passed its preliminary screening should be evaluated by the students for whom it is intended. Student previews often generate important information that affects purchasing decisions. Many organizations have published their own evaluation criteria; the following list is based on the standard evaluation form for the NWREL MicroSIFT Project.

Characteristics of good courseware

— content is accurate

— content has educational value

— content is free of racial, ethnic, and sex stereotypes

Instructional characteristics

— purpose of package is well-defined

— package achieves its defined purpose

— presentation of content is clear and logical

— level of difficulty is appropriate for target audience

— graphics/color/sound are used for appropriate instructional reasons

— use of the package is motivational

— package effectively stimulates student creativity

— feedback on student responses is effectively employed

— learner controls the rate and sequence of presentation and review

— instruction is integrated with previous student experience

— learning is generalizable to an appropriate range of situations

Technical characteristics

— user support materials are comprehensive and effective

— information displays are effective

— students can easily and independently operate the program

— teachers can easily employ the package

— program provides accounting features that allow teachers to track student progress

— program appropriately uses relevant computer capabilities

— program is reliable in normal use

EVALUATING TECHNOLOGY-BASED CURRICULUM MATERIALS

Technology alone will not improve the quality of education, but when integrated with curriculum and instruction, it can be a powerful educational tool. Technology that is fitted to curriculum and instruction can stimulate the development of higher-order thinking and problem-solving skills, and it can support collaborative, globalized learning.

A key concept in evaluating technology-based curriculum materials is authenticity. Is the technology used to bring real-world examples into the classroom? Do such examples enhance conceptual understanding of complex, naturally occurring phenomena by integrating technology and subject matter? Are activities such as simulations, Web experiments, and Web field trips used to enable students to understand the richness and variability of real life? Particularly with young learners, technology should help students learn "by doing, interacting, and exploring, rather than watching and/or listening".

To promote authenticity, learning assessment tools should pull students in desirable directions. Student products take the forms of portfolios, WebQuests, and reports to classmates. Proponents of these methods argue that they mirror what is expected of employees in the work world. When evaluation attends not only to what students must know but also what they must be able to do, assessments themselves can function as instructional devices.

Constructivism

Given the emphasis on authenticity, it is not surprising that the language of constructivism permeates the technology literature. Writers characterize technology as a tool that can help teachers and students become co-learners who collaboratively construct knowledge. Technology use that results in student engagement is characterized as successful. Engaged learners are: responsible for their own learning, energized by learning, strategic, and collaborative.

Comer and Geissler offer a framework for evaluating curriculum materials. They suggest that curriculum evaluators prepare their own assessment criteria tailored to the instructional context in which the curriculum materials will be used. Defining the instructional context requires evaluators to determine: (a) who the learners are; (b) who the instructor is and what constitutes the learning environment, of which the instructor is a part; and (c) the nature of the technical limitations. Once evaluators establish this context, they can begin to evaluate the following aspects of the curriculum materials: content, required technology and instructional tools, learning assessment, and teacher support, keeping in mind the need for authenticity.

"One of the most important distinctions in evaluating digital content is whether a product emphasizes open-ended exploration or drill-and-practice. Many experts, particularly those who support a constructivist approach to teaching, strongly prefer the former". When integrated effectively into the curriculum by skilled teachers, digital content enables students to seek and manipulate digital information in collaborative, creative, and engaging ways, all of which foster learning. For example, the JASON Project enables teachers and their students to participate in a year-round scientific expedition meant to encourage engagement—even excitement—about one or more of the earth's dynamic systems.

Students share data and are able to chat with scientists about their own experiments. On the Monterey Bay expedition, students did experiments in their own classrooms on the feeding of abalone and sea urchins. In another example, the Virginia Center for Digital History enables students to examine newspapers, letters, diaries, and maps of the historical period the students are studying. The Valley of the Shadow project, a story of two cities' histories during the Civil War, allows students to explore the lives of the families of soldiers and to reconstruct true-life stories.

Effective content focuses on information literacy skills to assist students in gathering, interpreting, and presenting information. "It turns out that successful searching and efficient electronic investigations must rest upon a carefully developed, structured foundation of information literacy skills that would include solid questioning, prospecting, translating and inventive abilities". Student projects such as WebQuests guide students through information gathering and make their searching more efficient.

Students become content producers. Products may take a variety of forms: video, software, CD-ROM's, web sites, e-mail, on-line learning management systems, computer simulations, streamed discussions, data files, databases, audio, and more. There are so many examples of student knowledge production that numbers and types defy description. A tour of the ThinkQuest site provides a flavor of what kinds of work students can do. The CEO Forum (2000) offers another example from students in Queens, New York, who created "YO! It's Time For Braces." This multimedia web production intends to inform and allay fears about orthodontic braces. The site includes advice, information, and pictures from 20 orthodontists and other specialists.

Technology and instructional tools

Evaluators must consider the hardware and software requirements of the curriculum and whether the teacher has ready access to them. In addition, how much time will the teacher need to invest in learning to use the technology? Hopefully, the technology infrastructure of the school or school district will accommodate access for students and staff both inside and outside classrooms. Evaluators should consider whether the technology helps students "understand the role and importance of technology in the real world". The technology skills required for success are taught in the context of the curriculum as just-in-time modules and not as isolated units. The technology should have the "ability to engage student interest . . . and to make use of computer capabilities". Evaluators should examine software in the same reflective way that they examine other instructional materials; that is, with children's learning in mind.

Assessment

The primary goal of technology assessment should be to measure student engagement as demonstrated by their observable performances. Students are most likely to perform in desirable ways when they engage in realistic and worthwhile tasks. Assessments in the JASON Project, for example, are hands-on, real-world exercises in data collection. "Performance assessments measure what is taught in the curriculum. There are two terms that are core to depicting performance assessment: (1) Performance: A student's active generation of a response that is observable either directly or indirectly via a permanent product. (2) Authentic: The nature of the task and context in which the assessment occurs is relevant and represents 'real-world' problems or issues".

Teacher support

No curriculum can be effective without high-quality, ongoing professional development. "The old approach of after-school technology training sessions does not work. Such sessions demonstrated the features of software applications but rarely showed how to use them in the classroom". Professional development should take into account the diverse learning styles and stages of the development of learners. Multiple teacher development options should be available—study groups, classes that emphasize teaching and learning strategies, online classes, and formation of teacher-support teams. Sufficient time should be allotted for teachers to participate.

There is no way to escape the fact that today's classrooms must provide technology-supported learning opportunities for students. Teachers must be prepared to use technology in ways that encourage student engagement ultimately student learning as measured in a variety of ways. Technology, used appropriately, can help students become active, independent learners with access to seemingly unlimited information. Only through evaluation of technology-based curricula can educators make informed decisions about the purchase and use of technology, and ultimately about the wisdom of their investments.

CONCENT MAPPING?

A concept map is a graphical representation where nodes represent concepts, and links represent the relationships between concepts. The concepts, and sometimes the links, are labeled on the concept map. The links between the concepts can be one-way, two-way, or non-directional. The concepts and the links may be categorized, and the concept map may show temporal or causal relationships between concepts.

Purpose of concept mapping

Concept mapping is a type of knowledge representation. Jonassen & Grabowski state that structural knowledge may be seen as a separate type of knowledge. "Structural knowledge provides the conceptual basis for why. It describes how prior knowledge is interconnected....Structural knowledge is most often depicted in terms of some sort of concept map that visually describes the relationships between ideas in a knowledge domain." Representing knowledge in the visual format of a concept map allows one to gain an overview of a domain of knowledge. Because the nodes contain only a keyword or a short sentence, more interpretation is required of the reader, but this may be positive. Concept mapping can be used for several purposes:

— To generate ideas (brainstorming);

— To design complex structures (long texts, hypermedia, large web sites);

— To communicate complex ideas;

— To aid learning by explicitly integrating new and old knowledge; and

— To assess understanding or diagnose misunderstanding.

Advantages of concept mapping

— Visual symbols are quickly and easily recognized;

— Minimum use of text makes it easy to scan for a word, phrase, or the general idea; and

— Visual representation allows for development of a holistic understanding that words alone cannot convey.

Applications of concept mapping

1) *Creativity tool:* Drawing a concept map can be compared to participating in a brainstorming session. As one puts ideas down on paper without criticism, the ideas become clearer and the mind becomes free to receive new ideas. These new ideas may be linked to ideas already on the paper, and they may also trigger new associations leading to new ideas.

2) *Hypertext design tool:* As the World Wide Web becomes an increasingly powerful and ubiquitous medium for disseminating information, writers must move from writing text in linear fashion to creating hypertext documents with links to other documents. The structural correspondence between hypertext design and concept maps makes concept mapping a suitable tool for designing the conceptual

structure of hypertext. The structure of both a hypertext document and a concept map can be seen as a directed graph or a knowledge graph. A concept map placed on the Web in hypertext may also serve as a Web navigational tool if there are clickable areas on the concept map that take the user immediately to indicated parts of the hypertext document. Designing hypertext is an activity with inherent problems. Some describe a dilemma faced by designers of hypertext authoring systems. In order to stimulate authors to write clearly structured hypertext, they have to decide when to force authors to reflect upon the structure of their work. Imposing a hierarchical structure from the beginning may result in too many restrictions for the author, while any effort to stimulate hierarchy afterwards is too late, and it may even be impossible for authors to restructure the jungle of nodes and relationships. Concept mapping may be a good intermediate step for authors to use to reflect upon their work when developing hypermedia.

3) *Communication tool:* A concept map produced by one person represents one possible way to structure information or ideas. This is something that can be shared with others. A concept map produced by a group of people represents the ideas of the group. In either case, concept mapping can be used as a communication tool for people to use to discuss concepts and the relationships between the concepts. They may try to agree on a common structure to use as a basis for further action.

4) *Learning tool:* Novak's original work with concept mapping dealt with learning. Constructivist learning theory argues that new knowledge should be integrated into existing structures in order to be remembered and receive meaning. Concept mapping stimulates this process by making it explicit and requiring the learner to pay attention to the relationship between concepts. Some argues that students show some of their best thinking when they try to represent something graphically, and thinking is a necessary condition for learning. Experiments have shown that subjects using

concept mapping outperform non-concept mappers in longer term retention tests. Concept mapping is also gaining inroads as a tool for problem-solving in education. Concept mapping may be used to enhance the problem-solving phases of generating alternative solutions and options. Since problem-solving in education is usually done in small groups, learning should also benefit from the communication enhancing properties of concept mapping.

5) *Assessment tool:* Concept maps can also be used as assessment tools. The research team around Joseph Novak at Cornell found that an important by-product of concept mapping is its ability to detect or illustrate the "misconceptions" learners may have as explanations of content matter. The conceptions students may have are often incomplete and deficient leading to misunderstanding of instruction. Concept maps drawn by students express their conceptions (or their misconceptions) and can help the instructor diagnose the misconceptions that make the instruction ineffective.

Advantages of concept mapping

Jonassen proposes that few of the computer tools used today for learning have been designed as learning tools. Usually educators use existing tools for teaching purposes. According to Jonassen, concept mapping computer tools belong to the rare category of computer tools that were designed specifically for learning. Some of the advantages of computer support for concept mapping include:

— *Ease of adaptation and manipulation:* Once you have a concept map on paper, try to fit in those forgotten concepts or the ideas you came up with overnight and you will know the advantages of computer assisted concept mapping. Anderson-Inman and Zeitz compare the use of the concept mapping program "Inspiration" (see below) with the paper-and-pencil approach and found that using this program "encourages revisions to the concept map because deletions, additions, and changes are accomplished quickly and easily."

— *Dynamic linking:* Most computer assisted concept mapping tools allow the user to point and drag a concept or group of concepts to another place on the map and automatically update all the appropriate links.

— *Conversion:* Once a concept map is created using a computer, the program usually allows the user to convert the map to different electronic formats. These can be vector or bitmapped images, a text outline, or even a hypertext structure. These electronic formats can then be stored, sent, manipulated, used, printed, and deleted just like any computer file.

— *Communication:* Advantages of digital communication are speed, high fidelity, and reliability. Having a concept map in digital format allows the user to send concept maps as attached files with e-mail messages, or include them in World Wide Web pages. Digitizing enhances the possibilities of using concept maps as communication tools.

— *Storage:* Computer assisted concept mapping allows for digital storage of concept maps. Digital storage takes less space, makes retrieval easier, and is especially important if concept maps will be used on a large scale.

Computer tools

Inspiration is currently one of the most popular computer software programs for creating concept maps. Organization of concepts, and brainstorming and mapping of ideas are mentioned in the User's Manual as primary functions of this program. The graphical capabilities of Inspiration make it an outstanding program for creating graphs for presentation purposes. Nodes may be shown in many different useful preset and user-defined shapes. Links may be straight or curved and may be labeled. Arrowheads may be placed on any side, and everything may be set to any color.

Anderson-Inman & Zeitz describe the classroom use of Inspiration and find that it encourages users to revise or change the maps. The graphical capabilities of Inspiration help users personalize concept maps. These capabilities also provide an incentive for users to manipulate concepts and revise conceptual relationships.

Concept mapping is a technique for representing the structure of information visually. There are several uses for concept mapping, such as idea generation, design support, communication enhancement, learning enhancement, and assessment. A wide range of computer software for concept mapping is now available for most of the popular computers used in education.

GRAPHING CALCULATORS IN THE MATHEMATICS CLASSROOM

As predicted by the National Council of Teachers of Mathematics (NCTM) in their series of reform documents, graphing calculators have presented a challenging task for mathematics teachers in today's classrooms. Faced with the power of a small and easy-to-use computer, teachers must reconsider the mathematical content, educational methods, and assessment strategies that they employ. In a world of accessible technology, the very nature of mathematics and what it means "to do mathematics" is called into question. Not unlike the painstaking infusion of four-function calculators into the elementary curriculum, graphing calculators are redefining the notion of demonstrated knowledge in secondary mathematics.

With calculators that can do so much more than simple arithmetic, increasing attention has been devoted to developing materials that enrich learning experiences in mathematics. Four distinct types of enrichment have been identified. Graphing calculators can be used as: (1) tools for expediency, (2) amplifiers for conceptual understanding, (3) catalysts for critical thinking, and (4) vehicles for integration.

It is not surprising that students miss the main objective of a lesson when they are caught in a trap of tedious computation or the point-by-point plotting of a complex graph. Without argument, the graphing calculator reduces the time and effort required to perform cumbersome mathematical tasks.

"A Look at Parabolas with a Graphing Calculator" describes an exploration involving quadratic equations. The TI-85 graphing calculator is used to solve routine problems associated with second-degree polynomials. In particular, the menu and matrices capabilities of the calculator are emphasized, highlighting the heuristic of solving a system of equations without the burden of multi-step calculations.

GRAPHING CALCULATIONS AS AMPLIFIERS FOR CONCEPTUAL UNDERSTANDING

Graphing calculators are capable of providing multiple representations of mathematical concepts. By building tables, tracing along curves, and zooming in on critical points, students may be able to process information in a more varied and meaningful way. To enhance understanding, it appears that working with representations that expose diverse aspects of a concept is critical.

Sharing teaching ideas: The Graphing Calculator and Division of Fractions" suggests using a graphing calculator to demonstrate that dividing a fraction is the same as multiplying by the reciprocal. The use of a graphic representation for each of the problems provides convincing evidence that these two arithmetic processes are identical.

GRAPHING CALCULATIONS AS CATALYSTS FOR CRITICAL THINKING

When wearisome computation and plotting tasks areminimized,

students can become engaged in answering "whatif" questions. The thought of changing the premises of amathematical argument grows more attractive if the chore ofexecuting those changes is easier. Moreover, the graphingcalculator promotes autonomy in asking questions,encouraging students to pose their own problems.

"Problem-Based Mathematics — Not Just for the College-Bound" contains an abridged description of The Interactive Mathematics Program, a comprehensive, standards-based high school mathematics curriculum. Aimed at replacing the traditional sequence of mathematics courses, IMP emphasizes using graphing calculators to enhance students' critical thinking skills. Produced by a National Science Foundation initiative, this four year program integrates content strands and focuses on problem-solving processes.

Using graphing calculations as vehicles for integration

Many math educators view "integration" as an ill-defined term. Does it mean to bridge the many content strands within mathematics? Is it the marriage of mathematics to other disciplines? Can it be used to describe connecting mathematics to the real world? Luckily, despite how the word is ultimately construed, the graphing calculator supports each of these aspects of integration. "Teaching Discrete Mathematics with Graphing Calculators" challenges the belief that graphing calculators are most useful in classes built around continuous topics, such as precalculus and calculus. In fact, rather than looking at smooth curves, the author provides examples of graphing calculator lessons that can help to connect ideas of algebra, geometry, measurement, and probability and statistics.

5

Interactive Communication Technology

INTERACTIVE MULTIMEDIA COMPUTER SYSTEMS

Interactive multimedia can be defined as "the integration of text, audio, graphics, still image and moving pictures into a single, computer-controlled, multimedia product". Most current definitions describe a powerful computer connected to a variety of other equipment: videodisc players, compact disc players, scanners, music synthesizers, high resolution monitors, etc. The workstation of the not-too-distant future will have all the multimedia effects—text, audio, graphics, images, sound, motion footage—digitized or converted into a code that the computer can store and manipulate. Some equate hypermedia with interactive multimedia, and here the terms will be used synonymously.

Hypermedia is the software framework for representing multimedia effects in a non-linear fashion, allowing user annotation, and providing navigational systems. Interactive multimedia refers to the interactive audiovisual aspect of hypermedia systems. The information is stored in nodes and connected by links (associations). Nodes and links are either built into the system or created by the learner as he/she traverses the database. Ambron sees computer-based multimedia learning stations allowing users to "browse, annotate, link, and elaborate on information in a rich, nonlinear, multimedia data base...explor[ing] and integrat[ing] vast libraries of text, audio, and video information".

Components

Interactive multimedia systems consist of several components: 1) the information or data system; 2) the software for accessing the information; 3) the hardware or technology; and 4) the communications system needed to connect all these parts. The information or data system (i.e., the contents of the multimedia database) can be any type of text, audio, or visual images. Currently, optical storage methods such as laser videodisc and compact disc are used largely for storage of audio and images (both still and motion), while traditional magnetic storage devices are used for text, graphics, animation, still images, and audio.

With the growing ability to reduce the storage space needed for motion and full color still images, and with the decreasing cost of memory, the trend is toward more storage in optical formats. Digital Video Interactive (DVI) is a developing technology that holds promise in this area. By allowing the compression and decompression of digitized images, it will increase the number of images that can be stored on a compact disc and improve the capacity of that medium to store motion video.

The software component consists of generic programs such as Hypercard, ToolBook, Linkway, Quest, Guide, and Notecards. These programs index, provide access to, and allow navigation through the text, visuals, and audio in the multimedia database. This component usually includes video and audio indexing and control software, an index, a map of everything stored, linkages to navigate through the database, and a way to build new links. The hardware component currently consists of a variety of discrete pieces of equipment which may include a CD-ROM player, a videodisc player, a voice synthesizer, an audio digitizer, a video digitizer, and a digital scanner all connected to a single computer system. The communications system consists of local and non-local networks connecting the hardware and multimedia databases, which may be stored in one place or scattered across locations.

Advantages

Hypermedia provides many advantages to the learner, especially through its abilities to adapt to individual differences and to allow the learner to control the path of his/her study. The learner can either be directed or wander through information. The system can provide customized interfaces for each user with varying levels of guidance. Some studies have shown that a learner-controlled environment can be more effective than a program that adapts automatically to learner differences. By providing information in a variety of modalities, providing a context for the information, and allowing multiple paths through this knowledge, the system allows the learner to select information in the format or formats best suited to his/her learning style, ability level, and information needs through one unified system of access. All of this will increase the learner's engagement with the learning situation as he/she elaborates on current knowledge. A hypermedia system can also be used in cooperative learning or group composition with a group of users contributing to a common database of information.

There are also several problems with hypermedia as it is currently conceived. Hypermedia systems can be both confusing and disorienting, especially for the less able student. One major problem is that current user interfaces are not "friendly" enough for the average user and too inconsistent across systems. Disorientation and distraction can be caused by jumping around throughout the database, the sheer quantity of data, and the lack of information on database size and extent. Some systems may be sacrificing depth of learning for breadth. Finally, there is still a technological lag between the hardware and software currently available and what is needed for efficient, effective systems. Further development is needed in optical and other storage methods and in equipment interaction.

Numerous design issues need resolving: 1) what authoring principles and methods work; 2) how misconceptions can be corrected and feedback provided; 3) how assignments can be created; 4) how the needed self-regulation can be developed in learners; 5) how both the materials and learning can be evaluated; 6) how links can be created and managed; 7) how assistance can be provided; and 8) how the learner can be prevented from feeling lost.

Research and development are needed for more powerful searching techniques, better graphic structure searching, and friendlier user interfaces. This technology is just beginning to develop. Watch for rapid developments as storage mediums which allow a reduction in the required storage space become more fully implemented; as optical storage formats gain wider acceptance; and as software programs for hypermedia become commonly accepted for accessing databases of visual and audio images. As the technology develops even further, the interactive multimedia computer system will move from a mixture of discrete storage formats utilizing various pieces of equipment to a fully digitized storage format contained on one system.

INTEGRATING TECHNOLOGY

Keeping pace with new technologies and integrating them into existing institutional structures is only one of many pressing problems facing community college leaders today. However, recent attempts to enhance learner-centered education through technology have resulted in successful holistic approaches.

Some views technology in higher education as being akin to a four-level tower in which each level is progressively more sophisticated than the one below it. The basement contains traditional technologies and the infrastructure for their use. These basic elements support the four traditional pedagogies on the first floor: directed instruction, learning by doing, real-time conversations, and time-delayed exchange. The second floor houses enhancements to these practices that require students to use instructional technologies. Finally, the third floor represents large-scale structures supporting new educational concepts, campus-based education and distributed learning. Moran and Payne suggest that successful integration of technology into community colleges hinges on the willingness of faculty to move beyond the basement and first-floor technologies with which they are most familiar and into the upper levels that incorporate information technology. The writers recount Kirkwood Community College's successful Instructional Technology Teaching/Learning Initiative in which faculty led the integration of technology into the campus.

With improving student learning as their primary goal, faculty members were carefully trained in the use of a variety of hardware and software programs. The initiative resulted in greater faculty integration of technology into their planning, teaching, and student evaluation routines. Recent activities include formation of an institute for studying the impact of technology on literature and development of a software program that allows downloading of student grades from instructor records into the student record system.

Additionally, faculty from the developmental education department mentor faculty in other departments in designing technology-based and technology-enhanced curricula. Results of these initiatives include a sequence of courses designed for specific vocational and college preparatory areas. Moran and Payne make it clear that when faculty assume a leadership role in integrating instructional technology, rather than administrators dictating that implementation, innovations that enhance student learning are the result.

PLANNING FOR TECHNOLOGY

Community colleges now operate in an age of diminishing budgets and resources as well as demands to expand their missions. Ehrmann identifies five policy issues with which all community college leaders need to be concerned when investing in instructional technology. Taken together, these concerns require decision makers to examine the underlying values that will affect their choices for where to invest scarce institutional dollars in order to yield the best return. Any successful attempt at integrating technology into existing institutional structures must begin with an evaluation of the current status of the college and a plan for improvement.

Gellman-Danley and Teague offer a 10-step guide to integrating technology throughout the community college. Based on their own experience at Monroe Community College that saw technological consolidation throughout both the academic and administrative sectors, the authors articulate the steps required to form an institution able to serve faculty, staff, and students more effectively and efficiently.

The cost of integrating instructional technology is another common concern. Some argues persuasively for new investment strategies that concentrate technology dollars in the top 10 to 25 courses that enroll upwards of 25% of students at most community colleges. He suggests concentrating technology investments in the introductory English, math, psychology, accounting, biology, fitness, and speech courses. He argues that improving access to these classes through technology will increase enrollments and potentially reduce operating costs.

Planning for technological innovation can be especially difficult for community college administrators during uncertain times, but it also provides them with opportunities for reinventing the institution. The creation of a "parallel college" at Sinclair Community College that seeks to, first, correct the mismatch between curriculum and modern technology and second, update current administrative operations systems with modern and efficient ones. Both objectives are part of that institution's efforts to produce more student-centered learning on campus.

When efforts to integrate technology into learner-centered teaching are successful, the results can be startling, as was the case with Project SYNERGY at Miami-Dade Community College in Florida. The project resulted in the creation and implementation of software designed to test, evaluate, and teach underprepared students at their own pace. An important initial phase of the project was the creation of a software "platform" that integrated a collection of faculty evaluated and selected educational software programs.

These existing programs in turn were integrated into a collection of diagnostic components. This new software platform was dubbed the Project SYNERGY Integrator (PSI). Using either LAN (local area network) or WAN (wide area network) computer technology, the PSI was designed to allow instructors to easily and effectively evaluate and track the competence of underprepared students in a wide range of basic skills.

The evaluation and selection of software was followed by the creation of questions by faculty that, when answered by students, would measure individual students' levels of preparedness in reading, writing, math, ESL, study skills, critical thinking, or other targeted areas. The questions, contained in a database called BANQUE, were integrated into the PSI, thereby allowing instructors to easily produce either topical or diagnostic tests custom designed for individual students. When faculty select questions for a particular test, specific learning objectives can be matched with the content of the topic covered.

Additional features incorporated into the PSI include e-mail, generation of reports for time-on-task, and access to software by individual students. These features allow the student and instructor to interact at the convenience of both parties and eliminate tedious grading and tracking functions. The system even provides students with computer games as rewards for effort and achievement.

Successes such as those experienced by Project SYNERGY can lead to additional, unexpected challenges. For instance, faculty typically are not compensated for the extra work they perform to enhance their instruction with technological innovations. Certainly they are entitled to fair compensation for these efforts although there are no easy answers. The obligations of both faculty and institutions need to be defined in this new environment. New competitors for community college students and their dollars pose another challenge. Doucette foresees the day when, in search of new markets, conglomerates such as Disney or Microsoft begin to compete for a sizable portion of students now taught by community colleges. He believes the challenge to community colleges will then be to once again discover new ways to "provide learning support services to help students learn, regardless of where they get their information".

No doubt other, unpredicted challenges will continue to arise as integration of technology into community colleges progresses. Efforts to find new and innovative solutions will become a common occurrence among those responsible for making technology decisions at the faculty, administrative, and staff levels. These challenges will force community colleges to revisit their missions, particularly in response to issues of access and service.

TOOLS FOR AUTOMATING INSTRUCTIONAL DESIGN

Instructional design (ID) is the systematic process of planning events to facilitate learning. The ID process encompasses a set of interdependent phases including analysis of learners, contexts and goals; design of objectives, strategies and assessment tools; production of instructional materials; and evaluation of learner performance and overall instructional design effort.

Automated instructional design (AID) tools assist instructional designers and others in creating instructional products to improve learning. AID systems aid in the production of courseware, or in the development of computer-based instruction (CBI), although some tools guide users in general decision-making that can apply to a range of instructional products and solutions. AID tools may eliminate some physical ID tasks such as storyboarding and test generation. However, the strength of AID tools lies in their ability to guide novices and non-ID professionals through the process of creating effective instruction. AID tools are especially useful in situations where instructional design expertise is lacking and subject-matter experts and others are responsible for developing instruction [as seen in military courseware development.

There are four types of tools that guide users through the ID process: expert systems, advisory systems, information management systems, and electronic performance support systems. Authoring tools are also mentioned as popular mechanisms for supporting the production of computer-based instruction. Some tools contain features representing more than one type of system.

— *Expert systems*: An expert system contains a domain-specific knowledge-base and performs decision-making and analysis functions for the designer using natural language queries. Expert systems for instructional design have been developed to provide advice to novice instructional designers and to facilitate the development process for experienced designers. ID Expert from the ID2 Research Group was created to develop and deliver computer-based instruction more efficiently. ID Expert is based on Instructional Transaction Theory, a "second generation" theory of instructional design. According to Instructional Transaction Theory, instruction is based on transactions (sets of interactions) between the system and the learner in order to accomplish a given task. ID Expert assists designers in creating transactions by presenting a set of decision-making steps involving instructional components, formatting, resources, etc. ID Expert is considered a prototype system and has not yet been released commercially.

The United States Air Force Armstrong Laboratory proposed two AID approaches that use expert system technology to provide expertise to novice instructional designers and subject matter experts in the design, production, and implementation of courseware used in Air Force training. Guided Approach to Instructional Design Advising (GAIDA) uses tutorials and context-specific advice and examples. Experimental Advanced Instructional Design Advisor (XAIDA) uses the Instructional Transaction Theory framework to encapsulate context-specific knowledge. Both of these environments are results of the Advanced Instructional Design Advisor (AIDA) research project.

Reactions to expert systems: While expert systems for instructional design can teach theory validation and function as authoring tools, they are limited by their inability to support analysis and design tasks. ID expert systems attempt to control the instructional design process, a process involving a large number of interrelated elements, and so must rely heavily on the knowledge and experience of the individual practitioner. Several instructional technologists have proposed systems that more subtly advise the instructional designer, rather than prescribe a set of solutions. Some examples are described below.

— *Advisory systems:* Duchastel challenges the expert system model by providing an advisory system model. Instead of controlling the problem-solving process with expert knowledge, advisory systems assist or coach users in accomplishing a given task. A prototype for the advisory system approach is the Instructional Design Advanced Workbench, an architecture for a computer-based workbench that supports the cognitive tasks of instructional design without constraining the designer.

— *Information management systems:* Instructional Design Environment (IDE) from the Institute for Research on Learning is a computer-aided design environment that supports an ID methodology for teaching the use of software in real-life problem-solving contexts. IDE helps document design and development options. It is intended for experienced instructional designers.

— *Electronic performance support systems*: Electronic performance support systems (EPSS) are self-instructional electronic environments that provide access to "software, guidance, advice, data, tools, and assessment with minimum support and intervention by others". EPSS have become popular in the 1990s for business and educational contexts that require "just-in-time" learning and a high level of a particular skill. Some examples of EPSS are listed below.

Building on Duschastel's "workbench," Paquette et al introduced a performance support system called AGD (a French acronym meaning Didactic Engineering. AGD provides procedural instructional design information to guide users in defining the learning system. AGD includes a rules-based advisory component that offers advice regarding specific design decisions made by users.

Other performance support systems tools include Designer's Edge from Allen Communication and Instructional DesignWare from Langevin Learning Services. Like AGD, these tools support the planning phases of instructional design, but contain a much more general advisory component.

In contrast to AGD, Designer's Edge and Instructional DesignWare lead designers through all tasks involved in instructional design, but place more emphasis on the ultimate production phase. Both tools provide a graphical representation of the instructional systems design model, thus leading to additional support for completing each step of the model. Data entered by users are cross-referenced with all steps to enhance continuity between phases. Usable reports and documents such as evaluation instruments, content outlines, lesson plans, and checklists can be generated by the users.

The primary difference between the two products lies in their intended audiences and purposes. Designer's Edge is for both novice and experienced instructional designers planning computer-based instruction. The product includes support for scripts, storyboards and other CBI production needs. Integration with external software applications is also supported. Instructional DesignWare is intended for course designers and trainers interested in producing either computer-based or classroom training. For this reason, more support is provided for decisions regarding media selection and course and presentation materials.

Authoring tools

Although they do not necessarily support the preliminary planning stages of instructional design, instructional designers use authoring tools in the development phase to produce computer-based instruction. Some authoring tools take advantage of the World Wide Web by providing features that integrate Web content into computer-based instruction and deliver instruction over the Web, authoring tools simplify the programming process and allow experienced users to create effective and visually-appealing instruction, but require a steep learning curve in order to take full advantage of their features. Current popular authoring tools include Macromedia Authorware 4.0, Aim Tech IconAuthor, WBT Systems TopClass, and Asymetrix Toolbook.

Some AID tools support instructional design by focusing on the cognitive aspects of instructional design (e.g., ID Expert, AGD, etc.). Some highlight the procedural steps of ID (e.g., Designer's Edge, Instructional DesignWare). Others support the production phase only (i.e., authoring tools for computer-based instruction). In general, AID tools that support the planning and evaluation phases of ID are not as widely used by practitioners as tools that focus on the authoring and media production phases. One exception may be Designer's Edge which has been cited as one of the most popular CBT authoring tools despite its intended purpose as a pre-authoring system. Regardless of its strength or approach, the value of a particular tool or type of system is measured by how well it can support a particular designer's task.

KNOWLEDGE MANAGEMENT IN INSTRUCTIONAL DESIGN

Instructional designers engage in activities related to the planning and implementation of instructional and performance support solutions. Available tools and technologies influence the way in which instructional designers accomplish their tasks. Knowledge management represents a technology that is changing how instructional design professionals work.

Instructional design (ID) professionals aim to improve individual and organizational performance. ID may be defined as a systematic approach to instructional planning that typically involves a project team analyzing a problem situation, exploring alternative performance support or instructional solutions, and then planning, implementing, evaluating, and managing solutions.

This process is often poorly-structured and iterative, involving people from different backgrounds and areas of expertise. In an instructional design project, different kinds of resources and artifacts are created: proposals, memos, analyses, solution strategies, lesson plans, evaluation plans, media support for lessons, performance data, and so on. According to the International Board of Standards for Training, Performance and Instruction, ID is an engineering discipline with principles, rules, and heuristics, many of which are sensitive to local conditions.

ID professionals are required to resolve complex issues, such as connecting learning and performance objectives with assessable outcomes. Several people are often involved in these problem-solving processes. Some team members may work on one task/aspect of an instructional or performance solution while other team members may work on a different ID problem (for example, storyboarding specific lessons). ID activities may be accomplished at different times as well as at different locations. In short, ID is a complex, collaborative enterprise, requiring careful planning and management in order for goals to be achieved.

KNOWLEDGE MANAGEMENT

Management involves a collection of activities (such as situation assessment, goal definition, team development, resource allocation, and so on) aimed at ensuring project/task progress and quality of processes or products. Knowledge is typically defined in terms of collections of rules, principles and structured information that enable people to make decisions and solve problems. Knowledge management (KM), then, is a technology that focuses on the knowledge involved in a set of problem situations or in a system. The notion of a system as a collection or combination of disparate, but identifiable, components organized to facilitate accomplishment of goals is essential in order to understand KM.

A system is a complex and dynamic collection of different things, including people, information, administrative processes, and so on. One aspect of management is to facilitate the effective and efficient functioning of system components. KM focuses on the knowledge components within a system; some knowledge may be explicitly represented (in the form of information databases, policies and procedures, for example) and some may be implicit (in the form of tacit knowledge, organizational culture, habits, etc.). One goal of KM is to facilitate the transformation of implicit knowledge into accessible explicit knowledge that can be brought to bear in relevant problem-solving situations.

Knowledge management systems (KMSs) are tools aimed at supporting knowledge management. KMSs evolved from information management tools that integrated many aspects of computer-supported collaborative work environments (CSCW) with information and document management systems. Key characteristics of a KMS are support for: (1) communication among various users; (2) coordination of users' activities; (3) collaboration among user groups on the creation, modification and dissemination of artifacts and products; and, (4) control processes to ensure integrity and to track the progress of projects.

Systems that support KM provide specific functions related to communication; coordination (shareable calendars and task lists); collaboration (shareable artifacts and workspaces); and control (internal audit trails and automatic version control). A user-centered KMS contributes to an organizational culture of sharing by providing a sense of belonging to a community of users and by supporting reciprocity among users.

KMSs extend the perspective of employees as knowledge workers by providing them with the means to create knowledge and to actively contribute to a shared and dynamic body of knowledge. A KMS provides support for many information functions, including: acquiring and indexing, capturing and archiving; finding and accessing; creating and annotating; combining, collating and modifying; and tracking. These KMS functions allow multiple individuals to organize meaningful activities around shared and reusable artifacts to achieve specific goals. In short, a KMS addresses the distributed nature of work and expertise.

Within business and industry, KM technology is being used to support organizational learning. The dynamics of the global economy place a premium on organizational responsiveness and flexibility. Partly as a response to the demands of a highly competitive global economy, KMS technology has emerged as a new generation of information management systems. In contrast with previous information management systems, a KMS is designed for multiple users with different and changing requirements.

Key enabling technologies include object orientation, broadband communications, and adaptive systems. Object orientation provides for the creation of knowledge objects that can be easily found, modified and reused. Broadband communication allows users separated in time or space to work on large data objects effectively as a team. Adaptive systems recognize that different users may have different requirements and preferred working styles.

A KMS can be viewed as an activity system that involves people making use of objects (tools and technologies) to create artifacts and products that represent knowledge in order to achieve a shared goal. Previous information management systems focused on a small portion of such a system, such as a narrow set of objects in the form of a collection of records or simple communication between team members. A KMS embraces the entire activity system but maintains a focus on the human-use aspects as opposed to the underlying or enabling technology aspects. KMSs have already met with significant success in the business sector and are spreading to other sectors, including education (Marshall & Rossett, 2000) and instructional design.

ID is a complex, collaborative activity involving teams whose members are often distributed in different locations. Consequently, it is natural to use a KMS to support ID. For example, the European Commission Fifth Framework AdaptIT Project involves the use of a KMS in the design and development phases of ID. Project Advance(r) at Syracuse University makes use of a KMS in all aspects of ID. The ability to provide communication, coordination, collaboration and control makes it possible for an ID team to minimize time spent on mundane tasks (such as tracking documents and reconciling different versions) and focus on higher-level problem-solving activities.

The enabling technologies associated with KM are also prominent, leading-edge educational technologies. The ability of KM technology to support school-based learning has been demonstrated. The ability of KM technology to promote collaboration among instructional designers has also been demonstrated, as indicated in the aforementioned projects. KM issues being addressed by ID researchers include: (a) the granularity of learning objects suitable for promoting effective learning and reuse; (b) the modes and types of communication appropriate for different users and tasks; and, (c) adaptive systems to support instructional design and development. The extent of transformation within ID communities of practice remains to be seen as the marriage of KM and ID is relatively recent, but the potential is enormous.

KM tools and systems are beginning to be used for the design and development of instructional systems and learning environments, and ID practice is changing as a consequence. For example, concurrent ID engineering is now more prevalent when KM is integrated with ID. There is a history of interaction between technology and instructional design. This interaction is evident in the design of learning environments.

The Web provides a recent and visible example of technology influencing how instructional designers structure courses and plan learning activities. KM technology can be integrated into an instructional delivery framework. However, there is far-reaching potential for KM technology to influence all phases of instructional design-analysis and planning as well as implementation, delivery and management.

KM tools and technologies have the potential to affect patterns of interaction among those who design and develop instruction, such as instructional designers, developers, content experts, system integrators, graphics artists, and media specialists. Specifically, a KMS enhances the communication, coordination, and collaboration among such a team while improving long-term productivity by facilitating access, archiving, retrieval and reuse of a variety of learning objects and instructional resources.

SUCCESSFUL K-12 TECHNOLOGY PLANNING: TEN ESSENTIAL ELEMENTS

Over the last 20 years, K-12 schools have spent millions of

dollars equipping their schools with the latest technologies, but often without a thoughtful plan of how their use would impact learning and teaching. Computers, like other technologies when they were new—such as radio, television, motion pictures, and video—were expected to substantially change education simply by making it more exciting and interactive. But technology use is not about the hardware, Internet connections, and so on. What is important is how the technology is integrated with the instructional program. The guiding question technology leaders must keep in mind as they develop their plan is, "Are students using technology in ways that deepen their understanding of academic content and advance their knowledge of the world around them?"

To ensure that technology dollars have an impact on students, staff, and the community, districts and schools must develop a thoughtful technology plan. Technology plans that help districts and schools to use technology effectively include all of the ten steps that follow.

1. *Create a vision:* Vision is the first step for technology planning. The district or school must have a picture of what a technology-enhanced program will look like in three to five years. Vision statements are compelling stories that describe how students will be using the technology and how teachers and other staff will be using it for data-driven decision making, increased productivity, and planning. A vision also includes how the learning environment will be enhanced to support technology use.

2. *Involve all stakeholders:* For any plan to be effective, all stakeholders should have the opportunity to have an input into the goals of the plan. Teachers, administrators, other employees, parents, and the general community all have a stake in the educational outcomes of students.

3. *Gather Data:* You must understand where you are in order to plan for the future, so gather as much data as possible about your present use:

— Conduct an inventory to determine what equipment and software you presently have and where it is located.

— Determine the present level of use in your classrooms. There are multiple ways to collect this information. One is to survey staff and student use by asking about both their skill levels and how teachers and students are using the technology. Develop your own survey or adapt one developed by another district. There are also several online assessments including, enGauge. The enGauge framework identifies six essential conditions critical to the effective use of technology for student learning.

Another resource is the Learning with Technology Profile Tool. This computer program presents indicators of engaged learning and indicators of technology. For each indicator there are three choices that educators can compare to their own practice. When finished, educators can view the results in a graphical format to help identify their strengths and weaknesses.

— Gauge the progress your school is making to improve student achievement. Each drawer within the Toolbox offers descriptions, examples, and specific in-school experiences to guide the many members of a school's community.

— Conduct site visits. It may be desirable to visit schools that demonstrate compelling reasons for using technology. This is particularly important if your school uses computers mainly for word processing and drill and practice. If your planning team has never seen student use of multimedia, digital video, or student web pages, it will be difficult for them to envision these uses. Visits can help to open one's mind to the possibilities.

4. *Review the research:* Knowing what the research says about the use of technology is important to guide your technology planning efforts. Research has found that some technology use impacts student learning while others make no difference. The research on technology's effectiveness is divided into two areas: (1) learning with computers, using

computers as tutors (most often drill and practice) and (2) learning from computers, which is when the student uses the computer as a tool in the learning process for communication, collaboration, research, or publishing. A summary of the research for both types of use finds that technology can impact student learning when the following conditions are evident:

— Students have easy access to the technology.

— Technology is in the classroom, where it can make a greater impact then when it is in labs.

— Ongoing teacher training is provided.

— Reform of teaching practices is evident, with a balance between traditional instruction, characterized by teacher lecture, and that of construction, characterized by the teacher serving as a guide and facilitator.

— The software is well matched with the teacher's assessment of student needs and the objectives of instruction.

5. *Integrate technology into the curriculum:* As the research demonstrates, technology impacts student learning when there is a match between content standards and the technology being used. Teachers face six barriers to effectively integrating technology with their curriculum:

— *Leadership:* The lack of leadership is the single biggest barrier to the use of technology.

— *Access:* One or two computers or a weekly visit to a computer lab do not impact student learning.

— *Time:* It takes time for teachers to review software and figure out how it fits with their instructional program.

— *Cost:* Schools often provide only minimal funds to purchase software. Teachers may not be willing to spend their own money to purchase multiple copies of software.

— *Training:* Apple Classroom of Tomorrow (ACOT) research found that it takes training for teachers to move from "How do I turn it on?" to where they comfortably and routinely integrate technology into their classroom.

— *Reform:* Technology makes its greatest impact when teachers use project-based learning practices to engage students.

Student proficiency standards embedded with instructional projects can help teachers to know which technology skills students need to demonstrate. The NETS project offers one model.

6. *Professional Development:* The plan must address the goals for professional development. Providing appropriate training is the key to effective use. Research has demonstrated time and again that an ongoing professional development program is required. The most effective staff development programs deliver to teachers when they need it, at their school, and on their own equipment. One-time "spray and pray" workshops do not result in any change in teacher behavior. The ACOT research found that teachers' growth goes through five stages: entry, adoption, adaptation, appropriation, and invention. Even with a strong professional development program, less than 50 percent of teachers reach level three. The plan should also address the technology proficiencies that teachers will be expected to demonstrate. The NETS Project, mentioned earlier, can also be a source for teacher proficiency standards if your state or district doesn't have them.

7. *Ensure a sound infrastructure:* For technology to impact student learning, the technology plan must ensure that appropriate resources are in place to support and maintain networks and equipment. Technical support is also essential so that all systems work 24/7. Techno-phobic teachers will quickly give up on technology use when it doesn't work

after they have spent many hours learning about the software and planning technology-enhanced lessons. Setting single standards for software, hardware, networks, and video equipment is crucial. Doing so will result in significant savings in staff development and support costs, including repairs, and will make it easier to upgrade and support district licenses. Technical support may be a nightmare otherwise, because incompatible systems can't "talk" to each other.

8. *Allocate Appropriate funding and budget:* The plan should be in line with your district or school's financial resources. It should not promise more than the budget can deliver. There are two parts to a technology budget. A recommended formula for the first portion is as follows: 40% of every dollar allocated should be for hardware, 20% for software, 20% for professional development, and 20% for upgrades and additional needs as teachers' expertise grows. If you spend all of the money on hardware, you will not see the return on student learning because there will be no funds for professional development, upgrades, and so on. These recommendations are not just for the first year, but for anytime you budget or receive one-time grant dollars. Budget separately for technical support expenses. Support must be available 24/7 so that teachers have confidence that the time they spend in reviewing software and planning will not be lost when equipment and networks fail to work. A thoughtful technology plan will not consider the purchase of more hardware and networks then the district can support with its technical support capacity.

9. *Ongoing Monitoring and Assessment:* The plan must address ongoing monitoring and assessment. Plan to collect data using rubrics, student artifacts, surveys and tests. Develop benchmarks and timelines for all components of the plan. Some questions the plan should address are:

— Is the technology being used effectively?

— What elements are missing?

— What needs to be added?

The plan should address how the results of this assessment will be communicated to all stakeholders. While planning for today, keep an eye on tomorrow by allowing for new and promising practices and technologies. Remember back ten years ago when "www" didn't mean the World Wide Web, laptop computers were big and called "luggables" by those who owned them, and when 48 k and a 24-baud modem were fast?

Would you have predicted back then the hardware, networks, and software you Have in your schools now? Probably not. Ten years from now will computers even Look like the computers we use now? How will Personal Digital Assistants (PDAs) And other handhelds change the way we organize and learn? And, finally will we All be totally wireless, able to communicate at anytime, anywhere? In preparation for the future, set some funds aside to encourage teachers to try new applications and determine what value, if any, these applications have for your program before you purchase items only a techie could love.

Technology can improve teaching and learning when a school or district develops a plan that incorporates these essential elements and provides appropriate funding to make its vision a reality.

BECOMING A TECHNOLOGICALLY SAVVY ADMINISTRATOR

At the turn of the century, technology has permeated public schools as it has the rest of society. Over 90 percent of schools have access to the Internet, and more than half of U.S. schools provide at least 90 percent of their teachers with an email account. Yet, as the critical issue of school computer utilization shifts from mere access to the more fundamental issue of how to effectively integrate technology into the curriculum, there has been little discussion of what role administrators should play.

As the world becomes more dependent on technology, students and their parents will continue to expect a public education to include the integration of computers and the Internet. Businesses are already demanding graduates who are technologically literate. Communities throughout the country will increasingly require effective leadership in the area of technology from insightful and forward-thinking school leaders. Given these expectations and demands, administrators who implement technology effectively in their schools and communities will contribute greatly to both education and the economy in the twenty-first century.

Forty-five states have in place or are creating state standards in the area of technology. Nine of these states require a technology-related exit exam for graduation. In conjunction with these initiatives, several states have passed mandates on teachers' competency; for example, by 2001, North Carolina and Idaho will require teachers to demonstrate technology competence for certification and licensure. In light of the current movement toward standards and accountability, it is likely that other states will soon create similar mandates. Such legislation or state-level policy will force school leaders to reflect on how best to promote the integration of information technology in their districts.

Technology is not an end in itself. The appropriate use of technology, Donovan reminds us, is to promote innovation toward school improvement. To reinforce this purpose in their schools, administrators should discuss with staff how technology can best be used to enhance teaching and learning. Throughout this process, school leaders should assure teachers that the goal of technology is to improve teaching and learning, not to replace teachers. Administrators must be prepared for a significant investment of time to move technology from a part-time tool to an active tool fully integrated into the curriculum. As Donovan suggests, to move an innovation to full integration, a reform must have many of the following characteristics: (1) be advantageous to current methods, (2) be compatible with needs and expectations, (3) be simple to use, (4) be easily tried without a huge commitment to change, and (5) be observable and modeled by staff who embrace technology. School leaders should concentrate on building a school context replete with as many of these characteristics as possible. When most of these factors are present, teachers will be more likely to embrace technology and begin to integrate it into teaching and learning.

As administrators have witnessed the introduction and implementation of information technology in their buildings, they have become acutely aware of the burgeoning expense associated with providing access to computers and the Internet. Between 1991 and 1997, $19.6 billion was spent on instructional technology in United States public schools. A recent survey of 400 school officials suggests that the total cost of ownership for a building with 75 computers was more than $2,200 per machine.

As school leaders move beyond the issue of merely ensuring access, they must develop strategies to sustain technology in their schools while taking into account the total cost of ownership. This clearly requires thoughtful planning based on how technology can be used effectively as part of a long-term school-improvement plan directed at improving learning and achievement goals (EDvancenet). One strategy is to develop a school vision statement of how technology can be utilized to achieve a school's objectives. School vision statements are most effective with a minimum of five sections:

1. *Vision and objectives to achieve the vision:* Engage school board members, faculty and staff members, students, and community members in the process of reflecting on, discussing, and articulating a shared vision of the future of the school or district.

2. *Assessment of current school environment:* Analyze the existing conditions of your school to more accurately

comprehend the terrain that must be navigated to achieve the articulated vision.

3. *Gap analysis:* Recognize the gaps between the current environment of learning and where the school wants to be in the future as the basis for an action plan to guide the school toward the vision through the utilization of technology as a tool.
4. *Evaluation:* Set in place appropriate methods for continually evaluating progress toward the vision and, based on this ongoing feedback, for reformulating the action plan.
5. *Strategy for altering objectives in accordance with formative evaluation data:* Articulate a change strategy that includes a plan for altering the objectives.

As a result of this articulated vision, a longitudinal technology plan is driven by the school vision rather than by the technology itself.

Technology raises many challenging issues for school leaders. To avoid litigation, administrators must become knowledgeable about at least the fundamentals of technology-related school law. The Council of School Attorneys and Technology Leadership Network (CSATLN), a subgroup of the National School Boards Association that includes 3,000 education-focused attorneys, states that "rapid development of new technologies has outpaced the development of related law, leaving educators in doubt as to how to manage issues of copyright, privacy, liability and security". CSATLN published Legal Issues & Education Technology: A School Leader's Guide to prepare administrators for the plethora of emerging legal issues associated with instructional technology. School leaders also can visit cyberlaw websites to remain abreast of developments in technology law that could influence school practice and policy.

More school leaders are becoming aware of corporate philanthropy as a supplement to district, state, and federal revenues. In 1997, corporations and other philanthropic organizations donated approximately $16 billion to individuals and groups in the United States. Of this total, nearly one quarter, or $3.84 billion, went to educational institutions. In 1998, total grant awards increased by 22 percent to $19.46 billion. By aggressively seeking out philanthropic gifts and grants for their schools, administrators can offset to some extent the high cost associated with introducing and sustaining technology in public schools.

The philanthropic process presents a dilemma for school leaders. The culture of schooling affords little time for such endeavors as grant writing. In addition, few school-level staff members possess the necessary experience, skills, and knowledge to engage in the formal and professional preparation of a grant. Although districts may have difficulty justifying a salary for a grant writer, can they afford not to hire one?

The decision to allocate funds for a grant writer can pay off handsomely. Those contemplating this step may want to review eSchool's School Technology Funding Directory and the Foundation Center's User-Friendly Guide to Funding Research and Resources.

The integration of technology in classrooms has been demonstrated to have a positive impact on student achievement. To gain this benefit, districts must couple technology with ongoing staff training. Once all teachers have access to the Internet and know the fundamentals of using computers, the Web itself can be a valuable source of professional development and curriculum materials.

Administrators should actively promote the use of the Web to obtain curricular ideas, as well as to find methods of more effectively integrating technology into classrooms to promote learning. One obvious step is to encourage teachers to take advantage of online professional-development networks, which can be a valuable component of their personal professional-development plan approved by the district or school. Teachers can use these networks to advance their professional growth without leaving the comfort and privacy of their classroom or home. One such community of K-12 teachers is the 21st Century Teachers Network. The online network is organized by state as well as by content areas, allowing for both virtual interactions on a national level and actual collegial opportunities on a local level.

On a more technical side, Tech Corps is a group of volunteers in each state whose goal is "to recruit, place, and support volunteers from the technology community who advise and assist schools in the introduction and integration of new technologies." Tech Corps can offer schools technical advice as well as provide recommendations regarding how to effectively integrate technology at the school level.

PREPARING URBAN TEACHERS TO USE TECHNOLOGY FOR INSTRUCTION

Since the early 1990s, the gap in the availability of computers and Internet access between schools in affluent and poor areas has decreased dramatically. While most schools now have computer and Internet access, many teachers still have difficulty with incorporating this new technology into instruction. This is particularly true in poorer urban school districts, where funding and time for teacher technology training are often lacking.

TECHNOLOGY SKILLS OF INSERVICE TEACHERS

Most teachers have some familiarity with computers and are able to use a variety of computer software. Further, 94 percent of all respondents to a recent National Education Association survey, and 99 percent of the respondents under 35, are able to search the Internet. Many teachers do not know how to incorporate computer skills into classroom instruction, however, according to a National Center for Education Statistics report. Almost two-thirds of all teachers reported feeling not at all prepared or only somewhat prepared to use technology in their teaching, but younger teachers, who grew up with computers and were educated with them, indicated they felt better prepared to use technology than their more experienced colleagues. Not surprisingly, teachers who reported feeling better prepared to use technology were more likely to make use of it than those who indicated they felt less prepared.

The use of technology in low-income schools

Educational technology, when used to develop higher-order thinking skills, can have a positive impact on learning, according to a study by the Educational Testing Service. But teachers in low-income schools often teach about the computer itself, and use computers for drill and practice, rather than for research, inquiry, and communication, as is often the practice in wealthier schools. This strategy is based on the assumption that children who lack basic skills need to learn them through drill before they can move on to higher-order thinking activities. Unfortunately, these children often do not get the opportunity to progress to higher-order problem solving. Furthermore, research has shown that in real-life situations lower-order and higher-order thinking are not separated; therefore, effective teaching should combine the two.

Current practice: A recent study by the Milken Exchange on Education Technology and the International Society for Technology in Education found that, "in general, teacher-training programs do not provide future teachers with the kinds of experiences necessary to prepare them to use technology effectively in their classrooms." It emphasized that since the United States will need a projected 2.2 million new teachers over the next decade, "the time to examine and re-engineer our teacher preparation programs is now." The study also pointed out several other deficiencies prevalent in teacher education programs:

— Approximately one-third of teacher education programs are limited by their information technology facilities.

— Most teacher training program faculty do not model the use of technology in teaching.

— Most teacher training programs do not have a written, funded, regularly updated technology plan.

— Most student teachers do not routinely use technology in their field experience and do not work with teachers who can advise them on its use, although information technology is available in the K-12 classrooms where student teachers get their field experience.

RECOMMENDATIONS FOR IMPROVEMENT

The most important recommendation of the Milken Exchange study is to integrate technology training into the entire teacher education program, since instructional time spent in other classes, such as methods and curriculum courses, is much more useful for educating student teachers about computer use than are formal stand-alone technology courses. The study also recommends that the following strategies be incorporated into teacher training programs:

— Focus institutional technology planning on the integration of technology in teaching and learning, not only on facilities.

— Provide student teachers with more opportunities to apply technology during field experience.

— Give school of education faculty the tools, incentives, and professional development they need to integrate technology into the teacher training curriculum.

The Web-Based Education Commission, established by Congress in 1997, recommends making professional development in technology a high priority. It cites several initiatives by Congress, the states, universities, professional organizations, and the business community which support intensive technology training for teachers:

— The Higher Education Act Amendments, passed by Congress and signed into law in 1998, hold institutions of higher education accountable for preparing teachers who are highly qualified not only in academic content areas but also in the effective use of technology in the classroom.

— The majority of states—42—now require that teachers demonstrate proficiency in technology as one component for receiving certification.

— The National Council for Accreditation of Teacher Education (NCATE), working with the International Society for Technology in Education, is incorporating technology standards into its accreditation process for teacher education colleges. While this effort is promising, NCATE is responsible for accrediting only 38 percent of the 1,300 teacher preparation programs in the United States.

— The CEO Forum developed a special StaR (School Technology and Readiness) self-assessment tool for schools and colleges of education. Over 240 institutions have undergone self-assessments to bring their programs from "low tech," with little or no technology use, to "target tech," the model for innovative use of educational technology.

Only four states require technology training for recertification of teachers, so much remains to be done in this area. The CEO Forum on Education and Technology recommends the following:

— Every state should develop standards for effective continuing education on integrating technology into the curriculum.

— Schools and districts should develop technology plans that include professional development in the use of technology and proficiency standards.

— Every teacher and administrator should have access to information technology.

— Resources for technology-related professional development should be increased.

— Every professional development program should integrate technology into its curriculum.

The Federal Office of Technology Assessment recommended that school districts devote at least 30 percent of their technology budgets to teacher training and support. However, only 6 percent of the $4.2 billion that K-12 schools spent on technology in 1996 went towards training. That figure increased to 17 percent for public school teacher technology training for the 1999-2000 school year, but it is still far below the recommended amount.

Government Support for Teacher Technology Training

A Presidential Panel report recommended that teachers need in-depth, sustained assistance to integrate computer use into the curriculum and reconcile new methods of instruction which use technology extensively with traditional methods. One program offering such training is the Teacher Led Technology Challenge (TLTC) in Berkeley, California, funded by the U.S. Department of Education's Technology Innovation Challenge Grant Program; it provides teachers with extensive support, tools, and professional development. A Classroom Technology Integration Specialist in each school plans and consults with teachers regularly during times set aside for this purpose. The TLTC was designed for adaptation by other school systems serving predominantly low-income and racially diverse populations.

The U.S. Department of Education's Preparing Tomorrow's Teachers to Use Technology (PT3) Program, begun in 1999, offers grants to support teacher preparation improvements—mostly in low-income communities, rural areas, and among minority groups and special populations. In its first two fiscal years the program has made a total of $300 million available to teacher preparation institutions. The funds will help them develop programs that prepare prospective teachers to use technology for improved instructional practices and student learning opportunities. By 2004, over one million teachers will have received technology training as a result of these grants.

The Federal government is also facilitating technology learning through support of online learning environments, since the Internet can help isolated teachers make new connections and expand access to new resources.

Specifically, the Internet can provide collaborative learning environments where teachers reflect on their practice, share expertise, and build a common understanding of new instructional approaches, by engaging with colleagues and experts in the field. An example is the Maryland Electronic Learning Community, also funded by the Technology Innovation Challenge Grant Program, which uses email, videoconferencing, digitized video, and Internet resources to support curriculum and professional development. Two among many online sites where teachers and students can engage in collaborative learning and reflection are TAPPED IN.

6

EDUCATIONAL TECHNOLOGY AND LEARNING OUTCOMES

In today's world, computer-based technology is not a frill, but an important component of any modern curriculum. During the last decade, technology expenditures tripled in K -12 schools in the United States; estimates suggest that over $6 billion was spent in 1999 -2000. Since no one wants these funds to be wasted, educators need insight into how to maximize the positive impact of their technology.

In order to understand the impact of technology on education, it is helpful to consider the purposes to which technology is applied. One distinction that we have found particularly helpful comes from Thomas Reeves who describes learning "from " computers as different than learning "with " computers. When students are learning "from " computers, , the computers are essentially tutors. In this capacity, the technology primarily serves the goal of increasing students 'basic skills and knowledge. In learning "with, "by contrast, students use technology as a tool that can be applied to a variety of goals in the learning process, rather than serving simply as an instructional delivery system.

Students use the technology as a resource to help them develop higher order thinking, creativity, research skills, and so on. Generally, more advanced technology is involved in learning "with. " These kinds of technology, we turn to the "lessons learned " from these studies and discuss a variety of key conditions that are necessary for technology to improve education. These factors, which repeatedly appear in the literature as crucial elements for successfully using technology, include the following:

— Technology is best used as one component in a broad-based reform effort.

— Teachers must be adequately trained to use technology.

— Teachers may need to change their beliefs about teaching and learning.

— Technological resources must be sufficient and accessible.

— Effective technology use requires long-term planning and support.

— Technology should be integrated into the curricular and instructional framework.

LEARNING FROM COMPUTERS

Learning "from " computers takes a variety of forms - including computer-based instruction (CBI), computer-assisted instruction (CAI), Integrated Learning Systems (ILS), and intelligent learning systems (ITS). All of these forms involve using the computer as a "tutor. " An examination of research studies that investigate the impact of technological tutoring systems on student achievement shows mixed results. While some suggest that CBI, CAI, and ILS can improve students 'basic skills in such disciplines as mathematics, others report that, in some instances, the use of computers to teach basic skills had a negative impact on academic achievement. Still others argue that many of the studies comparing CBI, CAI, and ILS with traditional instruction are so methodologically flawed that no conclusions can be drawn. Despite these cautionary findings, the literature provides considerable evidence for how to make the most of using computers as tutors.

Particularly in recent years, a number of studies have provided convincing evidence that such technology can be effective in teaching basic skills. For example, a study on the impact of learning technologies on student achievement in Illinois reported that scores on state assessments improved in many areas, such as 11th grade science and 10th grade reading, although gains were not uniform across subject matter areas. Similarly, a high school in Pittsburgh implemented a computerized "Cognitive Tutor " in its mathematics classes. . This tutor presented students with real-world, contextualized problems and built learning profiles of its users.

Evaluations showed that Algebra students who used this tutor outperformed students in traditional classes, having achievement gains of up to 25 percent in skill and up to 100 percent in problem solving. Retention in mathematics classes and attendance also improved among the students using the tutor. The West Virginia Basic Skills/Computer Education Program (BS/CE)was a large-scale, longitudinal study designed to focus on the State 's basic skill goals in reading, language arts, and mathematics. It began with a cohort of kindergarten students in the school year 1990 -91.

Each year the state of West Virginia provided every elementary school with enough equipment so that each classroom serving this cohort of children would have three or four computers, a printer, and a schoolwide networked file server. As the children of this first cohort moved through the elementary grades, their new teachers received technology training and the school received additional software, computers, and other technology tools.

Statistical analyses conducted by Mann and his colleagues (1999)show that, after the "technology-enhanced " cohort in West Virginia enrolled in grade three, statewide third grade Comprehensive Tests of Basic Skills (CTBS) scores went up five points in one year, after having risen only a total of six points over the previous four years. In 1997, the BS/CE cohort 's fourth-grade reading scores were the second highest among southern states. (In terms of per-capita income, West Virginia is 40th in the US; in achievement, it is 17th.)A study of the first fifth-graders to have had consistent availability of BS/CE showed gains in the Stanford-9 achievement test, with higher gains for the students with more BS/CE experience. After conducting a regression analysis, researchers concluded that BS/CE accounted for a significant portion of the total variance in the basic skills achievement gain scores of the fifth graders.

In another decade-long study, researchers investigating the impact of a computer-integrated instructional program called Project CHILD (Computers Helping Instruction and Learning Development)found that elementary students in project classrooms from kindergarten through fifth grade have consistently had "higher test scores and better discipline than their counterparts in traditional, self-contained classrooms". In CHILD classrooms, students engage in reading, writing, or mathematics tasks at learning stations, including a computer station with three to six computers. Positive results were found with students at both high-and low-achieving schools.

Moreover, longitudinal studies found that students who had been in Project CHILD classrooms during their elementary years had higher grade-point averages, higher standardized test scores, and more enrollments in advanced math courses at the middle school level than students who had not participated in the project. In addition to these longitudinal studies, a variety of meta-analyses conducted between 1985 and 2000 on the impact of CBI, CAI, ILS, drill-and-practice software, and computer tutorials on student achievement report that students using computers had higher test scores, typically as measured on standardized achievement tests.

In 1994, for example, Kulik aggregated findings from over 500 individual studies of computer-based instruction. These studies showed percentile gains on achievement tests of 9 to 22 percent over control groups. On average, students who used computer-based instruction scored at the 64th percentile compared to students without computers who scored at the

50th percentile. Kulik also found that computer-based instruction can decrease the amount of time required for students to learn basic skills.

As a result of these meta-analyses, many conclude that computer-assisted instruction and drill-and-practice software can significantly improve students 'scores on standardized achievement tests, in all major subject areas, preschool through higher education. Looking across these studies, it is clear that using computers in a tutorial capacity can be beneficial - particularly in today 's political climate - for schools and districts that are often heavily focused on increasing students ' scores on standardized achievement tests.

Moreover, some researchers argue that using technology to accomplish these kinds of goals requires less teacher training than more sophisticated uses and can often be accomplished with low-end technology. However, it would be shortsighted to focus only on how best to have students learn "from " computers - that is, , using technology to tutor students on basic skills.

LEARNING WITH TECHNOLOGY

While evidence indicates that computers can help students improve their performance on tests of basic skills, many researchers investigating the use of technology in education have found that technology is most powerful when used as a tool for problem solving, conceptual development, and critical thinking. In Reeves' terms, this kind of use consists of learning "with " technology. It involves students using technology to gather, organize, and analyze information, and using this information to solve problems. In this manner, the technology is used as a tool, and teachers and students (not the technology)control the curriculum and instruction. Tool applications can be used in a variety of curricular areas.

Using technology in this manner has become possible through increases in the sophistication and versatility of computer-based technology. As a result, early studies of CAI,

ILS, and other forms of computer tutoring offer little insight into the impact of students learning "with " technology. . Furthermore, early studies tended to focus on specific software or technology, severely limiting the generalizability of their results. In most instances, these early studies treat technology "as a discrete and isolated . . . input ", and fail to take into account the larger classroom, school, and district context in which the technology was being used.

By contrast, much of the research literature on learning "with " technology takes into account these larger issues of the learning context and educational benefits that are harder to quantify than basic skills. Current instructional technologies can give visual representation to higher-order concepts, use graphics and simulations to link mathematical concepts to real-world applications, provide tools for data analysis which can reveal subtle patterns in data, and supply contextual information through interactive dictionaries, encyclopedias, and similar resources.

With technology, students can spend less time doing calculations and more time creating strategies for solving complex problems and developing a deep understanding of the subject matter. Word processors have greatly simplified some aspects of writing, editing, and rewriting. Video has long been a way to present unfamiliar material that would be difficult to conceptualize when presented verbally, and today 's interactive video combines the power of visual presentation with the interactive and information-processing capabilities of the computer.

Computers may not provide the best means to read large blocks of text, such as complete books, but they are useful for scanning smaller sections of written material. Moreover, using hypertext links to browse through related material is a very efficient method for collecting information. With the Internet, students can have access to libraries many times more extensive than libraries in their schools or communities, and can take advantage of information that is up-to-date, not found in their textbooks, and perhaps unfamiliar to their teacher. Interactions through email have been shown to be motivating factors for students to improve their reading and writing skills. Email also allows students to collaborate with people not physically present, over large distances.

One of the most powerful uses of technology in education is to tailor instruction to students ' individual learning needs. Technology can provide the means for students with special needs to communicate via email and use the Internet for research, and can also help teachers accommodate students ' varying learning styles. Gifted students can work at their own pace and explore subjects in more depth than the basic curriculum. Technology can also analyze and provide immediate feedback on performance, and can suggest modifications in instruction where necessary to improve student achievement.

Impact on students

Technology used in these ways leads to outcomes that tend to be difficult to measure. The difficulty results not only from rapid changes in technology, but also because many existing assessments do not adequately capture the skills that this technology enhances, such as critical thinking, other higher order thinking skills, writing, and problem solving. As a result, studies examining the impact of students learning "with " technology are far from conclusive. Nonetheless, some studies exist that illuminate the conditions under which technology can improve student learning.

The Apple Classrooms of Tomorrow (ACOT)project, for example, was a 10-year study that set out to investigate how routine use of technology by teachers and students would affect teaching and learning. ACOT equipped project classrooms in five different schools throughout the country with computers, printers, scanners, laser-disc and videotape players, modems, CD-ROM drives, and a variety of software packages. ACOT teachers were provided with training on telecommunications, basic troubleshooting, and tool software such as spreadsheets, databases, and graphics programs. The project also helped fund a coordinator at each school site to provide technical and instructional assistance.

Researchers evaluating the impact of ACOT conducted a longitudinal study of project students, and reported that, when compared to their non-ACOT peers, they "routinely employed inquiry, collaborative, technological, and problem-solving skills uncommon to graduates of traditional high school programs ". In these ACOT classrooms, students routinely used tool software such as word processing, databases, spreadsheets, hypermedia, and multimedia. Interdisciplinary, project-based learning was commonplace at this site, where teachers worked in teams to integrate technology into the curricular framework. The skills ACOT students developed as a consequence were similar to those argued for by the U. S. Department of Labor.

According to the Commission, in addition to basic language and computational literacy, high school graduates must master the abilities to work with others; locate, evaluate, and use information; organize resources; understand complex work systems; and work with a variety of technologies. In another longitudinal study, researchers investigated the impact of project-based learning using multimedia. The project, funded through a federal Technology Innovation Challenge Grant, was aimed at helping teachers implement an exemplary model of interdisciplinary, project-based learning with multimedia, and thereby provide students with the opportunity to acquire content knowledge, as well as improve composition and presentation skills. In completing the projects, which were built around real-world problems, students used a variety of technological tools, including video cameras, digital editing, and Web authoring programs.

Data from teachers 'self-reports, as well as classroom observation data, suggest that project teachers were less likely to lecture than non-project colleagues, and instead took on the role of facilitator or coach. In project classrooms, students spent a greater amount of time than non-project peers in active, small-group collaborative activities or small group discussions. In short, project classrooms were much more student-centered than non-project classrooms, and were "organized around the collaborative construction of complex products ". Given the difficulty of measuring the effects of this kind of technology use, researchers designed a complex performance assessment to determine what students were learning.

The assessment required students to work in small groups for an hour to construct a brochure to inform elementary school principals and teachers about the problems that homeless elementary students encounter when they go to school. The assignment required students to document these problems, suggest solutions, and propose arguments about why these solutions would work. Brochures were rated on a variety of dimensions related to communication and presentation skills, including:students 'understanding of he curriculum content; students ' attention to an external audience; and design (e. g. , integration of text, images, and graphics).

Students from project classrooms as well as non-project classrooms completed the assessment. Their brochures were rated by judges who were blind to students 'affiliation (project or non-project). Results indicate that project students outperformed non-project students on all dimensions. Moreover, gains were not achieved at the cost of growth in basic skills, since researchers found that project students scored comparably on standardized tests to their non-project peers.

In addition to having a positive impact on the higher-order skills described above, numerous studies have reported that technology can lead to increased. student motivation and improved self concept. In 2000, for example, researchers commissioned by the Software and Information Industry Association (SIIA)examined 311 research reviews and reports from published and unpublished sources. They concluded that technology has been found to have a positive effect on student attitudes toward learning, self-confidence, and self-esteem.

In ACOT classrooms, teachers reported that students displayed increased initiative by going beyond requirements of assignments, and that students spent more time on assignments and projects when working on computers. Students often chose to use technology during free time, and before and after school. However, researchers noted that technology had an enduring, positive impact on student engagement in ACOT classrooms only under certain conditions.

Impact on and from education systems

In addition to examining the effect of technology on student outcomes, researchers have investigated the impact of technology on classrooms, schools, and districts. Results of a variety of studies suggest that, over time, technology can serve as a strong catalyst for change at the classroom, school, and district level. Glennan and Melmed point out, "Introducing information technology into the schools may provide the catalyst that enables and forces the restructuring necessary to meet our national education goals. " Conversely, evidence also exists that technology will have a stronger impact when technology integration is part of a broader-based reform effort.

In other words, the relationship between technology and reform appears to be reciprocal. Each can benefit from the other. Whereas using technology as a tutor tends to be associated with a focus on improving performance on standardized achievement tests, the type of instructional philosophy most consistent with learning "with " technology is constructivism. After the publication of A Nation at Risk, educational reform efforts focused heavily on raising course requirements and scores on standardized tests of academic achievement, for which computer-based instruction, Integrated Learning Systems, and similar forms of learning "from " computers were most useful.

In the early 1990s, educators and psychologists, as well as groups such as the National Council for Teachers of

Mathematics and the National Science Teachers Association, suggested a move toward more constructivist learning strategies, which calls for "teaching basic skills within authentic contexts ... for modeling expert thought processes, and for providing for collaboration and external supports to permit students to achieve intellectual accomplishments they could not do on their own ...".

The more advanced uses of technology support the constructivist view of learning in which the teacher is a facilitator of learning rather than the classroom 's only source of knowledge. In numerous studies of student learning "with " technology, , teachers have reported that technology encourages them to be more student-centered, more open to multiple perspectives on problems, and more willing to experiment in theirteaching. In technology-rich classrooms, students become more engaged and more active learners, and there is typically a greater emphasis on inquiry and less on drill and practice.

Technology also encourages student collaboration, project-based learning, and higher-order thinking. According to Means and her colleagues, "Technology supports exactly the kinds of changes in content, roles, organizational climate, and affect that are at the heart " of constructivist educational reform movements. Similarly, Bozeman and Baumbach report that schools that have embraced technological change in instructional delivery have seen dramatic improvements consistent with school restructuring.

Simpler Computer-based Tutoring Systems

Whether the technology involved is the simpler computer-based tutoring systems or the more advanced technology suited to student exploration, and whether the goal is to raise student achievement on standardized tests or to serve as a catalyst for whole school reform, research studies consistently point to certain conditions that favor productive outcomes. The following sections identify and explain the conditions that educators and policymakers should strive to put in place in order to make the most of their technology investments.

Technology as one piece of the puzzle

Although technology can support educational change, it will have little impact without accompanying reform at the classroom, school, and district level. For example, in Union City, New Jersey, a study was conducted of the impact of a school-business partnership designed to provide students and teachers with in-depth access to communications and information resources. Project students had access at home and at school to a variety of technological tools, including email, whereas non-project students had access only at school and were not provided with email.

Researchers examining the impact of the technology on student achievement found a substantial improvement in students 'standardized test results, particularly at the middle school level, where scores rose between 30 to 50 percentile points on a state-mandated test. While some of this improvement can be attributed to technology, researchers noted the importance of other restructuring efforts that were occurring simultaneously, such as a change in the reading curriculum from skill-based to whole language; the use of authentic literature instead of basal readers; block scheduling; extensive staff development; and increased parent involvement.

Researchers concluded, "The magic lay not exclusively in the technology, but in the interweaving of a systematic program of education reform with the judicious use of technology-based resources ". Researchers in the ACOT study noted that technology had an enduring, positive impact on student engagement only under certain conditions, particularly when the technology was integrated into other aspects of the students 'experience. For example, students were less likely to become bored with computers when teachers used technology as one tool among many in their instructional repertoire.

In such classrooms, teachers used computers only when they were the most appropriate tool for completing the assignment, not simply because they were available. Student engagement was more likely to endure in classrooms that emphasized the use of tool software rather than drill-and-practice applications. In order to maintain student engagement, teachers also needed to take into account individual differences in interest and ability. Finally, student engagement remained high in classrooms emphasizing interdisciplinary, project-based instruction. Other researchers have reported similar results related to student motivation.

Studies of IBM 's Reinventing Education program showed that students ' reading skills improved in schools that had leadership committed to a school reform plan as well as clear, meaningful educational goals. Walt Disney Elementary School in Burbank, California, used technology for the purpose of improving standardized test scores, but first organized the curriculum and teachers of the school for the effective integration of technology.

In ACOT classrooms, researchers found a strong complementary relationship between the adoption of technology and the creation of collaborative learning environments for teachers. And in a study of five technology-rich schools, goals for student learning were clearly articulated prior to the introduction of technology. These technology-rich schools were restructured (e. g. , longer class periods and project-based learning), were learner-centered, and had enhanced collegial relationships among adults (more consultation among teachers about curriculum and individual student learning).

In contrast, technology has been shown to be less effective when learning objectives are unclear and the focus of technology use is diffuse. Similarly, technology will not live up to its promise when teachers fail to focus on improving student learning.

Adequate and appropriate teacher training

A variety of studies indicate hat echnology will have little effect unless teachers are adequately and appropriately trained. Studies suggest that teachers who receive formal training use technology more frequently for instruction, and this use can lead to significant improvements in student achievement. In US, according to a report by the National Center for Education Statistics, teachers who report feeling prepared to teach using technology use it more frequently and in a greater variety of ways, and are more likely to have their students use technology as a tool in tasks that require higher-order thinking.

Specifically, the report states that students of teachers with more than ten hours of training significantly outperformed students of teachers with five or fewer training hours. Researchers investigating the BS/CE program in West Virginia also found that timely and comprehensive teacher training was a key factor in the program 's success. Evaluations showed that the use of technology was linked to higher scores made by eighth graders in problem solving and critical thinking, but only if the technology was used by trained teachers who use it in the most productive ways. Follow-up evaluations of this program also showed that the greatest gains in student achievement occurred when teachers were trained in the use of technology.

A study of the 1996 NAEP results in mathematics found that teachers who are more knowledgeable about the use of computers were more likely than their less knowledgeable colleagues to use technology for higher-order purposes, and that students whose teachers received professional development on computers showed gains in math scores of up to 13 weeks above grade level. In a wide-scale effort to improve the use of technology in classroom instruction throughout Rhode Island, 2, 400 teachers - 25 percent of all teachers in the state - participated in the Teachers and Technology Initiative. As part of this program, teachers spent 60 hours in training on hardware, software, and technology integration. In addition, teachers were provided with sample units and laptop computers to use both in the classroom and at home.

Researchers found an increase in the percentage of teachers using email and the Internet as a result of this training. Researchers conclude that the training gave teachers "a solid foundation in the use of technology as a core component of their instructional practices ". In Project CHILD, developers of the program clearly recognized the importance of teacher professional development. The CHILD model provides teachers with a full year of training and classroom coaching on using technology and on collaborative teaching strategies, as well as research-based materials to help teachers effectively integrate the instructional software.

Wahl suggests that organizations should spend 30 percent of their budget on equipment and 70 percent on the "human infrastructure " to support ongoing training and technical assistance. Since many schools and districts prefer to spend their limited funds on tangible goods such as hardware and software, it is not surprising that researchers investigating the impact of technology on education report that insufficient teacher training is a significant barrier to successful integration. Statham and Torell, for example, state that 80 percent of districts spend less than 10 percent of their technology budget on training, and that, on the average, teachers were offered only 21 hours of training in technology.

Research also suggests a lack of sufficient teacher training in technology use at the preservice level. As is the case with inservice professional development, the content of preservice education related to technology is "fundamental computer operation rather than preparation on how to use technology as a teaching tool and how to integrate it across the curriculum ". Moursund and Bielefeldt (1999) report that student teachers often do not have the opportunity to routinely use technology during their field experiences, and typically are not provided guidance by a master teacher on how to integrate technology into their instruction.

Given the lack of preservice and inservice training, teachers who want to hone their technology skills often do so on their own time. Statham and Torell, for example, indicate that 90 percent of teachers report that they are self-taught. A 1994 survey for the Office of Technology Assessment reports that less than 10 percent of new teachers felt prepared to use multimedia and communication technologies in their teaching, and only about half felt that they were competent enough with tools such as word processing or spreadsheets to use them in the classroom.

In 1999, the National Center for Education Statistics indicated that only 20 percent of teachers report feeling well-prepared to integrate technology into their teaching. Even those schools and districts that do provide teachers training typically offer after-school workshops that concentrate on the basic mechanics of hardware and software. Brief sessions on word processing, scanning, or using spreadsheets are commonplace. While many teachers have participated in this type of training, most report that it was too short in duration and too limited to be helpful. Although teachers do need to understand fundamental computer operation to have the confidence and expertise to use technology, they need to be taught much more.

Specifically, teachers need to be taught how to use technology to deliver instruction. Helping teachers to learn to integrate technology into curriculum is a critical factor in the successful implementation of technology in schools, but most teachers have not had training in using technology effectively in teaching. Even when professional development does focus on technology integration, teachers typically receive little follow-up training or support.

In an effort to create a model of staff development that overcomes the shortcomings of traditional inservice training, the Apple Classrooms of Tomorrow project, along with the National Science Foundation and three school districts, joined in 1992 to create teacher development centers at three of ACOT 's original sites. At the centers, visiting teachers observed and worked in ACOT classrooms for one-week practicums during the school year, or for four-week institutes during the summer. Unlike typical after-school programs, this model of staff development allowed participants to see expert teachers modeling instructional use of technology as they worked with students. Participants learned about integrating specific hardware and software into their instruction, and explored issues such as interdisciplinary instruction, alternative assessment, project-based teaching, and team teaching. ACOT coordinators also provided follow-up support for participants for one year after visiting the centers.

Researchers investigating the impact of the program found that when teachers are learning to integrate technology into their classrooms, the most important staff-development features include opportunities to explore, reflect, collaborate with peers, work on authentic learning tasks, and engage in hands-on, active learning. In essence, the principles for creating successful learning environments for children apply to teachers as well.

In addition to receiving training on how to use technology instructionally. research also suggests that teachers need additional help in learning how to assess products created using technology. Just as students sometimes focus too heavily on the technology-related aspects of assignments, teachers also can be distracted by the "glitz " of technologically sophisticated student work and lose sight of the "guts " or content. . It is not uncommon, for example, for teachers beginning to use technology to create grading rubrics where students are assessed on the number of different fonts used, or the number of different slides in a multimedia presentation, rather than on the actual content. Other reports indicate that in classrooms using multimedia, technology tends to be over-emphasized, while the underlying content is under-emphasized.

Changing teacher beliefs about learning and teoching

If technology is to be used in powerful ways - to support student collaboration, inquiry, and interactive learning - then teachers ' beliefs about learning and teaching often must change. For those teachers who firmly believe that the lecture-recitation-seat work model of instruction is the best teaching method under all circumstances, even the best professional development on technology will have limited success. Integrating technology into instruction is a difficult, time-consuming process; only those teachers who believe that technology use will lead to significant benefits for their students will undertake the associated challenges.

One study that carefully examined the changes in teachers ' beliefs as they integrated technology into instruction was on the ACOT project. Researchers found that the introduction of technology into project classrooms did not radically change teaching; instead, technology seemed to serve as a symbol for change, granting teachers a license for experimentation. To describe the changes that occurred over the course of three to five years in teachers ' instructional practices, researchers developed a five-stage model, which includes entry, adoption, adaptation, appropriation, and invention.

In the ACOT model, text-based curriculum delivered in a lecture-recitation-seat work mode was first strengthened through the use of technology, and then was gradually replaced by more dynamic learning experiences for students, such as collaborative, project-based, interdisciplinary learning. The instructional changes that occurred during these stages were closely tied to changes in teachers ' beliefs about classroom management, learning, teacher-student roles, and instructional practices. ACOT researchers believe that the shifts in teachers 'beliefs occurred when teachers began to see firsthand the benefits of technology use.

The development of ACOT Teacher Development Centers was based in part on the idea that if visiting teachers could see for themselves the potential benefits of using technology, then they, too, would confront and possibly change their beliefs about learning and teaching, and as a consequence more successfully integrate technology into their classrooms. Other researchers have drawn similar conclusions about the value of providing teachers with a vision of what is possible, and have noted that teachers who volunteer to be a part of a reform initiative can serve as models and mentors for those who are reluctant to adopt an innovation.

In Project Explore, for example, researchers felt that the project "benefited by capitalizing on teachers who were willing and motivated to bring about change and incorporate new technologies into the teaching and learning process ". Teachers who were involved during the early stages of the project opened their classrooms so colleagues could observe for themselves the impact of technology use on learning and teaching. Chang and his colleagues noted, "For more skeptical teachers, having an opportunity to look before they leapt was key to building momentum . . . ". These types of observational experiences can often serve as a strong impetus for changing teachers 'beliefs about learning and teaching and bolster their motivation for undertaking the difficulties associated with technology integration.

Sufficient and accessible equipment

Without sufficient access to technology, of course, even well-trained, highly motivated teachers will not be able to integrate technology effectively into instruction. Although studies are inconclusive about the optimal number of computers per classroom, research is clear that students and teachers are best served if they have convenient, consistent, and frequent access to technology.

For example, a RAND study of technology-rich schools suggested that the most successful of these schools had a high density of computers and high access to them. In these schools, the expenditure per pupil on technology was three to five times the U. S. average. Similarly, the West Virginia BS/CE study indicated beneficial effects from instructional technology are unlikely unless there is sufficient equipment and access to it.

A study of 55 schools in New York investigated the impact of increased access to technology. Results indicate that in schools that had more instructional technology -as well as teacher training -the average increase in the percentage of high school students who took and passed the state Regents exam in mathematics was 7. 5. Using principal and teacher reports related to technology access, researchers concluded that "42%of the variation in math scores and 12%of the variation in English scores could be explained by the addition of technology in the schools ".

Researchers also found a "strong relationship "between higher scores on the state 's Comprehensive Assessment Report on sixth grade mathematics tests and increased access to technology. Moreover, researchers reported a positive relationship between the amount of technology available and teachers 'self-reports of their skill using the technology. While recent surveys about the status of technology in schools suggest that the amount of technology is increasing, teachers continue to report that lack of access is a significant barrier to technology integration. Many schools have computers that are obsolete. It is not uncommon for schools to still be using machines that are over a decade old.

The results of a national survey of technology use conducted by Henry Becker revealed that fewer than 20 percent of schools have "at least one computer of any kind for every four students enrolled, one Pentium or Power Macintosh for every six students, one CD-ROM-equipped computer for every six students, and . . . at least half of all instructional rooms connected to the Internet by a high-speed, direct connection". Moreover, there are wide discrepancies in accessibility from state to state and from school to school, with high poverty schools typically having fewer technological tools.

Statham and Torell suggest that a 1:5 computer-to-student ratio would assure students "near universal access. " In the ACOT project, , researchers investigated the impact of "universal access " by providing all project students with a computer both at school and at home. Over the course of the project, researchers learned that, although computer access was important, access did not necessarily require a computer on every desk. Eventually, the configuration of computers in ACOT classrooms changed to require the sharing of resources. In the later years of the project, most classrooms had a ratio of about five students per computer, consistent with the recommendation of Statham and Torell.

Unfortunately, a 1:5 ratio far exceeds what is found in most classrooms. When ACOT began training teachers in their Teacher Development Centers in 1992, visiting teachers who participated in the program often found it difficult to transfer what they had learned in technology-rich classrooms to their own setting. Some felt limited by insufficient hardware and software in their own classrooms, but others learned how to use their one or two computers creatively. For example, some teachers used a "station approach, " where students rotated through a variety of different activities on a daily or weekly basis.

In such cases, teachers realized that they could manage effectively with only one or two "computer stations. " Despite the success of this approach, other researchers have argued that if students are to use computers to be better writers, researchers, and problem-solvers, they need to have access to computers when they are engaged in these processes, not only at some regularly scheduled time. Soloway and his colleagues believe that handheld devices (personal information managers or personal digital assistants)"are the answer to the access challenge in K -12 education".

Preliminary research with over 2, 000 students in a variety of schools around the country suggests that, despite their limitations, these devices can be effective tools in content areas such as physics and mathematics. Applications in reading, writing, and mathematics are currently available, and more are under development.

Classrooms versus computer labs

In addition to the number of computers available, the location of the hardware affects accessibility. Computers can be either in a centralized location (such as a computer lab), distributed (in the classrooms), or a combination of the two. All three models were used in the West Virginia BS/ CE program. The results from this program indicate that student outcomes are most improved by the distributed model. Students who had access to computers in their classrooms showed more improvement in basic skills than those who received instruction in computer labs. In addition, teachers who had computers in the classroom reported greater confidence and competence in using computers and more time using the computers.

In recent years, schools and districts have been working to connect students and teachers to the Internet. As is the case with computers, whether or not teachers use the Internet for instruction appears highly dependent on classroom connectivity. As researchers for the Software and Information Industry Association report, "Classroom connectivity to the Internet was found to be the best predictor of teachers ' professional use of the Internet.

Furthermore, classroom connectivity in general and, more specifically, connectivity with four or more computers were found to be important factors in predicting whether teachers directed student research involving the Internet. " Similarly, Henriquez and Riconscente, in a study involving almost 600 teachers in Rhode Island, concluded that a lack of computers connected to the Internet at the classroom level was the most significant barrier to the use of this important tool.

Computer access at home

In addition to investigating the importance of school access, researchers have examined the impact of students 'and teachers 'use of home computers. For example, in Union City, New

Jersey, researchers examined a cohort of project students who had sustained access to technology at home and at school, and compared their performance on standardized tests to non-project students who had a more limited, school-only access. Specifically, project students had access to tools such as word processing, spreadsheet, and database programs, as well as access to communication resources such as email and information resources such as the Internet.

Non-project students had access to similar resources at the school, but did not have access to email. Researchers found that project students did significantly better than the non-project students on standardized writing tests at the seventh, eighth, and ninth grade levels.

In Indiana, students participating in the Buddy project were supplied with home computers and modem access to the school. An evaluation comparing seven project classrooms to three non-project classrooms showed significant differences in a number of student outcomes. Specifically, project students "showed improvement in all writing skills, a better understanding and broader view of math, more confidence with computer skills, an ability to teach others, greater problem-solving skills, and greater self-confidence and self-esteem " than non-project peers.

In the ACOT project, for example, researchers found that teachers at the elementary level did not have time to develop appropriate homework assignments utilizing computers. Consequently, in later years of the project, ACOT continued providing home computers only at the high school site. Like students, teachers can often improve their skills with access to a home computer. Teachers typically do not have enough time on the job to learn to use technology, to practice what they have learned, and to explore further uses of the computer. Teachers who have computers at home have more time not only to learn to use technology, but to become more comfortable with it.

Long-term planning

Too often, technology is purchased without a clear vision of how it is to be integrated into the mission of the school or district. Research suggests that technology projects should be implemented only after a planning stage, where administrators and other stakeholders develop clearly articulated standards and goals for technology use. The most successful schools in IBM 's Reinventing Education program, for example, were willing to allocate time and other scant resources for planning how best to use the technology to improve instruction. Moreover, since hardware and software are constantly changing, schools and districts must revisit their technology plan on an ongoing basis and make revisions, as necessary, to take advantage of new opportunities and innovations.

Many schools and districts also make the mistake of spending most or all of their technology funds on initial purchases of software and hardware, and overlook the fact that replacing, maintaining, and supporting computer equipment will also require money. Unlike many items purchased for schools, such as library books or physical education equipment, computer hardware and software, as well as peripheral devices, quickly become obsolete. In some schools, printers sit idle because money was not budgeted to replace ink cartridges, toner, or paper. For this reason, costs of educational technology should be built into school budgets on an ongoing basis.

TECHNICAL AND INSTRUCTIONAL SUPPORT

Although adequate access to technology is a key factor in successful implementation, researchers investigating the impact of technology on student learning have found that a major barrier to technology use is the lack of technical support. Even teachers who enjoy using computers will stop using technology if the equipment is unreliable. Many teachers lack adequate troubleshooting skills - not to mention time - to fix equipment, , especially if it breaks in the middle of a lesson. Consequently, the effective use of technology requires an adequate school and district infrastructure and must include timely, on-site technical support.

Longitudinal research examining teachers 'use of echnology suggests that the support teachers need changes as they become more and more proficient in integrating technology into instruction. In the early stages of the ACOT project, for example, teachers needed basic technical support as they learned to use new hardware and software. Later, when teachers began experimenting with team teaching and interdisciplinary, project-based instruction, teachers needed professional development related to alternative student assessment strategies, such as performance-based assessments. Clearly, as teachers begin using technology for more sophisticated purposes, instructional support is as essential as technical support. At ACOT sites, a full-time coordinator gave teachers this crucial assistance.

The ACOT project also provided clear and striking evidence about the importance of principal and administrative support. In order for teachers to be eligible to participate in the ACOT Teacher Development Center project, their principals had to make a commitment to support them in three important ways when they returned to their schools. Specifically, principals were required to:1)provide time for teachers who had attended the center to plan together and to reflect on their practice; 2)give recognition for the teachers 'efforts; and 3)ensure that eachers had the authority and flexibility to adjust daily instructional schedules and to develop curriculum objectives that promote team teaching and interdisciplinary instruction.

ACOT staff also strongly encouraged principals to attend selected portions of the program with their teachers. Despite these commitments, administrators varied dramatically in their attitudes toward technology and in what actions they took to help teachers when they returned to their classrooms. Researchers found that the most crucial determining factor in whether teachers who participated in the program successfully integrated technology into their classroom was the level of support they received from school and district administrators. These findings are consistent with research conducted by the Office of Technology Assessment.

Technology integrated within the curricular framework

To use technology effectively, teachers must understand how its use fits into the larger curricular and instructional framework. Researchers at Educational Testing Service, for example, state that courseware (computer software designed to be used in an educational program)should reflect curricular standards, and should take into account research on how students learn. According to Statham and Torell, however, a survey in 1995 of elementary teachers reveals that schools used technology primarily to improve basic skills, rather than integrating it into the curriculum. They also report that only "nineteen percent of English classes, six to seven percent of mathematics classes, and three percent of social studies classes in high school integrated technologies into learning ".

According to researchers at the North Central Regional Educational Laboratory, CBI, CAI, ILS, and other forms of computerized tutoring are most likely to be effective when there is a match between the software, he objectives of the instruction, he students ' prerequisite knowledge and skills, and teachers 'understanding of he needs of the learners. And in the ACOT study, student engagement remained highest when technology use was integrated into the larger curricular framework, rather than being an "add-on " to an already full curriculum. Advocates of technology use in the classroom sometimes cite the importance of developing students 'job skills, and teachers often respond by "teaching technology, " such as keyboarding or word processing, rather than using it as a tool to teach the curriculum. However, research suggests that when technology is integrated into the larger instructional framework, students will not only learn how to use the equipment and software, but will also gain content knowledge.

Moreover, using technology within the curriculum framework can enhance important skills that will be valued in the workplace, such as locating and accessing information, organizing and displaying data, and creating persuasive arguments. Other research has shown the importance of integrating technology into the curricular framework. For example, West Virginia 's BS/CE program integrated technology into instruction rather than isolating computer skills from content learning. Researchers identified this characteristic of the program as one reason for its effectiveness.

Research on the Middle School Mathematics through Applications Project (MMAP)provides a striking example of how powerful technology can be if its use is embedded in content-rich activities. MMAP was created to help students learn mathematics as they designed solutions to real-world problems with the use of technology. At first, both students and teachers were so deeply engaged with the technology itself that little attention was paid to content learning. With proper support from project staff, however, mathematical content became more of a focus and the use of technology became more transparent. Specifically, project staff structured MMAP problems, activities, and assessments to enhance the subject matter content. Eventually, a balance was achieved:Students continued learning about and using the technology and many also reached middle-school mathematics standards.

EDUCATIONAL TECHNOLOGY AND SCHOOL IMPROVEMENT: GUIDLINES FOR TEACHERS

Technology helps people to learn, to be creative, and to become players and communicators in a global village. Technology, tied to the Internet, allows students and teachers of all ages to engage in knowledge building on a worldwide stage as never before possible. Many learning opportunities may never reach students in high-poverty or isolated schools except through the use of technology.

In many settings, educators, family members, human service providers, and other business partners are considering how technology can assist in implementing schoolwide improvement plans. Across the nation, these improvement efforts set high standards for all students, draw on challenging content, and require engaging instructional strategies. Technology can be used to individualize instruction and to provide learning experiences ranging from remediation to enrichment. Technology also can provide easy access to vast resources. Teacher, parent, and community partnerships are key to facilitating school improvements, including planning for and implementing technology. Schools, through technology resources and telecommunication, can make those partnerships more informed, immediate, and meaningful. In addition, research and best practices show that the relationship between technology and student learning involves understanding the following concepts:

- — Technology empowers new solutions and opens doors to learning opportunities previously unavailable.
- — The design of the technology tool and the instructional methods surrounding its use need to be congruent.
- — Hands-on access to computers and ancillary equipment for all students on a regular basis is a determining factor in the success of technology.

Developing a Personal Vision for Uses of Technology

Create a personal vision that aligns with school improvement efforts to use technology to prepare students for lifelong learning. It is important that plans for using technology in the classroom be guided by a personal vision about school improvement and technology. A personal technology vision also needs to align with the school community's vision about the desired learning outcomes for students and school-family-community partnerships. A good vision takes into account findings from research and best practices as well. Emerging trends indicate that technology can:

— Accelerate and enrich basic skills development in reading, writing, mathematics, and the sciences.

— Engage students in real-life applications of academics and encourage ownership of one's own lifelong learning.

— Help teachers meet the individual learning needs of their students more effectively, and connect teachers with each other across distances and time for professional collaboration.

— Serve as a catalyst for educational reforms, helping learners explore the world beyond the classroom and enhancing home-school connections.

In your vision, you may picture your students using electronic networks to access cultural resources and to interact with experts providing new kinds of primary sources. You may see yourself involved in an online learning community-consisting of other teachers-using technology to acquire new skills and knowledge to meet the challenges of teaching in the 21st century.

Stories about a school community's past successes and failures imple-menting technology indicate the importance of technology within the school. A good vision creates a new story pointing to a future that is better than the present or past, yet is achievable within a reasonable timeframe.

INTEGRATING TECHNOLOGY INTO THE CURRICULUM

Objective

Identify common uses of technology to foster student achievement in alignment with state and local learning standards. The poem illustrates what can happen when students rely too heavily on electronic tools, such as a spelling checker, and not enough on thinking skills. Without guidance on how to use electronic tools appro-priately, students will not know how to interpret preprogrammed advice that may appear on the computer screen. Teachers can help students develop the thinking skills necessary to use technology tools effectively.

DEVELOPING LIFELONG LEARNING SKILLS

In addition to good reading and math skills, the basic skills for the 21st century include the ability to solve semi-structured problems, work in diverse groups, and communicate effectively. The processing capabilities of today's technology push the envelope on all of these, as well as other lifelong learning skills, including informa-tion literacy skills. The American Library Association has defined nine information literacy standards in the following three categories:

— The ability to access, evaluate, and use information appropriately

— The ability to use information for independent learning or to follow personal interest

— The ability to be a socially responsible consumer of information

Today's interactive technology tools often require the learner to develop and apply these higher-order thinking skills, along with the necessary hands-on technology literacy skills to access online communities and manipulate electronic information. The newly released National Educational Technology Standards (NETS) define a set of technology literacy standards for students in the following six categories:

— Basic operation and concepts of technology systems

— Social, ethical, and human issues related to technology

— Uses for productivity tools

— Uses for networked communications tools

— Uses of research tools

— Uses of problem-solving and decision-making tools

Those involved in the NETS initiative indicate that these standards are only a starting place. They are working further to develop standards addressing technology integrated into specific curricular areas, at developmental learning levels, and for student assessment purposes. Nonetheless, technology standards for students have been set by the majority of states that are also developing ways to measure student progress when learning with and from technology.

The types of technology resources that give students access to curricu-lar content are expanding. On both state and national levels, policy-makers are infusing technology into content standards and learning goals. A good example of this trend comes from the Wisconsin Educational Technology Plan PK-12 (WETP). WETP is based on the belief that "curriculum and technology will play an unquestionably crucial role in the futures of individual children and our world. Experts from many disciplines advise that technology should and can play an important role in curriculum planning, development, delivery, assess-ment, and administration". In addition, teachers are finding ways in which technology can facilitate developmentally appropriate learning experiences at all levels of education.

Technology in Science Instruction

Science is very conducive to the use of hands-on technologies. In real life, scientists are heavy users of technology and are highly dependent on it to conduct their work. In US, the National Assessment of Educational Progress Survey showed that except for social studies (8%), science teachers were the lowest users of technology among the major content areas. The report indicated that only 12 percent of college bound students reported using computers in their science courses. This number is in sharp contrast to 72 percent using computers in schools for word pro-cessing, 44 percent for English classes, and 27 percent for mathematics.

A coalition of organizations under the auspices of the National Research Council, released science education standards for the nation. They included technology standards, such as being able to use technology to study scientific processes, explore new scientific knowl-edge, and understand the impact of technology on living organisms. Network Science Models represent a promising use of technology to meet the science standards. Through telecommunications, usually the Internet, students at several schools work collaboratively to collect data. They then organize and analyze the data and share their findings with others.

For example, one testbed pro-ject called for students' exploration and data collection of wetlands, providing hands-on learning experiences with the scientific research methods. Students disseminated data given by other schools through satellite broadcasts. They explained the results of their inquiry and compared them with the results of other schools working on the same unit. "Much of the research of the student teams depended on the infor-mation that was downloaded and discussed during interactive broad-casts" (Feldman & Nyland, 1994, p. 3).

Some concerns about using technology in science revolve around costly safeguards for high-end technology equipment, including specialized computers; probes; temperature, motion, color and other sensing devices; data analysis; and display tools. Additionally, many excellent applications of technology in science require ready access to the Internet, which is not yet available in many classrooms. However, most schools have an Internet connection available in the learning resource center and/ or computer laboratory. While weary of outdated drill-and-practice technology in their science classes, many educators are not aware of the educational software built for scientific inquiry and dis-covery.

Types of technology commonly used for science include:

— Simulation and demonstration tools that show how concepts apply to real-world phenomena.

— Exploration and guided practice tools that assist students' use of scientific knowledge.

— Online data-sharing communities involved in scientific inquiry.

— Reference CD-ROMs and Web sites for information research.

— Problem-solving tools that foster scientific thinking.

— Creative activity tools that encourage students to imagine probabilities.

— A range of digital and electronic instrumentation.

Technology in English/Language and Arts Instruction

In US, the new English/Language Arts Standards, developed by the National Council of Teachers of English and the International Reading Association, reflect the influence technology is having on the discipline. Standard one acknowledges the need for students to be able to "read a wide range of print and nonprint text". The definition of text now explicitly includes multisensory forms of communication as well as print.

In reading instruction, electronic books, often on CD-ROM, turn read-ing from a static, print-based activity into a multisensory, interactive experience. Most print-based books embody a story grammar or rhetor-ical structure that assumes the reader will start at the beginning and read through the page sequence to the end. Hypertext (characterized by links that one can click on with the mouse to go to another section) adds depth and elaboration to content through associative, audio, dynamic visual, and video texts that affect the nature of reading and writing across the curriculum. When reading an electronic text, the reader can decide from among a number of reading paths which one to follow.

Electronic books often allow readers to adapt texts to their vocabulary level or prior knowledge through the use of audio, animated demon-stration, and/or video clips that elaborate on meaning. In his review of the literature, Park found evidence that the adaptive features of electronic texts can individualize learning approaches and techniques according to the needs of individual learners.

Some students find writing skills particularly difficult to acquire because of the cumbersome process of having to revise their writing over and over again. However, today's word-processing tools allow students to edit their work efficiently and proficiently as long as stu-dents have solid keyboarding, software, and analytical skills. Word-processing technology supports such writing tasks as brainstorming, analyzing audience, defining a purpose, organizing content, structuring an argu-ment, and evaluating one's own or another's writing.

Some of the popular types of technology used for English/ language arts instruction include the following:

- Drill and practice in reading and writing to improve basic skills.
- Record keeping for self-monitoring.
- Word processing to support generating and organizing text.
- Software to support writing, including electronic grammar, spelling, and style checkers
- Authoring tools for creating multimedia presentations
- Multimedia reference tools, such as encyclopedias or the Internet, for student research
- Instructional vocabulary, phonics, and story mapping games
- Software for teaching reading strategies, including electronic books with multisensory stories

— Networked computers for participation in online learning communities with collaborative writing spaces

Technology in Mathematics Instruction

The US National Council of Teachers of Mathematics (NCTM) was the first professional organization to create national standards for appropri-ate uses of technology in a content area. NCTM recommends that:

— Appropriate calculators be available to all students.

— A computer be available in every classroom for demonstration purposes.

— Every student have access to a computer for individual and group work.

— Students learn to use the computer as a tool for processing information and performing calculations to investigate and solve problems.

The NCTM report, *Curriculum and Evaluation Standards for School Mathematics* (National Council of Teachers of Mathematics, 1989), states that exposure to appropriate experiences gives students mathe-matical power. Mathematical power is defined as "an individual's abili-ties to explore, conjecture, and reason logically, as well as the ability to use a variety of mathematical methods effectively to solve nonroutine problems. This ... is based on the recognition of mathematics as more than a collection of concepts and skills to be mastered; it includes methods of investigating and reasoning, means of communication, and notions of context. In addition, for each individual, mathematical power involves the development of personal self-confidence". The hands-on learning experiences fostered through today's interactive technology applications empower students with a level of mathematical power they cannot achieve without technology.

Mathematics teachers were early users and champions of technology because much of the initial software that was available to schools assisted in the teaching of basic mathematics skills. Since then, many schools have reported that students who supplemented teacher-led instruction with individualized computer-assisted drill-and-practice did better in mathematics than students who received conventional instruc-tion. But perhaps even more significant is that because the new technology made calculating and graphing easier, it changed the very nature of the problems that mathematics can solve and the methods mathematicians use to solve them. Generally speaking in mathematics education, technology serves as a tool for:

— Acquiring, evaluating, and processing numeric information.

— Performing calculations and interpreting trends.

— Graphing and communicating numeric information.

— Investigating and solving problems with mathematical premises.

— Creating and running models and simulations.

— Scaffolding higher levels of abstraction.

Technology in Social Studies

Technology is also valuable in social studies. For example, WETP advocates using geographical, mapping, and history-based software applications, as well as age-appropriate simulations with elementary students who are expanding their understanding of the world beyond themselves and their families. "Simulations offer students the opportu-nity to participate in historical events or major decision-making events by virtue of role playing. Whether studying the 50 states or debating the pros and cons of declaring American's independence from England, students will find a wealth of excellent technology-based applications to make exploring social studies themes exciting" Following are the types of technology tools for social studies include:

— Databases and graphing and charting software for conducting comparative studies of demographic trends.

— Electronic atlases and laserdiscs, videos, and CD-ROM images for developing an understanding of geographical and physical characteristics.

— Telecommunications, especially the Internet, for conceptualiz-ing self, family, and community contexts around the world and for demonstrating characteristics of our global village.

— Simulations for role-playing activities of historical events.

— Statistical programs for conducting quantitative research and for analyzing results.

Existing technology applications support all areas of curricula, includ-ing world languages, business, vocational education, fine arts, and special education. Today, the momentum behind putting technology into classrooms requires teachers to consider all aspects of their curriculum to identify places where technology can benefit students by enhancing their learning experiences.

PURSUING PROFESSIONAL DEVELOPMENT

To identify areas for personal professional growth aimed at enhancing one's teaching practices and uses of appropriate technology resources. Successful professional development in technology happens both on a personal level and on a systemic, schoolwide level. Many teach-ers can take advantage of professional development opportunities offered at the district level, such as software or Internet workshops and incentives for taking graduate-level courses in educational technology. However, teachers are responsible for their own progress in integrating technology into their daily practices.

Taking a Learner-Centered Approach

Technology often plays the role of catalyst within a district, ushering in educational reforms that call for learner-centered practices. The American Psychological Association has established a set of learner-centered principles that focus on psychological factors primarily internal to and under the control of the learner. The learner-centered approach is based on the understanding that each learner is unique. When integrating technology into a learner-centered classroom, stu-dents' individualized learning styles and strategies become apparent.

Reviews of research conclude that low-achieving students or those with little prior content knowledge are likely to require more structure and instructional guidance than students at higher levels of achievement. Thus, a rule of thumb for selecting technology resources is that students with different levels of achievement and content knowledge require a range of technology resources.

Technology resources can range from close-ended drill and practice to the open-ended World Wide Web. Drill-and-practice software can rein-force specific types of skills or mastery of knowledge. Technology advancements, however, have moved educational technology beyond the limits of drill and practice to interactive technology tools designed around learner-centered principles that call for engaged learning roles. Engaged learning changes the teacher's role from information gate-keeper to facilitator, guide, and co-learner, with the student as explorer, producer, cognitive apprentice, and sometime teacher. In addition to educational reform methods, teachers must also reskill in the following four technology-related proficiencies areas.

Basic Uses of Technology. Teachers acquire basic "know-how" for operating computer hardware, software, and ancillary equipment, such as scientific probes or telecommunications cameras, as well as trou-bleshooting abilities to address technical problems that may arise. The novice characteristically uses preset, surface toolbar features of tech-nology to automate established practices. The intermediate user explores layered toolbar features of technology to increase productivity and efficiency. The advanced user customizes toolbar features to trans-form his or her daily workflow.

Instructional Uses of Technology

Teachers increasingly individualize their instructional practices with technology to support various learner strategies to meet achievement standards. The novice begins to under-stand from a specialist how technology applications align with learning standards. The intermediate user consults with a mentor to successfully integrate technology in learner-centered ways that lead to overall stan-dards' achievement. The advanced teacher plays an active facilitation role within a community of learners, using technology to help students meet achievement standards on an individualized basis.

Administrative Uses of Technology

Teachers develop data-driven practices and manage individualized learning with the support of tech-nology tools. The novice responds to mandated uses of technology for record keeping and scheduling. The intermediate user regularly enforces technology usage policies and draws on established management features of technology for monitoring and reporting students' progress, as well as managing daily practice. The advanced user per-sonalizes and/or creates technology tools for managing data-driven practices, helps develop usage policies, and models ethical technology practices.

Professional Development Uses of Technology

Teachers use telecommunications and networked computers to access online courses and information resources, as well as collaborate among colleagues. The novice begins to use technology as a supplemental resource for accessing professional information. The intermediate user accesses technology for up-to-date professional information and to communicate one-on-

one with colleagues. The advanced user relies on a paperless, interactive information system for professional growth and purposeful collaborations among students, colleagues, mentors, parents, and busi-ness partners.

Teachers need to reach an agreement on which technology proficiency criteria are most pertinent to their grade level or content area. Teacher teams can create their own technology proficiency chart to identify lev-els of technology use relevant in their school context. Teachers can then use the chart to assess their own progress and mentor others in area(s) where they have excelled.

Equitable Use of Technology Resources

Students who are ready for the future know how to use technology effectively for a variety of purposes. Students who miss out on the opportunity to learn to use technology effectively miss out on vital life skills. Most schools, however, do not have enough technology resources for every student and require rotating schedules for the use of computers in order to maintain equitable access for students. Important to a teacher's professional growth is learning how to integrate technology resources equitably.

Some activities require that all students have hands-on time with a key-board/ mouse. Other activities call for learning through technology-enriched demonstrations or collaborative group work wherein team-mates rotate the hands-on use of technology tools. Vojtek and Vojtek state that technology integration happens when the teacher knows "when a technology is the most appropriate tool to help students learn or demonstrate a particular concept or skill. . . Only when we truly integrate technology into instruction, using it as a tool to help all students improve their learning, will we finally score". Equitable expectations vary from school context to school context, depending on the amount and types of technology available. Nonetheless, all schools and districts should have procedures for moni-toring technology equity practices. Teachers need to familiarize them-selves with and enforce these procedures when using technology in their daily practices.

School-Family-Community Partnerships

Today's families come in many different shapes and sizes. Nonetheless, many researchers and school personnel agree that parents (or guardians) are a child's first teachers and that the home is his/her first classroom. Teachers who know how to use technology to facilitate parent involvement can build valuable school-family-community connections that will enhance a child's growth and development, especially in today's fast-paced culture. Family uses of technology appear to differ when income, parental educa-tion, and ethnicity differ. These familial differ-ences can have considerable consequences for student achievement at school. Access to technology that supports extended time on learning tasks outside the normal school day enriches learning and expands access to resources.

Parents, as school partners, can guide the use of technology resources in the home and/or through the public library or other community centers. But parents need to be aware of and supportive of educational change. Teachers can help by keeping parents informed and knowledgeable about how and why technology is used for learning.

Education in a technology-rich environment is a dynamic, interpersonal learning experience for both teachers and students. Teachers become more familiar with each of their students' learning styles, personal interests, and achievements. Students have the opportunity to explore personal interests and abilities and to interact more closely with their peers, parents, and community members interested in their academic and personal development. Students learn vital lifelong learning skills, such as how to generate and access valuable assessment data about themselves and how to share their knowledge with others in meaning-ful ways.

Technology, when used effectively to empower the learner to achieve a learning goal, has great potential. Teachers hold the key to determining how the learning standards and goals, instructional mode, tasks, and technology resources align with individual learner needs. Teachers in technology-rich learning environments make decisions that require time for meaningful reflection on their personal practices to help students achieve required learning standards.

ON-LINE COLLABORATIVE LEARNING ENVIRONMENTS

The impact of new technologies on Society and their corresponding influences on Educational Systems has stimulated interest in studies which reveal interesting and effective practice incorporating computer-based techniques, and research which can guide such pedagogy. Developments in multimedia materials, in networking that encourages and supports collaboration within the teaching/learning process, and in software tools that enable students to become knowledge authors not only improve instruction, but can take on innovative roles that have the potential to transform educational practice. This *Special Issue,* which has these perspectives, features over forty papers covering aspects of collaborative on-line learning environments and is organised rather loosely into six inter-related themes.

These themes raise issues such as how collaborative learning can be engineered to encourage active participation and engage deeper levels of thinking: system facilities which are effective in supporting such interactions: the pedagogies employed in instructional designs and the patterns of interactions which result: the range of applications employing collaborative learning methods and the benefits and particular problems arising in these studies. Other papers consider if the innovations have lasting effects on new courses and the transformation of educational practices; and how these techniques should influence teacher education and staff development.

In Collaborative System Design the papers include topics of how designs adapt to different communities of practice; agent techniques for interlinking individual learning paths as a prelude to collaborative interchanges; various web-based systems for supporting educational transactions via shared documents and multimedia facilities; systems and tools for a Virtual Classroom that supports mentoring; and a system that discusses and employs organisational and technical principles of knowledge management.

A second topic considers the Pedagogies that underpin Collaborative Learning. These include techniques of concept mapping and scaffolding, of supporting collaborative writing in ways that concurrently lead to individual development, and discourse schemes that emphasize structure and moderation of interactions in building up communities of practice. Role play simulations on the Web provide a further approach and these papers, though discussing the pedagogy, illustrate experience through case studies that can result in changes to teaching philosophy as well as to learning.

Collaborative Interactions is a third theme. Some studies report on the patterns of interactions in computer conferencing applications in a variety of contexts, including Languages, the Humanities, Science, Teacher-Training, and Law. Reports on the importance of task settings and structure, and the types of student contributions and feedback in relation to learning should hold the interest of readers, while a paper entitled *The Body Matrix* examines how the interactive experience is perceived by students, the metaphors which are used in their accounts, and the pedagogical issues which these raise.

A wide range of *Applications* is discussed in a fourth section, which has case studies from Primary, Secondary and Higher Education in subject areas including Mathematics, Language Learning and Writing, Business Studies, and Education. But each has a viewpoint, for example, broadening students' perspectives and improving critical thinking; using parents, volunteers and experts to provide support for tutorial and for problem-solving scenarios; employing Virtual Reality and gaming techniques; coping with large classes; and methods of planning and task structuring. Three papers at the end of this section place emphasis on Evaluation, considering student differences in interactions, learning preferences, and how the evaluation experience influences new courses.

A fifth topic is entitled *Building Learning Communities*. Here the emphasis moves towards engineering communities of practice. One paper examines Wenger's requirements of mutual engagement, joint enterprise and shared repertoires; another suggests encouraging and making roles and responsibilities explicit via group 'contracts'. A study with Primary schoolchildren also registers a need for some privacy for participants; while a fourth paper recounts how a learning community system has been established, in addition to traditional teaching methods, within a Business School.

COMMUNICATIONS TECHNOLOGIES IN EDUCATION A THREAT TO FACULTY

As the use of technologies increases in all phases of our society, community college faculty are bombarded by terms related to computers, computer-based education, broadcast television, satellites, point-to-point microwave, telecomputer networks, and interactive videodiscs. Faculty are frustrated. There is an expanding, somewhat unfamiliar vocabulary. There are expectations for greater productivity on the part of faculty: expectations which come at times of stabilizing or declining resources. New technologies are often touted as the answer to classroom problems.

A growing number of community college instructors have embraced computer technologies enthusiastically and have been effective in incorporating them into their courses, while others have flatly rejected such technologies. Faculty are still uncertain about the communications technologies as partners in instruction, and they are asking, "Should I fear these new technologies in education?" Some answer, "Yes, " but more answer, "No. "

Communications technologies have the potential to transform the educational process. They also have the power to change the roles of faculty in community colleges, even to the point of reducing the number and status of teachers. Although the transformation is not occurring overnight, the likelihood of it strikes fear in the hearts of some faculty. On the other hand, some faculty approach communications technologies openly, expectantly and impatiently, wishing that progress in the direction of their ideals for improving education could occur more rapidly.

In addition, many faculty see in communications technologies an opportunity for greater role differentiation and specialization. For example, some teachers might become actively involved as instructional designers while others might develop specializations in assessment, small group facilitation, computer programming, media development, cross-cultural education, or distance learning. Since new technologies have the potential for spreading learning more pervasively throughout our culture, there is the likely possibility of a greater need for faculty as educational specialists. Thus the answer to the question, "Are communications technologies a threat to faculty?" is more accurately "No" than "Yes. "

The introduction of new technologies into the teaching and learning process initiates a change in power relationships. These technologies give students more control over their own learning. According to Shirley C. Smith, Drexel University, "the locus of control for the educational process is shifting from professors to students. Students now have more power to experiment and play 'what if' games". In fact, some technologies give students total control over their learning. For example, a freshman level mathematics course on an interactive videodisc can present the material to be learned, drill and test the student, record responses, and compute the grade without the assistance of a teacher. Such a course can be made available to students without an instructor's supervision in learning resource centers, public libraries, or the learner's own home.

Thus, technologies have the potential of upsetting traditional power relationships in the learning process, a process in which teachers have traditionally held authority and control. On the other hand, the technologies have the potential for freeing faculty from many roles that they often describe as dreary or unprofessional, such as drill, repetition, and other learning situations that require systematic responses. Moreover, computers already play a variety of roles in recordkeeping, and thus aid faculty in course management.

Communications technologies in education allow for much greater individualization of learning. Students are able to progress at their own speed: to start learning when they are motivated and stop when they are saturated. Since community college faculty have long sought to individualize instruction, communications technologies are a real asset toward that objective. Moreover, these technologies allow the instructor to individualize instruction without having to make individual prescriptions for each student in each class during each term. Material presented on well-designed software which is branching rather than linear can free the instructor of repetitious analysis and prescription and produce opportunities for more creative tasks. Such tasks could include assisting students as they are following their learning prescriptions, defining and measuring the outcomes of education, or structuring learning environments. Should teachers fear communications technologies in education? The answer may be "Yes" for some, but it should be "No" for most community college faculty.

Reducing the Threat

The development of communications technologies and their application to learning has brought about the diffusion of higher education's monopoly on formal learning beyond high school. Long ago, a learner had to enroll in a course in order to learn how to write better business letters, compute more accurately, or read more rapidly. Now, however, with individualized instruction available in colleges, in public libraries, and in video outlets, the learning environment is changing. Nudging that change is the development of many forms of distance learning, including electronic universities. All of these allow students to learn within the settings of their own choosing and to acquire credentials for their achievements, if they so desire.

The outcome for formal postsecondary education could seriously constrict on current providers. On the other hand, community colleges, and other components of the formal learning system, can benefit because, as research has repeatedly shown, the more education people have, the more likely they are to participate in further education.

Faculty may feel less threatened by technologies once they see their potential for furthering professional development. If colleges are going to expect productivity gains as a result of the incorporation of communications technologies into the learning process, administrators and policy makers must help faculty develop new skills. It is important for administrators and faculty to remember that the biggest expense involved in incorporating new technologies into any process is the expense for staff training. It is not uncommon for 75 percent of the cost of such a conversion, if it is successful, to be related to staff development. People who are trained merely to apply a new technology to their specific jobs do not learn enough about it to go beyond the current application. And it is in the potential for future applications that productivity gains can be the highest.

Roger Kershaw, the director of the Educational Testing Service Technology Research Group, worries that if administrators are not willing to provide adequate support, both with release time and other resources, then communications technologies incorporated into education "will go the way of such failed innovations as the teaching machine". Of such unsupported technologies, George Bonham cautions, "They will come dangerously close to education's earlier failed flirtations with television and computer-aided instruction".

Thus if faculty and communications technologies are to become true partners in community college learning endeavors, administrators and policy makers must be fully committed to staff development. This means planning and allocating adequate resources for courseware development and review, plus the development of the new skills required to incorporate the technologies into the course and to transform the learning environment into one in which technology enhances learning.

7

PRINT MEDIA AND HUMAN LEARNING

Print is the foundation of education and the basis from which all other delivery systems have evolved. The first distance-delivered courses were offered by correspondence study, with print materials sent and returned to students by mail. While technological developments have added to the repertoire of tools available to the distance educator, print continues to be a significant component of all distance education programs.

ADVANTAGES OF PRINT

— *Spontaneous*. Print materials can be used in any setting without the need for sophisticated presentation equipment.

— *Instructionally transparent*. The medium of delivery should enhance, not compete with, the content for the learner's attention. If the student reads well, the print medium is the most transparent instructional medium of all.

— *Non-threatening*. Reading is second nature to most students. As a result, they are easily able to focus on the content, without becoming mesmerized or frustrated by the process of reading itself.

— *Easy to use*. Given adequate light, print materials can be used any time and any place without the aid of supplemental resources such as electricity, viewing screen, and specially designed electronic classrooms. The portability of print is especially important for rural learners with limited access to advanced technology.

— *Easily reviewed and referenced.* Print materials are typically learner-controlled. As a result, the student rapidly moves through redundant sections, while focusing on areas demanding additional attention.

— *Cost-effective.* No instructional tool is less expensive to produce than print. In addition, facilities abound for the inexpensive duplication of these materials.

— *Easily edited and revised.* In comparison to technically sophisticated electronic software, print is both easy and inexpensive to edit and revise.

— *Time-effective.* When instructional print materials are created, the developer's primary focus remains on content concerns, not the technical requirements of the delivery system.

LIMITATIONS OF PRINT

— *Limited view of reality.* Print, by its reliance on the written word, offers a vicarious view of reality. Despite the use of excellent sequential illustrations or photos, for example, it is impossible to adequately recreate motion in print.

— *Passive and self-directed.* Numerous studies have shown that higher learner motivation is required to successfully complete print-based courses. To a certain extent, the passive nature of print can be offset by systematic instructional design that seeks to stimulate the passive learner. Still, it takes more motivation to read a book or work through a written exercise than it does to watch a television program or participate in an audioconference with an instructor encouraging student participation and response.

— *Feedback and interaction.* Without feedback and interaction, instruction suffers, regardless of the delivery system in use.

By nature, print materials are passive and self-directed. Even with print materials incorporating feedback mechanisms and interactive exercises, it is easy for learners to skip to the answer section.

— *Dependent on reading skills.* Thanks to television, most students have developed fairly good viewing skills by age four. These same children, however, often fail to develop adequate reading skills by age 12. Reading skills must often be improved. Lack of ability in this area cripples the effectiveness of even the most instructionally sound print material and must be overcome if print is to be used effectively.

FORMATS OF PRINT MATERIALS

Various print formats are available, including:

— *Textbooks.* As in traditionally delivered courses, textbooks are the basis and primary source of content for the majority of distance-delivered courses. While textbooks should always be critically reviewed before adoption, this is especially critical when the learner and the instructor are not in daily contact.

— *Study guides.* Typically, distance educators use study guides to reinforce points made during class and through the use of other delivery systems. They will often include exercises, related readings and additional resources available to the student.

— *Workbooks.* In a distance education context workbooks are often used to provide course content in an interactive manner. A typical format might contain an overview, the content to be covered, one or more exercises or case studies to elaborate the points being made, and a quiz or test (with answer key) for self-assessment. In addition, there is typically some form of feedback, remediation, or "branching" loop to recycle students through the instruction as needed.

— *Course syllabus.* A comprehensive and well-planned course syllabus is the foundation of many distance-delivered courses. It provides course goals and objectives, performance expectations, descriptions of assignments, related readings (often by session), grading criteria, and a day-by-day overview of the material to be covered. The syllabus must be as complete as possible in order to guide the students through the course in the absence of daily contact with the instructor.

— *Case studies.* If written imaginatively, case studies are an extremely effective instructional tool. In fact, case studies are often designed around the limitations of print and intended to spark the students' imaginations as they place themselves in the particular case under consideration. Many case studies present a content-based scenario. They raise questions, pose alternative solutions, and then branch students to different sections of the text. There, the consequences of the selected alternative are described.

DESIGNING INSTRUCTION FOR PRINT

Because print is largely a one-way communication medium, the challenge is to design instruction to maximize the amount of interaction in distance education print materials. Consider:

— *Writing style.* Misanchuk suggests that distance educators write instructional materials with language more like that used for speaking than for writing journal articles or books. His tips for writing instructional materials include:

- — Use short sentences.
- — Avoid compound sentences.
- — Avoid excess information in a sentence.
- — Use the active voice.
- — Use personal pronouns.
- — Keep equivalent items parallel.

- — List conditions separately.
- — Avoid multiple negatives.
- — Use point form.
- — Use familiar examples.
- — Write as you would speak.
- — Avoid unnecessary and difficult words.
- — Avoid jargon; use technical terms only when necessary.
- — Put sentences and paragraphs into a logical sequence: first things that affect many, then things that affect few; first the general, then the specific; first permanent provisions, then temporary ones.
- — Avoid cultural and gender stereotyping.
- — Focusing on content organization before developing content. Prior to content development, create an outline of the material to be covered. Print materials are often too wordy because the author is planning, organizing and writing at the same time. Instead, organize content based on the identified goals and objectives. At first, focus on systematically and creatively ordering the flow of topics, not polishing a finished product. The end result will be a well-organized content outline from which the written content will easily flow.

— *Developing a course introduction.* Misanchuk suggests developing a written course introduction that will be the very first thing a distant student sees. The course introduction can include biographical background information about the instructor, a course overview, course goals and aims, a listing of any textbooks or ancillary learning materials that will be needed, and information about assignments, examinations, and grading.

— *Staying with a consistent format.* Learner anxiety with the unknown can be reduced through consistency in instructional presentation. Develop an effective format and organizational scheme and stick with it. Use adequate headings and subheadings to visually guide the reader through the material.

— *Using advance organizers.* Advance organizers are a means to connect new material with a learner's prior knowledge and cognitive structure. They should be of a more general and abstract character than the learning matter that follows and help the learner to relate different parts and concepts of teaching material to each other. Place the most general and comprehensive ideas at the beginning of a lesson and progress to more structured and detailed information.

— *Using examples and analogies.* In a traditional classroom, teachers spontaneously provide examples and analogies to illustrate a point that students are having difficulty understanding. Because distant students and their teachers may not have this type of interaction, include lots of good examples and analogies in print-based materials. Be sure, however, that these examples address the various cultural groups, ages and experiences of the students.

— *Including questions.* Questions in print material can stimulate the learner to be more active and to deal more intensively with the learning matter. Use questions that aim at understanding rather than merely reproduction and memorization of facts.

— *Adding a table of contents.* A detailed table of contents can help the learner to quickly refer to the appropriate section.

— *Incorporating a glossary of terms.* A glossary summarizes all the new, often technical terminology encountered in a document. It may be helpful to delineate glossary entries in the instructional material by putting them in boldface type.

ROLE OF NEWSPAPERS IN EDUCATION

Special supplements or regular items in national newspapers—sometimes inconjunction with radio and other mass media—have often been used inlarge-scale distance education programs in such subjects as health care andrural development or in national in-service teacher training programs. Using newspaper distribution networks is often the most cost-effective way of gettingeducational material to large numbers of readers. Newspapers are also used as avehicle for communication and contact between and among students, coursedevelopers, tutors, and instructors, and in-house student newspapers aresometimes used to provide general information on an institution's courses.

ROLE TEXTBOOKS IN EDUCATION

Most school and college textbooks are written for classroom use and thus maynot be appropriate for a distance education course. The exceptions are textbookswritten in a personal style that include self-assessment questions, and reviewtests or questions at the end of each main section or chapter. For the distancelearner, many standard textbooks would need to be complemented by a study guideor course guide with commentary and notes. Some on-line courses based on a"wrap-around" model use standard textbooks or course readers (edited compilations of articles) as a basic resource, giving on-line guidance on whichsections, chapters, or articles to read for later discussion through theconferencing system.

Criteria for Choosing Textbooks for External Students

The main criteria for choosing textbooks are:

— Appropriateness

— Readability

— Availability

However, these criteria still leave a great range of choice, so some further comments may be helpful. No single text can be ideally suited to the interests and abilities of all students taking a subject. Furthermore, reliance on a single source of information, ignorance of contrasting views and a belief in the infallibility of the printed word should not be encouraged at a tertiary level. If initiative and self direction are to be encouraged, the selected text will need to be supplemented with additional sources, readings and lecturers' notes.

Appropriateness

It is difficult to generalise across different subject areas, but there are some widely applicable criteria.An appropriate text should, in the first instance, relate to the described content and objectives of the subject it is recommended for. Unfortunately, many recommended texts do not have this close relationship. Consequently, either the subject gravitates away from its official description, or the text is only used peripherally, despite its often considerable expense.

If the match between subject and text is assumed, then all other things being equal, a text should be chosen which:

— Has a logical scope and sequence.

— Reflects recent developments in scholarly research.

— Attempts to interpret the methods and results of research as they apply to theories and statements of fact.

— Has a conceptual framework that gives it direction and purpose whilst achieving to a consistent theoretical perspective.

— Has a content based on identifiable and acceptable assumptions and factual information relevant to any concepts examined.

— Is consistent in the use of terminology and concepts without ambiguities, vague terms, and unclear meanings.

— Has a defensible scheme for the selection of material.

— Attempts to focus on or identify problems and hypotheses that can serve to stimulate student thought and inquiry.

— Encourages students to question various observations and related interpretations of reported phenomena.

— Promotes the creative discovery of relationships by students and provides 'creative encounters,' in the form of cases, experiments, episodes, dilemmas etc.

— Deals freely with controversial issues and where feasible, identifies all points of view, and if one point of view is preferred, makes clear on what grounds the conclusion was reached.

— Has definitive, detailed and annotated bibliographies, with fully identified statistical data sources.

Some of these criteria are more applicable to particular subjects than to others, and there are no doubt addition factors to be considered in some cases. However, the importance of choosing texts after some informed and rational examination of alternatives, cannot be denied.

Readability

When choosing a text particular consideration should be paid to its readability, notwithstanding all arguments about the need to use the language of the discipline being taught and not some ersatz version. If students fail because they cannot read a set text, the book is being used for the purpose of selection rather than instruction. Unreadable texts increase uncertainty in the minds of students. Tolerance of uncertainty varies from student to student, but eventually all will give up reading if a text is too difficult.

It follows that to choose a suitable text it is desirable to attempt to predict its readability and consider just what makes a text difficult. Unfortunately individual judgements have been shown to be unreliable, probably because of lecturers' differing academic experiences. It is strongly advised that judgements about the readability of texts are made in consultation with your colleagues. Even though trialling of texts is virtually impossible, by working together and paying attention to some specific factors, it is possible to extend and make more reliable your professional judgement.

Some points to note when considering readability are:

- It is a combination of reader factors and textual factors so keep the potential reader in mind.
- College students are generally less able readers than lecturers expect them to be, so don't just choose texts for 'A' students.
- Reading ability varies according to task, so take advantage of situations where the students are already familiar with the content of a text.
- Motivational factors tend to be overestimated, so even if the content is inspirational, it can still cause reading difficulties.
- Readability is in part a consequence of textual factors such as:
  - legibility of print
  - illustrations
  - vocabulary
  - conceptual difficulty
  - syntax
  - organisation.

Textual Factors Influencing Readability: It is fruitful to examine these in more detail, as even though they cannot indicate the most appropriate text, they can help in the elimination of those texts which are likely to cause reading difficulties.

— *Legibility of Print*: As there are about 2,000 types of print it is hard to pick the best type, but remember, unless you have a vastly different cultural background to your students, if you have any difficulties in reading a book, you can be sure they will.

— *Illustrations*: Contrary to popular belief, copious illustrations do not necessarily make texts easier to read. If illustrations, notably in the form of diagrams are an integral part of the text, they will enhance readability by facilitating comprehension. However, illustrations such as photographs may contain much information irrevelant to the learner and may distract him from a highly organised text with carefully selected verbal material.

— *Vocabulary*: This is generally considered to be the best single predictor of textual difficulty. Word length (letters or syllables) and word frequency (in common usage), are statistics often used in readability formulae. Some common sense should be used here; texts with unnecessarily complex vocabularies are best avoided where possible, but small words may have obscure meanings.

— *Conceptual Difficulty*: As hinted at above, easy words may be used for hard concepts. For example, 'a black hole in space' is easy enough to read, but a difficult concept to grasp at an appropriate level of analysis. Unfortunately there are no criteria for the reliable judgement of conceptual difficulty. Predictions in this area can only be based on knowledge of the nature of students and the academic discipline involved.

Try to bear in mind that there is a theoretical optimum conceptual density for any text. The implications of this involve the ability to distinguish between general texts which can be read systematically and reference texts, invaluable for some purposes, but having a conceptual overload which makes them unsuitable for sustained study.

— *Syntax*: Bearing in mind the need to extend the competencies of the student, texts are more easily read if they have a syntactical style similar to that already familiar to the reader. Texts to avoid are those with an unnecessary degree of complexity, typified by long sentences, large numbers of clauses per sentence, frequent qualifying and probability words. Conversely, compression and excessive abbreviation inhibit comprehension.

From this point of view, the best texts are those which use the formal language of the discipline in as simple a form as possible; without undue loss of meaning.

— *Organisation*: It is helpful to most students if set texts have a clear conceptual structure which is reflected in the layout and indexing system. It seems that learning is also enhanced by the inclusion of so called 'Advance Organisers' which are simply such things as summaries of content and structure, pre and post questions, which are interspersed in the text.

Using Formulae to Predict Readability: There are about ten commonly used formulae which have various degrees of validity and reliability. Some are much easier to administer than others, and they all have limitations when applied to James Joyce, Gertrude Stein or highly codified scientific material. Generally speaking, it is only valid to apply a formula to narrative or expository prose, and whilst it is not suggested you should do so, it is useful to know how material from some subjects have emerged from such analyses.

— *English*: At tertiary level there is little justification for choosing literary works on the basis of their readability, except perhaps when they need to be ranked in terms of degree of difficulty.

— *Maths*: Generally maths texts are relatively easy to read as the words stress operations, whilst the concepts are portrayed in figures and mathematical symbols.

— *Science:* Be careful to choose books which are consistent in their level of readability. Inexplicable variations may occur especially if texts are poorly edited. Investigators have revealed high degrees of inconsistency.

— *Social science*: Students have great problems with readability because of frequent:

  — conceptual complexity and density of material

  — Poor style

  — structural complexity and vocabulary and syntax

  — lack of precision in the use of words

  — changes of meaning of words in Particular contexts

  — heavy burden of new vocabulary.

So, once again, it is advisable to choose a text which deals with difficult concepts in as clear and simple a way as possible.

In addition to textual factors, the reader himself must also be considered in any discussion of readability. The students enrolled in a subject will have a range of individual prior reading experiences, so gross categoriations of readability may have to be reconsidered in the light of individual differences.

Furthermore, readability should not be regarded as a static phenomenon. It varies as a consequence of the experiences, skills and motivation of the reader. To illustrate this, consider the farmer who can analyse market conditions from studying farming newspapers and journals, but has difficulty in reading novels. Similarly, many lecturers experience a marked drop in their reading effectiveness when confronted with legal documents, technical manuals and budgetary information. In neither case would the uneasiness, lack of confidence, painstaking analysis and limited comprehension experiences when dealing with unfamiliar specialised material, be transferred to all reading situations.

So, if effective learning is to take place, there must not be a mismatch between the demands of the literature of the subject and the competencies, experience and motivation of the student.

The following checklist may help you in choosing texts from the readability point of view, subject, of course, to the content being suitable for your purposes.

Readability Checklist:

— Is the print legible?

— Do the illustrations assist or detract from comprehension?

— Is the vocabulary as simple as is permissible?

— Is the level of conceptual difficulty and density appropriate?

— Is the syntax familiar enough to facilitate reading?

— Is the material organised and indexed in a logical manner?

— Do the students have experiences, competencies and motivations which suggest they can and will read the chosen texts?

Availability

At the risk of stating the obvious, if students cannot obtain texts they cannot read them. The non-availability of texts is a recurring problem which seems to result from:

— The small size of the market in specialist texts;

— Unreliability of shipping;

— Lack of communication between suppliers;

— Failure to place orders with suppliers;

— Remoteness of students.

In view of these problems, the utmost care must be taken to ensure that students are provided with as few difficulties as possible. It is advisable to:

— Check the availability of books with the bookshop, before making a final choice;

— Check with publishers/suppliers if the chosen book is both new and highly specialised;

— Beware of the availability claims of publishers representatives.

In addition to the problems of purchasing compulsory texts, students often encounter problems in obtaining library copies of recommended references.

Therefore, try to:

— Ensure books recommended for occasional reference are available from the College library;

— Indicate to students which texts are available from the College library;

— Inform librarians of anticipated demands for texts.

Finally, having made an appropriate choice of text, some thought should be given to its use. Books clearly serve a variety of purposes, an edited series of readings will have a different function to a catalogue of factual information. However, it is important that whatever the style of the chosen text, it is integrated with the accompanying notes. A booklist and series of exam questions is inadequate for the majority of students. If the aim is to attempt to replicate for the external student all the learning experiences of the on-campus student, then the text will usually only be a substitute for the formal lecture. Seminars, informal discussions and other aspects of active student learning need to be substituted for with an appropriate set of notes.

Where possible, these notes should contain comprehensive guidance about the use of set texts. Questions may be asked so the student can check his comprehension, also summaries are helpful in assisting students to extract the main points. The choice of texts and their proper use are crucial factors in relation to a student's ability to complete his studies. It is in all our interests to ensure he does so.

The choice of textbooks can be a complex and time-consuming matter. However, in view of the relatively unsophisticated reading abilities of students, it is apparent that considerable numbers of students are hindered in their progress by being confronted with inappropriate texts.

ROLE OF CORRESPONDENCE UNITS OR WORKBOOKS

Correspondence units or workbooks are written for independent distance studyby the course designers or instructors, and tailored to the course and students.They are generally written in a personal style, as if the writer were speakingdirectly to a student (a "tutorial in print"), and are structured so that thestudent's reading corresponds to the agreed study schedule for the course (eachunit might correspond to eight hours' work or a week's work, for example). Awell-designed unit contains explicit study objectives, a clear table ofcontents, a glossary of any new or technical terms introduced, completedexamples, and many in-text activities, such as exercises and self-assessment andreview questions. Students may be encouraged to annotate the units with theircomments and answers to exercises and quizzes, and then compare their responseswith model answers or instructor's comments at the end of the unit.

ROLE OF STUDY GUIDES AND COURSE GUIDES

A printed course guide or study guide is an essential part of any distanceeducation course, even one in which nearly all the teaching is conducted throughnonprint technologies such as TV or conferencing. A guide introduces the course,specifies the objectives, and provides information and guidance on study skillsand assessment (such as homework assignments and examinations). It also mayinclude preparatory and follow-up reading for TV broadcasts or audiocassettes,and guidance notes and follow-up activities related to material in a textbook orcourse reader. It would also include contacts, technical information, lists ofreferences and resources, and details about the course designers, instructors,and tutors and, in some cases, about the other students.

Study Guides for Textbooks

Textbooks are rarely written for the precise group being taught and never for the individuals who are being taught. Therefore, the material in the text must be referred to in a manner which makes it palatable to at least the group being taught and preferably to individuals within that group. This can be achieved by considering the following functions of the learning material. The suggestions offered are by no means exhaustive; they are a sample of ideas which may help make standardised texts more appropriate for your particular students.

Arouse the student's interest and provide motivation for further study

The design and layout of the materials have already been fixed by the publisher, so the lecturer should focus on personalising the materials for his particular aúdience.

Suggestions:

— Point out why the text is relevant to both the professional concerns of the student and the course content.

— Ask the student to relate general ideas in the text to his own experiences or pre-existing knowledge.

— Explain which parts you found stimulating and why.

— Add information linking national conditions and the perspectives of the text.

Clearly define what is expected of the student

It is helpful to make clear why it is necessary for the student to study the text, and more specifically what will be expected of him in terms of knowledge, behaviours and attitudes.

Suggestions:

— Make a checklist of knowledge skills and attitudes that the student can use to monitor his own progress.

— Outline what the student should focus on in each section of the text.

— Summarise what the student should have learned after each section.

— Relate the content of the text to the formal assessment.

Make clear the overall structure of the material to be studied

Ideally the text chosen will have an appropriate structure, however, it may need to be classified and related to the relevant course or subject structure.

Suggestions:

— Draw up structures based on both the description of the subject and the contents of the text. Then link them together.

— Explain the logic of sectionalising the text.

— If the structure of the text is inappropriate, provide a better one, in which the content of the text may be located.

— Ask the student to make a diagrammatic representation of the conceptual network of the subject.

Guide the student carefully through the subject matter in the text

This involves guiding the students through the subject. The degree of prescription of the signposting procedure may vary greatly, both in response to the type of student and the nature of the subject.

Suggestions:

— Provide a study schedule showing order and duration of study for each section.

— Offer suggestions as to how each section may be best dealt with.

— Link together contents, objectives, assignments and activities.

— Relate all physical components of the subject e.g. notes, readings and texts.

Give the students something to do other than read

The majority of texts require only passivity on the part of the learner. Hopefully this passivity is an illusion, as the learner is supposedly actively relating new knowledge to pre-existing conceptual frameworks. Nevertheless, in many cases learning will be enhanced if a text is accompanied by some device meant to promote more obviously active learning.

Suggestions:

— Test the student's recall and comprehension.

— Ask the student to analyse parts of the text and write a personal synthesis.

— Encourage evaluation of the text.

— Require the student to relate ideas in the text to concrete examples and personal experiences.

— Make outrageous or controversial statements and demand reactions.

— Present fallacious arguments for the student to verify or refute.

— Require the matching of case studies with sections of the text.

— Present cloze exercises for completion.

— Ask for diagrammatic representations of verbally expressed material.

— Ask for matrices of concepts.

— Arrange postal simulations.

— Provide problem solving exercises.

Keep the students informed about their progress

Students require feedback in the areas of tuition, academic, administrative and personal counselling. Tuition and academic counselling are the lecturer's main responsibility and are unlikely to be catered for by textbooks.

Suggestions:

— Encourage regular contact.

— Provide numerous self testing exercises to check progress through the text.

— Include easily-marked quickly-returned assessment items.

— Demonstrate remedial feedback loops related to self testing exercises.

— Provide feedback on audio tape in the form of comments on any work attempted.

Help students retain information and transfer it to novel situations

It is unlikely that the chosen text relates to the experiences and needs of your particular group of students.

Suggestions:

— Set work to link experiences with text.

— Ask for additional examples.

— Attempt to empirically support or refute arguments in the text.

— Ask repetitive questions, building up complexity.

— Demand problem solving approaches, using textual information.

— Be aware of student progress and the worthwhileness of your subject

— Such considerations are rarely included in texts, yet we need to know about the student's level of competence and the effectiveness of the course.

Suggestions:

— Ensure assessment is based on content of the text, i.e. is it valid?

— Begin with short easily-completed, easily-marked, lowly-weighted assessment items.

— Use variety of assessment procedures all based on the same content.

— Consider assessment in relation to student's total workload.

— Ask questions about degree of difficulty and perceived relevance of sections of the text.

— Ask for suggestions for improvement.

8

AUDIO AND VIDEO MEDIA

Teachers have explored the use of radio in the classroom almost since radio technology entered into the mainstream of society, yet radio remains a relatively unused mode of instruction. Students may begin their study of communications technology by reading about some early devices and their inventors. Radios and telegraphs are part of early communications technology history, and Samuel Morse, Guglielmo Marconi, Lee DeForest, Philo Farnsworth, and David Sarnoff were communications pioneers. The first popular radios were called crystal radios because they used crystals to receive the broadcast signals.

Building a crystal radio, either from a kit or from parts, is an engaging, hands-on science activity. In addition to building the crystal radio, earth science and chemistry teachers might consider making the galena crystals that receive the signals. Many early crystal radio listeners made their own galena crystals before radios were sold in stores.

Teachers can also use radio assembly projects to help students learn about electricity, wave energy, the electromagnetic spectrum, the earth's atmosphere, and the sun's effects on the earth's atmosphere. Many popular electronics stores have a full range of reasonably priced, easy to assemble electronics and radio kits.

AM-FM RADIO: HANDS-ON GEOGRAPHY AND LANGUAGE ARTS ACTIVITIES

Depending upon your geographic location, you may hear many AM-FM radio stations from Canada, Mexico, Central America, and the Caribbean. If you are near those regions, you will hear broadcasts by English, French, and Spanish native speakers-a special opportunity for foreign language learners. Some AM-FM stations now maintain Web sites and offer their listeners real-time programming and audio archives. Listening to online audio resources requires computer software such as RealAudio, a sound card, and speakers.

Many U.S. AM stations may be heard across the country. Listening to broadcasts from other U.S. locations makes an excellent activity for learning U.S. geography. The term DX means long-distance, so listening to faraway stations is known as "DXing". among radio hobbyists. In the evening, AM radio broadcasts are heard over great distances because atmospheric conditions allow AM radio waves to bounce between the atmosphere and the earth. Students might hear AM broadcasts from several hundred miles away if they listen to AM stations after dark.

INTERNATIONAL SHORTWAVE BROADCASTS

Just as an AM-FM radio is a tool for students learning about local and regional geography, a shortwave radio is a good tool for learning about world geography. Every country in the world has shortwave radio broadcast stations, and most stations have programming in English, as well as their native language. Beginning with 6th-grade social studies curriculum, the study of geography may be enhanced by listening to international shortwave broadcasts. Students will hear news and cultural programming that will enhance the information found in books, encyclopedias, and on the Internet. Topics such as latitude and longitude, time zones, continents, hemispheres, and the tropics may all be highlighted through radio listening activities.

Writing letters to international stations to give listener reports is a long-standing shortwave listening hobby activity. The writing assignment combines listening and language arts skills. Stations usually reply with letters or special postcards, brochures, posters, key chains, and bumper stickers. Teachers may use these items to prepare interesting displays in a classroom learning center.

National weather service broadcasts

Many people listen to a radio to hear weather reports; however, in a classroom it's not always convenient to wait for a radio station's weather report. With a weather radio, you don't have to wait. Weather radios are tuned to the National Oceanic and Atmospheric Administration (NOAA), weather channels that provide broadcasts 24 hours a day. Most NOAA broadcasts range about 50 miles from their main location. Many AM-FM radios, scanner radios, and CB radios include NOAA channels for listeners' convenience and safety. NOAA also coordinates a national program for trained volunteer weather watchers called Skywarn. Teachers may wish to consider Skywarn training for a class weather project or for individual science projects.

Scanner radios: hearing the world of work

A scanner radio will bring the world of work into the classroom. These high-speed scanning receivers monitor government, businesses, and nonprofit organization's frequencies in your local community. Unlike the shortwave radio, a scanner radio receives local FM communications and broadcasts within a range of about 50 miles.

Since the conversations you hear on a scanner radio are between people, there is no way to know when they will occur. A scanner radio scans through many frequencies and stops when a transmission signal is detected. The listener will hear many transmissions, and it is important to program the scanner radio to listen to the public service agencies desired. Some occupations that use scanner radios include: police, fire, hospitals, ambulances, aircraft, schools, universities, factories, warehouses, boats, taxis, city buses, delivery trucks, utility companies, TV and radio news crews, the FBI, mall security, hotels, and construction crews.

Amateur radio

Many students today build their own web pages; however, students in the 1950s and 60s, built stereos and radios with kits from companies like Heathkit. Many students earned amateur radio licenses from the Federal Communications Commission (FCC) and built their own ham radio stations. Today, most ham radio operators buy ready-made radio equipment, and many enthusiasts listen to packet radio or participate in ham satellite communications. Other ham radio operators communicate with the NASA Space Shuttle and the Mir Space Station via amateur radio. Not long ago, the FCC eased the requirements for the entry-level ham license by eliminating the Morse code requirement. Students and teachers can now become No-Code Technician Class operators by passing two multiple-choice exams.

Study guides for these exams include the entire FCC question pool, as well as full explanations for each answer. Kindergarten-age students have earned licenses, however most young hams are in the middle and high school grades. Many schools across the country and around the world have amateur radio stations. Students can practice speaking, interviewing, listening, and writing skills in an amateur radio school club or classroom activity. Some teachers use the amateur radio as the communications link for school-to-school projects. Real-time radio conversations allow students to practice listening and speaking skills-a valuable experience that is not found with an e-mail connection.

Radio technology offers a unique way for K-12 teachers to integrate technology into the curriculum. Elementary teachers can help students learn basic electricity and regional geography in entertaining ways using AM radios. Social studies teachers will appreciate shortwave radios as a tool for teaching U.S. and global topics. Science, physics, and earth science teachers can use radios to demonstrate the properties of electricity, wave energy, weather, and the earth's atmosphere. English and language arts teachers will be able to use radios to reinforce listening, writing, and speaking skills. With a shortwave radio, foreign language teachers can provide advanced students with an opportunity to hear the authentic language demonstrated by native speakers. Teachers without Internet connections will find radios an accessible technology for bringing the world to their students.

CABLE TELEVISION IN THE CLASSROOM

What an instructional opportunity! Using cable television in the classroom as an integral part of instruction now makes it possible to include the latest news and current events in a classroom discussion of world happenings.

Cable television is already in the classroom...or at least the potential exists for cable to be integrated into classroom instruction. Federal grants and local cable companies' access initiatives make televised programming available to school districts with even the most modest operating budgets. Major television companies such as Cable News Network (CNN) and Whittle Communications have pioneered cable television connections for classroom instruction since 1989. Prior to the advent of cable in the classroom, most television programming intended for instruction was delivered in one of three forms: Community Antenna Television (CATV), Public Television (PTV), and Instructional Television (ITV).

The potential for instruction provided by cable in the classroom is eclipsed, however, by the number of educational practitioners who remain uninformed about the concept or who lack proficiency in the use of protocols and strategies necessary to optimize the benefits of cable in the classroom as a form of instructional telecommunication. Teachers, trainers, and educational administrators nationwide would benefit from structured opportunities, rather than trial-and-error, to learn how to maximize the potential of the medium.

Cable television in the classroom is a form of distance education. The benefits of distance education have made converts out of many rural school administrators. Through communication satellites, rural schools are able to gain access to the most advanced courses for students and staff, while still maintaining their rural characteristics and personal touch. Regarding urban and suburban schools, some suggests that satellite television is globalizing classrooms by exposing students to world events and cultures other than their own.

The expenses associated with linking schools to cable television vary depending on mode of transmission and available resources. Instructional Television Fixed Services (ITFS) systems, which provide terrestrial microwave (point-to-point) transmission, range in cost from $200,000 - $300,000 for service to five different locations. A fiber optic system servicing five different locations in a moderately sized city could cost in excess of $800,000 plus a monthly service charge of $35,000. Microwave equipment to up-link and down-link programming costs from $280,000 to $600,000 per station. Additional hourly charges for connecting range from $300 to $500. Cable television systems are the most economical. Installation of coaxial cable costs about $7,500 per mile. Thus 50 to 60 miles of cable for a group of schools, for example, would cost approximately $450,000. School districts pay for the service.

Cable network

Most cable network school collaborations are regional such as the Eastern Educational Television Network (EEN), the Southern

Educational Telecommunications Association (SECA), the Central Educational Network (CEN), and the Pacific Mountain Network (PMN). These groups service member stations from Maine to Virginia, Maryland to Texas, Ohio to the Dakotas, and the Rockies to the West Coast respectively. Non-commercial syndicators such as the Agency for Instructional Technology (AIT), Great Plains National (GPN), and Western Instructional Television (WIT) develop innovative classroom programs as well.

However, a substantial portion of cable instructional television programming is done at the local level. Fifteen percent of all instructional programming for public television is produced locally, with PBS providing 63.9%, regional networks providing 14%, ITV suppliers generating 6.1%, and commercial syndicators providing 4.4%. Other instructional television productions represent 5.2% of the total broadcast hours. Approximately 14.5% of all PTV broadcasting is devoted to instructional programming. News (16.4%), information (29.5%), cultural (20.5%), general children's (6.5%), Sesame Street & Electric Company (11.4%), and other (1.2%) represent the balance.

A first year composition course was broadcast twice each week over a local cable television service. Despite technical problems and complicated record keeping procedures, the instructors found that students who watched the broadcasts improved their writing skills as much as their counterparts in traditional classes.

A Spanish teacher interacted with 3,959 elementary students at nine different sites through the use of studio and classroom cameras and televisions. The instructional television programming was interactive. Mathelps, produced by the Logan City (Utah) School District, is an hour-long interactive tutoring program aired on local cable television. Each concept is followed by a brain-teaser contest, to which students phone in their solutions.

In 1987, over 18 million students watched instructional television each week. Four rural school districts used interactive cable television to link classrooms and teach advanced high school courses which would have been prohibitively expensive for any one system to offer alone. The future success of cable television in the classroom is largely dependent upon continued congressional mandates which reserve a portion of the air-waves for non-commercial and educational uses. Additional revenues must also be allocated or identified from private sources to offset the rapidly rising costs associated with programming, production, and advances in technology.

Cable in the classroom can introduce real events into instruction by reporting the news from a perspective with which young people are familiar and are capable of understanding. Broadcasts transceived by television satellite can present issues as opportunities in which young people can play an active role, rather that as overwhelming problems no one can solve. By incorporating current events and televised symposia into instructional strategies, learners are exposed to perspectives beyond their teacher's own view and can explore truth without sensationalism or condescension. Thus cable television access to the classroom allows learners to make informed judgments about the content under study.

INTERACTIVE VIDEODISC

Students in English have been directed to write an essay about the culture and major events during the time of John Steinbeck's classic GRAPES OF WRATH. They have also been given a computer-based interactive video system with which to search for relevant information. Controlled by a computer, a major database of textual information is available through CD-ROM and computer disc; in addition, a database of visual and audio information is accessible through a videodisc.

During their eager search through the information, the students run into problems with one of the concepts and press "lesson" to be tutored on the topic. The tutorial uses both text and visuals to make important points. For a final small group exercise, the students engage in a life-like simulation to check their understanding of the issues of the day. The unit concludes when the teacher uses the interactive video system in front of the class to summarize features of the exercise. Video and text are at the teacher's fingertips with the simple press of a few buttons. Discussions are lively because the experience has enticed the students by immersing them in the sights and sounds of earlier times.

As demonstrated in the above scenario, interactive video can be a very complex learning system, or it can be a simple tool for teachers to use to enhance their instruction. The term has been used broadly in the literature and includes three major aspects: 1) interactive video as storage, 2) interactive video as hardware, and 3) interactive video as learning concept.

A videodisc storage unit is a 12- or 8-inch disc that looks like a large version of an audio compact disc. It is also read by a laser beam and, since no stylus ever touches the disc, it does not wear out and is not affected by fingerprints. This videodisc has two formats, each offering different capabilities: Constant Angular Velocity (CAV) and Constant Linear Velocity (CLV). Each side of a 12-inch CAV disc can hold up to 54,000 slides, 30 minutes of motion video, or a combination of the two. In addition, there are two tracks that can store a total of 30 minutes of random access audio. An 8-inch disc can hold about half as much data.

On a CAV disc, information is stored in tiny pits pressed in concentric rings on thin, shiny, reflective metal which is then sealed between protective layers of plastic. The rings each contain a "slide" and have their own "address." Information in each ring can be accessed in less than three seconds. Besides compact storage, a major advantage of interactive video is this rapid, precise access to any bit of information on the disc.

A CLV disc spins at a constant linear velocity, much like a long play record. Because of this, CLV discs can hold much more data than CAV discs: up to one hour of straight play motion video for a 12-inch disc and 20 minutes for an 8-inch disc. This format allows random access through time code rather than frame number. Because time access is not as precise as frame access, the major advantage of a CLV disc is its compact storage capability.

Interactive video as hardware

Interactive video hardware is needed to run a videodisc. The Nebraska Design/Production Group developed a widely adopted classification scheme which groups the hardware by "levels of intelligence". The higher the level, the greater the ability for internal computer control. Contrary to expectation, the more control the system has, the easier it is for the learner to operate and ignore the hardware.

— *Level 0:* This describes a stand-alone videodisc player that is used for simple linear playback. Many movies are stored on CLV discs and are played in this fashion.

— *Level 1*: A Level 1 player is also a stand-alone videodisc player, but it has additional built-in functions for rapid and precise frame searching, variable motion, mono or stereo audio control, stable freeze frames, and scanning. A Level 1 player allows the teacher to display any information in the visual and audio database to an entire class. A Level 1 player can also be used by students, individually or in small groups, with a keypad and printed directions.

— *Level 2:* A Level 2 player has all the functions of a Level 1 player plus a built-in microprocessor and user-programmable memory. This type of player is most useful when programming is encoded right on the second audio track of the videodisc. Level 2 players allow more internal control through this programming on the disc. They are often seen in malls, information booths, or science displays where the customer is invited to press simple, one-key responses. While this system has its greatest use outside the classroom, it can be used by the teacher for individualized or small group enrichment exercises.

— *Level 3:* A Level 3 player has all the capabilities of a Level 2 player and is connected to a microcomputer. Current combinations of videodisc players and computer systems offer a choice of one or two screens. In a two-screen system, one displays the video while the other displays the computer text. In a one-screen system, video and computer text are displayed on the same screen. A one-screen system, with an appropriate overlay board, displays computer images and videodisc images simultaneously. Often the hardware comes with a variety of components for interaction, such as a touch sensitive screen, mouse, or light pen. Because of the computer "command center," Level 3 interactive video offers the most flexibility for use as a large group, small group, or individual learning device.

Since the development of this classification scheme, some have defined another level. Level 4 has come to mean any Level 3 player with additional hardware such as a second (or third) videodisc player, a CD-ROM drive, or other electronic equipment.

Interactive video as learning concept

Fleming and Levie classify the difference between instruction and learning according to the locus of the activity—instruction occurs outside the learner, but learning is something only the learner can do. As shown in the opening scenario, interactive video can be a true learning device since it is not something that is done to the learner but, rather, is an activity the learner does himself or herself. Some states that in order for learning to occur, learners must be, at a minimum, mentally active in the learning process. All computer-based instructional systems can mentally engage learners by directly involving them in learning. But because of the added dimension that video offers, interactive video surpasses other computer-based systems in its ability to involve the learner and engage him or her in a two-way dialog. Well designed interactive video lessons invite learners to interact with the visuals by enabling them to interrupt, identify, sequence, and select from alternative actions. Students can interrupt visual scenes when they identify problems in the scenario. They can stop sequences if they can't follow the logic or get lost. They can practice with concepts by matching pictures to words, identifying critical visual elements of concepts, or matching sounds to words. For sequencing activities, learners can select appropriate psychomotor sequences or select options and be shown consequences visually and dramatically.

Interactive video has been used in almost all content areas from literature to mathematics and science. The literature is full of case accounts of its effectiveness for a variety of uses. It must be remembered, however, that it is not the medium which makes interactive video effective, but the way in which it has been implemented. Some state that interactive video is "more than a new trick, a new device or even a new technology".

Interactive video as storage and hardware blends the elements once available only as separate media. Interactive video as learning concept creates an environment where the two-way dialog essential for learning has become a reality. Because costs are falling and research has demonstrated the importance of interactivity, interactive video is destined to play an important role in the future of education and training.

How have videodiscs been used for special education instruction?

One of the first interactive videodisc projects in the field of education was the Media Development Project of the Hearing Impaired at the University of Nebraska. The discs included instruction in social studies, language development, and finger spelling. A Level III disc series called "Thinking It Through" taught interactive thinking skills. Students could explore decision-making processes and the consequences of different responses to a problem or situation.

The California School for the Deaf at Riverside developed an interactive videodisc for teaching language and reading skills to hearing impaired students. The purpose of the program was to increase exposure to motivating language and reading experiences. An authoring system component provided ten interactive formats. s were branched through the instructional sequences on grammar, syntax, categorization, capitalization, spelling, and punctuation.

At Utah State University, three projects were conducted under the auspices of the Interactive Videodisc for Special Education Technology (IVSET) program. Hardware and software components were developed to produce CAI (computer-aided instruction) materials for mentally handicapped students, a bilingual assessment instrument for mathematics skills, and an instructional program to teach social skills to behaviorally handicapped students.

A current investigation at the University of Pennsylvania involves a new method for teaching young children to read and write. The study incorporates the use of microcomputer and videodisc players to initiate communication at the very onset of instruction. Deaf and multiply handicapped children are included in the program. Preliminary results demonstrate a significant improvement in word and phrase identification, reading comprehension, and basic sentence construction.

At the University of Iowa, an interactive videodisc system is being used to train teachers and clinicians in classroom observation skills. The program provides complete training in the use of the Classroom Behavior Record (CBR) with children referred for psychiatric services. The training side of the disc contains motion samples of classroom behavior and glossary information. The practice side provides extended motion samples of classrooms and can be used for practice and reliability testing.

Interactive videodisc in vocational education

As new technologies transform the workplace, workers must have the ability to cope with change, take responsibility for their learning, think critically to solve problems, and work cooperatively in a team environment. Instructional technology can prepare students to meet these workplace challenges while keeping them motivated and interested. In the past, some instructional media failed to fulfill their promise. However, interactive videodisc offers a combination of media—computers, video, audio, and graphics—which has greater potential to:

1. Increase opportunities for individuation, diagnosis, and self-pacing
2. Give access to a wide variety of information resources
3. Bring resources to isolated or limited-mobility populations
4. Stretch instructors' capabilities to reach more students
5. Accommodate different learning styles
6. Provide better ways to measure skills than standardized testing

Proclaimed "the hot new teaching tool of the nineties", videodisc systems can be simply a disc player and monitor for play back, or they can include a microcomputer to allow the user to interact with the program. Compared to videotapes and other media, interactive videodiscs provide enhanced picture and sound quality; extended longevity of both the discs and the players; faster, random access to individual frames; high quality freeze-frames; huge storage capacity; and connectivity to other devices.

Interactive video can instill confidence and enthusiasm, reinforce self-directed mastery learning, make instructional management easier, and motivate special needs and at-risk students. The multisensory mixture of video, text, sound, and graphics increases learner interest, attention, and retention. The visual and auditory cues engage different learning modalities. Branching enables a closer match with individual learning styles and speeds. Student progress through lessons can be monitored.

IVD can be used in different settings. Individual use offers the most scheduling flexibility and self-pacing. In a group situation, video is projected on a large-screen monitor and viewing can be stopped to allow discussion and debate. A cooperative setting with two learners provides opportunities for teamwork and collaboration. Among the instructional applications are video glossaries that replace slides; simulations and demonstrations; desktop publishing of curriculum materials; individual and group testing with computerized grading and recordkeeping; student projects such as video term papers; and video encyclopedias. With bar codes incorporated in textbooks, video segments related to the text can be conjured up with an optical scanner.

Effect of learning

Studies of the effectiveness of interactive video have compared it both to traditional methods and to other types of instructional technology. Nursing students who used a videodisc on patient assessment independently showed no significant differences in cognitive achievement in comparison with a group who received lectures. However, the IVD group had significantly increased positive attitudes toward learning and more time for individual work with instructors. Another study used both videotape and IVD for safety instruction of auto workers.

Higher achievement, fewer errors, and more favorable attitudes were found among the laserdisc users. Three groups of junior high industrial arts students were taught shop safety rules in these formats: videotape only, computer-assisted tutorial, and interactive video. Although the tutorial was somewhat more effective for this type of task, interactive video significantly improved attitudes.

At Miami-Dade Community College, students using supplemental interactive video and/or computer-assisted tutorial scored higher on an academic skills test than those given lecture and textbook instruction. Although not appropriate for every learning situation, IVD clearly has strengths that justify its use. Student control of the interaction gives them ownership of the success and consequences of their actions. "Feedback is instant, realistic, nonthreatening, and helpful". Well-designed interactive video creates a two-way dialogue that engages the learner mentally and physically.

Vocational educators have applied IVD in various ways:

1. Harrison School District in Colorado Springs created an employability skills videodisc that has four modules: dependability, responsibility, human relations, and teamwork. It dramatizes on-the-job situations, allows students to choose solutions, and illustrates the consequences of the choices.
2. In Wisconsin, Interactive ModuMath provides remedial instruction for technical students with low math skills without holding back more able students. Typical lessons include presentation of theory, drill and practice, word problems with remedial branching, and review and posttesting. With the recordkeeping and authoring system, the "live" instructor can monitor student interaction with the video tutor and make alterations.
3. Westinghouse provides training in safety, security, and quality standards through videodisc simulation of workplace problems—a practical way to give real-world experience without the dangers that wrong safety choices would entail. "The Total Quality Approach to Job Performance" also seeks to affect work ethic and attitude.

4. The Academy of Aeronautics Welding Simulator includes an extensive tutorial and a realistic simulation that puts a video welding torch in students' hands. A three-dimensional touch screen becomes a welding environment that responds to the position and movement of the torch.

The key factors in using IVD in vocational education are related to instructional design, the role of the teacher, and costs.

— *Instructional issues* : A basic question is whether IVD is the appropriate medium for the subject or the situation. Demonstration and hands-on practice are traditional vocational education techniques that videodiscs do very well, but there are other instructional situations in which another medium might be better. The catalog of commercial educational videodiscs grows larger every day, but editing and adaptation are difficult and production can be time consuming and costly. However, systems are becoming available that permit educators to create, store, and update their own courseware; Apple's HyperCard is one example. Another strategy is "repurposing" existing films or videotapes by transferring them to disks and combining them with a branching and interactivity package. A concern expressed in initial studies of IVD's effectiveness is the extent to which the novelty of the medium accounts for improved attitudes and motivation. Because video is similar to television, it has the advantage of familiarity; whether this transfers to learning is the question. Another factor is the effect of previous experience with technology on students' ability to benefit from the medium and their interest in using it.

  Teacher role : Technology definitely changes the role of the teacher. IVD is a highly learner-centered medium, and the teacher acts more as a resource person or facilitator, meeting such learner needs as continued contact with peers, increased guidance and feedback, and opportunities to apply newly acquired skills. Teachers may have less flexibility in instructional choices in order to accommodate the medium's characteristics, but they have more time to give individual attention, answer questions, and stimulate creativity. Teachers will need more training in the effective use of the medium and stronger instructional management skills.

Costs : Although cost seems to be a barrier to IVD use, most equipment is modular and additions such as image processors and authoring systems can be made over time. Van Horn asserts that videodiscs last longer than other media and in the long run are cheaper than film and videotapes. Production costs can also be high, stresses that IVD is not significantly more expensive to produce than other well-designed instructional systems. "Interactive video and traditional instruction are different means to different ends" and a different frame of reference should be used in analyzing the costs and benefits of IVD.

Some urges educators not to be deterred by the supposed barriers of novelty, cost, and lack of availability of videodiscs. More than 750 educational titles have been issued, according to the videodisc compendium for education and training.

USE OF LOCAL AREA NETWORKS IN SCHOOLS

"The days of the standalone computer are drawing to a close. Networks will dominate the educational technology scene into the 1990s." So goes the prevailing wisdom in many educational technology circles throughout the country. And, judging from the numbers, that wisdom just may be right. According to Quality Education Data's 1987-88 survey of the 173 largest school districts, 64% were networking, and 36% of those not networking planned to use the technology by 1990.

Advantage of networks

Why are networked computers making greater inroads into

schools than ever before? The answers are many and varied, but most educators agree that networks offer them the following advantages:

— They eliminate the handling of floppy disks.

— They cut down on computer printouts, making it possible for students' work to be viewed on-screen, sent to teachers' workstations, or even channeled into "electronic gradebooks."

— They support management programs that give teachers detailed reports on a student's progress, even pointing out areas where improvement is necessary.

— They allow several students in a class to use one program at the same time, or to work on different programs or different parts of the same program at the same time.

— They eliminate the need to buy several copies of one software program, thereby often reducing costs.

LANS

A local area network, or LAN, is a data communications network, covering a limited geographical area, like a school. LANs can connect a large number of electronic devices, including computers, dumb terminals, tape drives, modems, file servers, and various printers. Most LANs in schools, especially for curriculum use at the K-8 level, consist of a roomful of computers connected to a file server, such as a Mac Plus with a hard disk that acts as a large storage center for all software. The file server also controls the flow of information, such as software, messages, or homework, between central storage centers and each computer, and also between computers and printers. Connecting and communicating is made possible by (1) a network interface card at each computer, file server, etc., (2) a cable connection between these components, (3) a network controller, and (4) a network-access method.

Network Software

In the past, one drawback to networking was the lack of software to run on the network. Today, almost all the major software companies offer network software, though not all of their programs are networkable. Furthermore, site licenses for some programs, like word processors, are not cheaper than individual copies because the company charges a network and a per user fee. Site licenses themselves still present some problems for educators who shy away from what they consider to be confusing legal or technical details. But early lamentations over software inadequacy are dying down as publishers scurry to satisfy the voracious appetite for networkable software.

Island Park School District, Nassau County, New York has three labs. One is a full lab for students in grades K-3, designed to concentrate on reinforcing basic skills. In the upper school, there are another two labs. One is for grades 4-8 and focuses on teaching and skills reinforcement, as well as keyboarding and word processing. The other is in the library and is open for "creative uses." All labs have 50 Apple IIe's or GS's and a Corvus network. According to Dr. Erich J. Stegmeier, assistant superintendent, "We couldn't function without the networks. It would take 1,000 diskettes to handle all our software and disk needs."

Plano School District, Plano, Texas is a large district (28,000 students) emcompassing 21 elementary schools. Each school has two labs, and each lab has 30 computers and one file server. Bill Adkins, director of instructional technology, says "We began networking in order to pull student information from each of the student stations and communicate from machine to machine. Our goal is to have, by 1992, a network that will channel everything a student does into one core electronic gradebook." Another goal of the Plano program is to tie courseware into curriculum objectives and make it possible to automatically track student progress towards these objectives.

Eight Tips for buying a Network

1. *Ease of use:* Teachers and students have to be able to send and receive software, messages and schoolwork easily. Management programs should be easy to use.

2. *Compatibility:* Most computer manufacturers now produce their own networks, so compatibility shouldn't be a problem. Increasingly, however, other companies are selling LANs, mostly for IBMs or clones. These might be cheaper or more appropriate.

3. *RAM use:* How much random access memory does the network need for each computer? With the minimum amount, you should still be able to run all your essential programs and more.

4. *Size, distance, and expandibility:* How many computers can the network accommodate, and can it be expanded? Although it may seem unlikely now, you may want to add more computers in the future. In addition, discuss closely with the manufacturer how you intend to use the network. Placing computers far apart can affect the network's efficiency.

5. *Security:* If you need security, how does it work? Does the network provide the security you need while still allowing you to run the programs you need?

6. *Maintenance:* Unfortunately, too many districts leave maintenance to their computer coordinators or even teachers. Ask the manufacturer about management contracts. It may be cheaper to train a few technicians to service networks.

7. *Bandwidth, speed, throughput; interfaces and gateways:* These are technical words which apply to the kinds of information you plan to send (text, pictures, graphs) over the network. Have the manufacturer demonstrate how well the network handles them.

8. *Ease of installation:* Installation might come with the package, or it may be easy enough to do yourself. Some LANS, however, require extensive wiring or software installation. If you're not prepared to manage this, pay the installation charge.

CD-ROM DATABASE SERVICES

CD-ROM is a new storage medium that can serve as a quick, economical source of information for students, researchers, writers, and professionals in many fields. CD-ROM is a form of optical disk or laserdisk technology that is similar to the popular digital audio compact disk, or CD. As their name implies, CDs are written to and read by the concentrated light beam of a laser. The laser creates tiny pits, representing bits of digitized information, on the plastic surface of the disk. An optical disk can contain information in any form, including audio, video, text, graphics, or a combination. Unlike magnetic media (audio and videotapes, floppy and hard computer disks), optical disks are almost error-free and indestructible.

CD-ROM is a compact disk with read-only memory: information stored on it cannot be changed. The most conspicuous advantage of CD-ROM is its large storage capacity. One disk with 550 megabyte capacity can store 220,000 pages of text, or the equivalent of about 1,500 floppy disks. Used with a microcomputer, CD-ROM greatly expands the microcomputer's ability to deliver information in an interactive environment. CD-ROM databases can be accessed directly by users, thus freeing them from the necessity of consulting (and paying) an expert to do online mainframe searches. Information from many CD-ROM databases can be downloaded to floppy disk for later use with a word processor or other software, or printed on paper.

CD-ROM does have several disadvantages. Its greatest drawback is that information cannot be added or erased by the user. And CD-ROM still does not have the storage capacity to handle full-text documents in very large databases: many are indexes containing citations with abstracts. A number of databases are updated monthly or quarterly, but for current information such as news, this may not be sufficient. And while CD-ROM is capable of storing mixed media, most publishers offer text because text requires the least storage space. Full-motion video is not yet economical. Finally, the hardware does not allow a full range of flexibility and compatibility for those who wish to use more than one CD-ROM product.

CD-ROM versions of nearly all popular reference sources are showing up in libraries, schools, colleges, and professional institutions. One of the earliest and most popular products is Grolier's Electronic Encyclopedia, which packs the entire text of the 20-volume The Academic American Encyclopedia onto one CD-ROM. An impressive resource for writers is Microsoft Bookshelf, which contains 10 classic reference books on one CD-ROM.

These include a dictionary, thesaurus, spellchecker, almanac, Bartlett's Familiar Quotations, the Chicago Manual of Style, and a zip-code directory. Other CD-ROM products include InfoTrac II (Information Access Company), with listings from The New York Times Index and many other newspapers and magazines, and the Readers' Guide to Periodical Literature. Two visual resources are Facts on File Visual Dictionary and On the World.

On the World contains maps and lets the user create graphics, symbol overlays, and text. Substantial portions of enormous reference and research databases for business, law, medical and life sciences, social sciences, and engineering and hard sciences are available on CD-ROM, sometimes from more than one publisher.

Most novices find CD-ROM easy and fun to use. Microsoft Bookshelf, for example, operates like a desktop utility. The writer uses just a few keystrokes to display a menu of reference books across the top of the screen, open a "window" for the desired resource, find the information (such as a zip code) and, if desired, download the information directly into the text he or she is writing. Using many CD-ROM databases, however, requires learning some basic computer searching skills. Fortunately, most CD-ROM search software allows users to develop these skills naturally as they access information. Help is available through help screens and printed manuals. Many publishers also offer onscreen or print, and toll-free assistance numbers.

Usually the search proceeds through a series of menus, beginning with choices of search fields, such as author, title, or subject. Users type in keywords and the system tells them how many items in the database contain those words. They call up and read the items and, again using menus, decide whether to print the information they want or download (save) it on a floppy or hard disk for later editing with a word processor.

As users become more accustomed to searching, they can begin to use more sophisticated functions. For instance, they can use partial words as search terms (truncation), impose conditions such as "and," "or," or "not" (Boolean operators) between search terms, or combine different search fields in a single query. The software also offers different ways to browse through the indexes or the database itself. The new Grolier's illustrated encyclopedia has a hypertext feature that allows the user who is curious about a highlighted term in the text to access a definition or cross-reference instantly.

Novice users who are already familiar with computers and with library searching will find it easier to learn to search a CD-ROM. The tendency is usually to retrieve too much information: users must be able first to state their requests in specific terms, then to manage and synthesize the information they obtain. Institutions that have installed CD-ROM systems have found that another tendency is to rely too much on the CD-ROM database and forget that (1) other, traditional, reference sources are available, and (2) the library may not have all the materials described in an index database. Finally, one drawback of searching CD-ROMs is that not all search programs are created equal: users who access more than one database may need to adjust their skills for different software.

Cost

A CD-ROM system can easily cost thousands of dollars. Disks run from a low end of about $200, to $2,000 or more for specialized research databases. Databases that are available on a subscription basis include regular updates and require the payment of an annual licensing fee. Minimum hardware requirements are a microcomputer and a CD-ROM drive. An interface card placed inside the computer connects it with the CD-ROM drive.

Many systems call for IBM or compatible microcomputers with hard drives and at least 512K capacity, and most users also want color monitors and printers. Some research is necessary: not all CD-ROM drives read all CD-ROMs, and none read audio CDs. CD-ROM drives are sold at typical computer, electronics, and department stores. Package deals, including equipment leases and upgrade kits, are available. Microsoft, for example, is working on an agreement with Sears to sell its Bookshelf product with a CD-ROM drive for about $1,100. While these costs may be discouraging for the individual, there is a bright side. Libraries and schools, which tend to find CD-ROM more convenient and less expensive than online searching and printed materials, are offering CD-ROM services for little or no charge. They also offer personal assistance in the form of librarians or instructors. This allows the novice user to become familiar with the technology before making a purchase. In the meantime, new products are being developed, existing products improved, and prices coming down in this highly competitive market.

Future of CD-ROM

As enthusiastic as users have been toward CD-ROM and other

optical disk technologies, the most exciting news is yet to come. Designers are currently developing media that can be written to and erased, including WORM (write once-read many) and DRAW (direct read after write). They are also exploring ways to increase the capacity of compact disks further, which would allow storage of more full-text databases such as newspapers. New chips compress audio and video data, thus making it more feasible to combine graphics and text for user-generated documents, desktop publishing, and presentation graphics, and to offer more full-motion video.

Greater storage space increases the potential for more powerful software, including highly interactive programs, natural language interfaces, and artificial intelligence. Research efforts include CD-I (compact disk interactive) and DVI (digital video interactive). Databases are only the beginning. Optical disk applications include education and training at all levels from kindergarten to corporation.

With enhanced interactivity and creative combinations of text, audio, and video, education in general will become more like entertainment. Children, for instance, will teach themselves reading and math skills while playing "games" with joysticks. Other products include intelligent games and simulations, drawing and painting, filming and animation, musical composition, and of course much improved capabilities for document writing and data analysis.

Inconveniences of current CD-ROM systems are being addressed. "Jukeboxes" now allow users to access many disks without manually changing them, and "daisy chains" allow more than one drive to be linked together. Hardware in general will become more standardized, less expensive, and more transportable. Multipurpose CD players will be able to stand alone without microcomputers. Portable units in cars, for instance, will provide maps and tourist information, mechanical diagnostics, and music.

While optical disk technologies are still very young—audio CDs were introduced in 1982 and CD-ROMs in 1984—their potential is revolutionary. New products are being marketed so fast that almost the only way to keep up is to read articles and advertisements in periodicals such as Byte Magazine, CD-ROM Review, Database, Electronic and Optical Publishing Review, Optical Information Systems, and PC World. Product reviews and publisher directories also appear in professional journals for educators, library and information specialists, and researchers in areas including management, law, economics, medicine, and agriculture.

9

BENEFITS OF INFORMATION TECHNOLOGY

More than three decades ago, computers and related information technologies were introduced to educators as educational tools. Today, there are computers of various descriptions in nearly all schools in the United States. Teachers, school administrators, government officials, and others faced with the costs involved in technology implementation must constantly evaluate the educational benefits of technology. Is there research or other evidence that indicates computers and advanced telecommunications are worthwhile investments for educators?

Using educational technology for drill and practice of basic skills can be highly effective according to a large body of data and a long history of use. Students usually learn more, and learn more rapidly, in courses that use computer assisted instruction (CAI). This has been shown to be the case across all subject areas, from preschool to higher education, and in both regular and special education classes. Drill and practice is the most common application of CAI in elementary education, the military, and in adult educational settings. Some notes that in the military, where emphasis is on short and efficient training time, the use of CAI can cut training time by one third. In the military, CAI can also be more cost-effective than additional tutoring, reduced class size, or increased instruction time to attain equivalent educational gains.

APPLICATIONS OF TECHNOLOGY TO ADVANCED SKILLS

The application of educational technologies to instruction has progressed beyond the use of basic drill and practice software, and now includes the use of complex multimedia products and advanced networking technologies. Today, students use multimedia to learn interactively and work on class projects. They use the Internet to do research, engage in projects, and to communicate. The new technologies allow students to have more control over their own learning, to think analytically and critically, and to work collaboratively. This "constructivist" approach is one effort at educational reform made easier by technology, and perhaps even driven by it.

Traditional lecture methods are often left behind as students collaborate and teachers facilitate. Students, who often know more about technology than the teacher are able to assist the teacher with the lesson. Since this type of instructional approach, and the technologies involved with it, are recent developments, it is hard to gauge their educational effects. The Apple Classrooms of Tomorrow (ACOT), a 10-year project where students and teachers were each given two computers, one for school and one for home, illustrates some of the gains made in students' advanced skills. ACOT notes that students:

— Explored and represented information dynamically and in many forms

— Became socially aware and more confident

— Communicated effectively about complex processes

— Became independent learners and self-starters

— Worked well collaboratively

— Knew their areas of expertise and shared expertise spontaneously and

— Used technology routinely and appropriately. Another effort called the Buddy Project supplied students with home computers and modem access to school. Positive effects included:

  — An increase in writing skills

  — Better understanding and broader view of math

  — Ability to teach others, and

  — Greater problem solving and critical thinking skills.

Effects of technology on student attitudes

Numerous studies over the years that other benefits enjoyed by students who use technology. These benefits involve attitudes toward self and toward learning. The studies reveal that students feel more successful in school are more motivated to learn and have increased self confidence and self esteem when using CAI. This is particularly true when the technology allows the students to control their own learning. It's also true across a variety of subject areas, and is especially noteworthy when students are in at-risk groups (special education, students from inner-city or rural schools).

On-line technologies

The Internet and advanced networking technologies are comparative newcomers to the classroom. Efforts such as Net Day and e-rate discounts enacted by the Telecommunications Act make it easier for many classrooms around the country to connect to the Internet. Although a large body of research on the effects of the Internet in the classroom does not yet exist, recent studies illustrate some observed positive effects. A study by the Center for Applied Special Technology shows significantly higher scores on measures of information management, communication, and presentation of ideas for experimental groups with on-line access than for control groups with no access. Also, students in the experimental group reported significantly increased use of computers in four different areas—gathering information, organizing and presenting information, doing multimedia projects, and obtaining help with basic skills.

Use of technology by teachers and administrators

Teachers and administrators use computer and information technologies to improve their roles in the educational process. Some examples include:

— Using computer tools to streamline record keeping and administrative tasks, thereby helping to free up time for instruction or professional development

— Decreasing isolation by using e-mail and the Internet to communicate with colleagues, parents, and the outside world, and

— Increasing professional development activities by taking distance education courses, accessing educational research, and accessing classroom materials such as lesson plans.

Some of the observed benefits associated with educational technology have been reviewed above, but what are the factors that help technology succeed in bringing about these benefits? Glenna & Melmed and the Technology Counts analysis suggest the following factors observed in successful technology-rich schools:

— Evidence of a detailed technology plan. Such a plan should consider funding, installation and integration of equipment, ongoing management of the technology. The plan should also express a clear vision of the goals of the technology integration.

— Teacher training and continuing education. Teachers should know how to operate the technology and how to integrate it into the curriculum.

— Support from administration. Administrative support can come in the form of funding, or in restructuring schedules and physical space to reflect the new learning environment.

— Support from the community. Parents, businesses, and community members can use technology as a springboard to become more involved in the activities of neighborhood schools. All can help with wiring or technical support. Parents can use e-mail to facilitate communication with teachers and administrators. Businesses can use e-mail to help mentor students and help them prepare for the workplace.

— Support from government. Adequate funding and appropriate policy making can help to assure that technology is accessible to all schools on an equal basis.

These factors suggest that to succeed, trchnology, like any educational tool, cannot exist in isolation, but must be made an integral part of the entire instructional process.

The impact of technology

Traditional methods of evaluating the effectiveness of educational technology present a number of problematic issues. Glenna & Melmed state these succinctly:

— Most available tests do not reliably measure the outcomes being sought. The measures that are reported are usually from traditional multiple-choice tests. New measures need to be developed which would assess the higher-level skills and other effects often affected by technology.

— Assessments of the impact of technology are really assessments of the instructional processes enabled by technology, and the outcomes are highly dependent on the quality of the implementation of the entire instructional process. Crucial elements include instructional design, content, and teaching strategies associated with both the software and the classroom environment.

— The very dynamic nature of technology makes meaningful evaluation difficult. By the time long-term studies are completed, the technology being evaluated is often outdated.

The U.S. Department of Education and Educational Testing Service (ETS) notes that new methods of evaluation that look at technology in context are being investigated. These methods will focus ideally not on the question "Does technology work?" but rather on how it impacts the various components of the educational process.

Technology has been shown to have positive effects on the instructional process, on basic and advanced skills. Technology is also changing the instructional process itself. To be effective, technology cannot exist in a vacuum, but must become part of the whole educational environment. New measures of evaluation are under development which would help to better define the role of technology in its wider context.

INFORMATION: SEARCH STRATEGIES, TOOLS AND RESOURCES

In the current Information Age, the speed at which we work makes us increasingly dependent on high-quality, accurate information. However, information is becoming more voluminous, fragmented into different formats and media, and duplicated in multiple physical locations. In order to access and use these myriad sources effectively, people must be information literate. As defined by the American Library Association (ALA) in its mission statement for the global information society, 21st century information literacy is the ability to seek and effectively utilize information resources, including knowledge of how to use technologies and the forms in which information is stored. This means that asking a good question, as well as accessing, locating, evaluating, and using information, is critical not only in scholarly activities but in making daily decisions.

Having accurate, up-to-date information determines the difference between the rich and the poor in the Information Age. Community colleges can make a vital contribution toward closing this gap by equipping their students with the ability to access, retrieve, and utilize information.

As we strive to understand information literacy issues in a more holistic manner, the Information Literacy: Search Strategies, Tools & Resources (ST&R) Program developed by Ercegovac can provide invaluable guidance in a variety of information literacy environments.

GROWTH OF COMPUTER NETWORKS AND INFORMATION SERVICES

The growth of computer networks and information services has already enabled learners at all levels to share resources, collaborate with one another, and publish their results electronically. To use information sources effectively, we need both technology infrastructure (TI) and information literacy infrastructure (ILI) in place. While TI has been well-funded and developed, ILI is poorly applied in teaching and learning, and requires educators' attention. Information technology is a tool for writing papers, communicating with colleagues worldwide, and exchanging experiments, ideas, and programs internationally. As community colleges are considering distance learning and adding new technologies to their curriculum, ensuring students' information literacy becomes vital. However, this shift may challenge existing campus dynamics.

The proliferation of information sources and educational technology have created a dysfunctional relationship between community college faculty and librarians that is based on an outdated teaching/learning paradigm. Traditionally, teaching has been the purview of faculty while librarians were viewed as merely custodians of printed information resources. In the current Information Age however, librarians have become the primary instructors in community colleges to teach research methods and critical thinking skills as applied to information access. As such, there is increasing support for community college librarians to be seen as key instructional team members and as partners with faculty.

Especially as libraries are transformed into integrated library/high technology centers, resource-based learning and information literacy can be adopted as goals across academic disciplines. At Central Seattle Community College, for example, faculty linked an English composition course with one in library science to teach students how to use information literacy skills in the context of cultural pluralism. By working together, librarians and faculty were able to teach content as well as the valuable skill of navigating through complex data bases and information resources.

While faculty may know how to teach English composition or other standard courses, they may not be as comfortable teaching information literacy. Fortunately, an abundance of resources has emerged from sources including the Department of Education, the ERIC Clearinghouse on Information and Technology and independent authors. These publications state information literacy goals, review literacy tools, provide case studies, and present adaptable models of information literacy curricula.

The ST&R programme

One recently developed aid is the Information Literacy: Search Strategies, Tools & Resources (ST&R) Program that can be tailored to the local needs of colleges. It is comprised of three integrated instructional components: the ST&R book, a PowerPoint presentation for classroom use, and an HTML version of the book for installation on institutional servers.

Implemented at the intersection of learners and Web-ready information resources, ST&R can initiate students to the world of information literacy. It is a comprehensive and flexible tool that has been developed to enable students to become self-sustained seekers and users of information sources and digital libraries. This can be especially useful in the community colleges where many students are from disadvantaged or lower socio-economic backgrounds and previously may not have had access to such sources.

The program has been designed for anyone interested in the critical and effective use of all types of information sources regardless of their format and medium. ST&R takes a user-centered perspective and focuses on the intellectual aspects of locating, evaluating, interpreting, and communicating information sources rather than on the technical aspects of these activities.

Furthermore, ST&R is comprehensive because it contains references to a variety of sources and digital repositories, introduces effective search strategies and tools for the use of these sources, and covers critical evaluation of these sources. In this one-stop "literacy mall," ST&R also offers exercises, a glossary of introduced terms and concepts, and Internet addresses of numerous sources available on the Web. In particular, the electronic version of ST&R allows students to connect automatically with Internet addresses and explore various search engines in an orderly and guided manner. Instructors are equipped with the "ST&R Show," based on the Microsoft PowerPoint 97 presentation program, that features links to selected Internet digital libraries and resources.

The ST&R Program also is flexible because its content is divided into a series of nine interrelated yet independent chapters. Students can expand each chapter by doing more exercises and searches, tracking new Web addresses, updating the existing ones, and developing their own portfolio of annotated information sources.

This program is the first attempt to translate research from the fields of information seeking, information retrieval, and educational psychology into a practical information literacy program. It can be utilized in a variety of academic settings including libraries, media centers, and classrooms. In addition, different academic departments may wish to incorporate individual parts of ST&R into their curricula to fit their own information literacy mission, students, and collections. Also, the program is scalable to the different academic abilities of community college students.

In summary, ST&R represents an accumulation of over 10 years of teaching, in-class testing with undergraduates at the University of California, Los Angeles, and feedback from real learners and users. It is based on understanding the user, active learning, a conceptual approach in teaching, and modularity. While the program is a very practical information literacy tool, it also is based on solid research and conceptual foundations. For example, it recognizes the importance of the information life cycle as well as the user.

In this Information Age, we browse and query the world's repositories without ever having to leave our workplaces and communities. Thus, it is not surprising that the traditional sense of a library as a confined space with local dimensions has introduced ambiguities to the way people interpret library collections and uses. As a result, the value of a library as a store has been questioned, and the library's role as a service is largely misunderstood.

Another concern is the ease with which untrained users can directly search sources, resulting in their continued difficulty with utilizing information retrieval systems. Furthermore, definitions of access and information are not agreed upon universally. All these changes have created the need to rethink information literacy and to educate students in the lifelong quest for knowledge. ST&R helps in this regard.

SAY "YES" TO TELEPHONE LINES IN THE CLASSROOM.

In June 1994, a Texas Center for Educational Technology (TCET) "customer" requested information/documentation that could persuade the school district administration, the school board, and the community that telephones in K-12 classrooms are necessary. Since TCET did not have information on file concerning the use of telephones and telephone lines in education, the request for information was forwarded to educators worldwide via the Internet.

Several educational listservs and conference groups on the Internet posted a request for comments, observations, and opinions from educators having experience with telephones in the classroom. TCET received responses to the information request from large and small schools. Geographically, responses came from school districts all across the United States and from Australia. Although reports included a few cautions and negative observations, the vast majority of comments were resoundingly positive favoring the installation of telephone lines in classrooms.

Respondents agreed overwhelmingly that in an age of information and communications, it is essential to equip K-12 classrooms with modern communications tools including telephone lines. Students and teachers need to learn how to use communications tools to gather information to support learning in various curricula. The telephone lines are used in classrooms in predominately two ways: voice communications and computer communications. A couple of respondents mentioned the use of phone lines for the exchange of FAX messages.

Voice communications

As expected, most respondents indicated that improved parent/teacher communication was the primary advantage of voice communications. Many also reported improved intra-campus and inter-campus communications. Telephone installations improved office to classroom communications in many schools. With classroom telephones it was not necessary to disrupt the whole class with an announcement over the PA for a student to come to the office. The office can contact the teacher by phone and the teacher can quietly tell the student to go to the office.

Ken Phillips, Principal at Taylor Elementary School in Cleveland, Tennessee, installed a key electronic telephone system as a flexible, versatile solution to the need for an intercom system. Three telephone lines come into the school. The phone rings only in the office. If a call for a teacher is determined to be important enough, it is transferred to the teacher's phone. The system can also be an intercom and they can even pipe background music into the classrooms.

Many respondents found that a telephone in the classroom helped considerably with discipline management. Some school districts have also reported a considerable decrease in absenteeism because of phones in the classroom.

Many reported an increase in teachers' morale. Apparent increases in efficiency and productivity have accompanied increases in morale. Quoting Leeanne Needham, Technology Specialist with the Issaquah School District in Issaquah, Washington, "What a difference the phone made! We were much more productive as educators. The most beneficial part was the improvement of teacher/parent communication." In an article in "Education Technology News", Lockwood Elementary School, reported that having telephones in the classrooms improved student morale. When students complete outstanding work, they are encouraged to call their parents and relate the good news.

In some high schools with classroom telephone installations, the teachers put information in their voice mail about homework and assignments for the week, easily retrievable from a student's home. This has resulted in considerable improvement in communication between teachers, students, and parents. Announcements for sports and other events are sometimes posted on voice mail. At some schools, students use classroom telephones to obtain local research information and to contact content experts. These activities enhance learning and add current knowledge to many curricula.

In the Reader Exchange column of "Learning94" , Beverly Blackman Dornburg of Bill Brown Elementary in Spring Branch, Texas, reported that she used a speaker phone in her classroom to let her students communicate with their pen pals in Australia! Similarly, Lockwood Elementary School teachers had their students talk long distance with President Clinton during the presidential campaign to get, first hand, his position on various issues. Students also talked with an executive of Taco Bell to obtain information about the corporation's new automatic taco-making machine.

Gellerman discusses many applications of various telephone systems that are now in K-12 schools. Major uses include: (1) making important school information available to the community, (2) allowing connection to electronic grade book programs, (3) ability to check on a student's progress (homework hotlines), (4) obtaining test schedules via voice mail, and (5) checking attendance records. A few high schools have installed telephone registration similar to that used at many universities.

Potential negatives of having telephones in classrooms include abuse of the communications tool by teachers and/or students. Proper use of the system needs to be part of orientation for students and teachers. A phone ringing in the classroom can be disruptive, but probably no more so than the teacher from across the hall coming in to borrow something. Most of the schools are preventing this by answering all calls in the office. Calls are then forwarded to the classroom only when the teacher has a free period or if the call is an emergency.

COMPUTER COMMUNICATIONS

Computer communications via telephone lines (telecomputing) allow teachers and students access to information for conducting research in almost any area of the K-12 curriculum. It opens connections to content experts from around the world via E-mail, E-mail lists, and newsgroups and allows for the exchange of document and data files. Survey respondents reported that the best way to connect classrooms to the Internet (and other information highways) is to establish a local area network (LAN), a computer network throughout the school. Once the LAN is in place, equip it with a communications server that allows any computer on the network to connect to the outside world.

The negatives of telecomputing are few but include the fact that the telephone line is not the best connection (access) to the Internet, although it is the most economical. The worst negative might be the "garbage" that is accessible through the Internet. Some means will need to be established to control what information students access. Flanders (1994) discusses various aspects of this issue.

FAX

Yet another mode of communication via telephone lines is the FAX machine. In his response to TCET's request for information, Gary Bowers of Region X Education Service Center in Richardson, Texas, reported that Lawrence Livermore Laboratories in Livermore, California, faxes answers to questions from middle school students in the Livermore area. Gellerman also reports that some schools will now FAX course information, enrollment forms, and student grade reports.

For many school districts, the principal hindrance to installing telephones or telephone outlets in classrooms appears to be the cost. Many districts have found ways to minimize the expense, however. Several schools have four or five lines coming into the school that are connected to a key telephone system or a PBX system from which lines are run to each classroom. Other schools have found different ways to split one line into four or five to similarly cut down the cost of phone bills yet provide the classrooms with this essential communications tool.

In a presentation at TelEd '93, Fergus revealed one sizable school district's solution for putting phone lines in classrooms. The Des Moines Public School District chose to install its own telephone system to serve the entire district. Although it was a large financial investment in the beginning, money was saved in the long run, and there is a telephone in each classroom. The district phone system was installed in 1985. They are currently wiring eight schools per year and should have all sixty schools in the district wired and telephones in all classrooms by the end of 1995.

LAPTOP COMPUTERS IN THE K-12 CLASSROOM

Over the past decade, many schools have investigated the educational possibilities of mobile computing. More recently, an increasing number of K-12 schools are implementing the use of laptop computers. Improvements in portable computing technology and examples of successful pilot programs using laptops and other portables have inspired many K-12 schools to consider laptops for their students.

Organized laptop programs in higher education date as far back as 1988 when Drew University in Madison, New Jersey, began providing notebook computers to all incoming freshman. Now more than 50 postsecondary institutions worldwide require at least some of their students to use laptops. Throughout the 1990s, a number of private schools in the United States and abroad began requiring ownership of laptops.

In 1996, inspired by the successful use of laptops in Australian schools, the Microsoft Corporation and Toshiba began one of the most high-profile programs now underway, currently known as Microsoft's Anytime Anywhere Learning (AAL) Program. Technology corporations, such as NetSchools, NoteSys Inc., Apple, and others are promoting the use of laptops in K-12 education, providing hardware packages for schools, and in some cases, software and technical support as well.

How are schools integrating laptops into their technology infrastructure? Microsoft commissioned an ongoing study of Anytime Anywhere Learning, published as the Rockman Report. In their study, Rockman identified five models of laptop use currently in place at the K-12 level:

— Concentrated-each student has his or her own laptop for use at home or in school

— Class set-a school-purchased classroom set is shared among teachers

— Dispersed-in any given classroom, there are students with and without laptops

— Desktop-each classroom is permanently assigned a few laptops for students to share

— Mixed-some combination of the above models.

Each model has potential advantages, either in terms of instructional benefits, ease of implementation, or savings. In the concentrated model, teachers are free to integrate technology fully into instruction as well as assignments, since all students have access to a computer for homework, study, and projects. In the class set and dispersed models, teachers are free to integrate laptops during the school day; however, there may still be students within the same class who lack access to a computer in the home, so integration options are more limited. In the desktop model, although the computers are owned and maintained by the school, a student working on a computer-based project during the school day might be allowed to take the laptop home to complete their work. Also, teachers are better able to reconfigure their classroom setup to suit their technology integration needs.

Laptops can also take the place of desktops in a traditional lab setting. For example, the Cuba-Rushford School District in Allegheny County, New York, created a 70-computer laptop lab. These computers are available for checkout to their middle and high school students. For many schools, the primary advantage of laptops over desktops is in creating opportunities for all students to have access to a computer both during and outside of the school day.

Portable alternatives

Traditional laptops are not the only portable computers appearing in elementary and secondary institutions. Some schools uncomfortable with the high cost of laptops have explored the advantages of lower-priced portables designed for K-12 students. The AlphaSmart and DreamWriter, for example, make it possible to provide each student with a rechargeable portable that can be used for word processing or keyboarding instruction at a fraction of the cost of a traditional laptop.

Some mini-portables do more than word processing. Casio's Cassiopeia Computer Extender, for example, includes the graphing program Maple as well as Geometer's Sketchpad, a dynamic geometry program. This mini-portable can therefore be used in math and science instruction at the high school level. In addition to scaled-down portables, manufacturers are also designing full-scale laptops with younger students in mind. The StudyPro is a durable infrared wireless laptop with few moving parts marketed specifically for K-12 use. Also, Apple's AirPort wireless network hub is another wireless technology designed to meet the needs of laptop schools. With wireless networks, schools can allow multiple users to share a single network connection, as well as avoid some of the hassle and expense of physical cabling.

Educators who work with laptops have begun to explore their unique advantages. The 1999 Laptop Learning Challenge sponsored by Toshiba and the National Science Teacher's Association recently recognized innovative uses of laptops in K-12 mathematics and science education. Some award-winning ideas showed students using laptops to facilitate group work, to analyze data immediately during a lab exercise, or to conduct scientific investigations in the field rather than in the classroom.

Evaluators of the Copernicus Project, a multi-district laptop pilot program in Seattle, Washington, found laptops to be especially suited for writing activities, student projects, and presentations. Other uses for laptops include creating spreadsheets to solve math homework problems; creating book reports that inspire student creativity with presentation software such as PowerPoint or HyperStudio; or having students routinely hand in assignments via floppy disk or connect to the school network and save their work to a central file server for the teacher to review, add comments, and leave for the student to retrieve.

Several studies suggest educational benefits related to laptop use. Specific benefits noted include increased student motivation, a shift toward more student-centered classroom environments, and better school attendance than students not using laptops. In his study of a laptop pilot program in Beaufort, South Carolina, Stevenson also reported that students with laptops demonstrated a "sustained level of academic achievement" during their middle school years, as opposed to students not using laptops who tended to decline during this same period. He also noted that these academic benefits were most significant in at-risk student populations.

In their study of laptop use in middle school science classrooms, some found that those laptop classrooms in which skills and the process of inquiry were emphasized had the most positive impact on student learning and attitudes. According to Rockman, a majority of teachers in laptop schools reported an increase in both cooperative learning and project-based instruction. Other research has not supported the educational benefits of laptop use.

Some found that the impact of laptops after one year was "at best marginal" on achievement in mathematics, science, and writing. Also, some reported a more positive relationship between laptops and student attitudes than between laptops and academic achievement. Research into the educational use of laptops has only begun; relatively few K-12 schools have had laptops in place long enough to generate longitudinal studies of their impact on student achievement. It remains to be seen what additional research will reveal about the long-term impact of laptops on student achievement and outcomes.

Equity controversy

With growing concern over equity in access to technology, laptop programs have become increasingly attractive. Whether through leasing programs, purchasing refurbished hardware, or obtaining technology grants, many schools hope to reduce their student-to-computer ratio by considering some form of laptop program. Critics point out the possibilities of theft, vandalism, and accidental damage. Newer "student-friendly" laptop models address some of these issues; not only are they more durable, but some have included theft-deterrent technology as well.

However, despite the creative educational possibilities of laptops and promise of equitable access for all students, added costs in the form of hardware, network costs, technical support considerations, and faculty training remain the greatest obstacles. The presence of laptops in a school does not necessarily imply student ownership; however, some schools are advocating or requiring student purchase or rental. Partnerships between schools, nonprofit organizations, and corporations can defray costs, but ultimately parents share the expense with schools that hope to put a laptop in the hands of every child.

For this reason, there is concern among some that laptop programs may worsen technology inequities among students for families who are unable to assume these costs. The controversy over laptops is not limited to issues of equity and cost, however; the Texas Board of Education recently made headlines by suggesting the state replace all textbooks with CD-ROMS and fund a laptop leasing program for all 3.9 million students with the estimated $1.8 billion in savings over six years. Despite these issues, many educators hoping to bring the benefits of educational technology to more students continue to look for creative ways to overcome these obstacles.

The future of mobile computing in K-12 education is still uncertain. Laptops may never become as common in classrooms as hand-held calculators. Solutions for issues of cost, technical support needs, security, and equitable access are challenging for many schools. Many schools with laptops, however, remain positive and enthusiastic about the changes observed and benefits their students derive from access to portable computers.

Although many laptop programs are young and studies are still in progress, research has shown educational benefits from the use of laptops, particularly with respect to increasing student motivation and creating more student-centered classrooms. Continuing improvements in student portable computing technology as well as models of successful programs may make laptops an increasingly attractive option for K-12 educators and technology planners.

COMPETENCIES FOR ONLINE TEACHING

Information technology is changing the way people live and learn. Not surprisingly, information technology (IT) is also transforming the nature of teaching. These remarks provide a framework for thinking about such changes and exploring work in progress that is relevant to the development of competencies specific to teaching online.

Competence refers to a state of being well qualified to perform an activity, task or job function. When a person is competent to do something, he or she has achieved a state of competence that is recognizable and verifiable to a particular community of practitioners. A competency, then, refers to the way that a state of competence can be demonstrated to the relevant community. According to the International Board of Standards for Training, Performance and Instruction (IBSTPI), a competency involves a related set of knowledge, skills and attitudes that enable a person to effectively perform the activities of a given occupation or function in such a way that meets or exceeds the standards expected in a particular profession or work setting.

The structure and assessment of competencies may differ from one community of practice to another and even within a community. To facilitate a common understanding of competencies in the\context\of online and distributed learning some specifications have been elaborated. Typically, a competency is divided into specific indicators describing the requisite knowledge, skills, attitudes and context of performance.

There are different ways to validate that a person has demonstrated the relevant competencies. One of them is through a certification process. Teacher certification is a common practice, and the notion of teacher competencies is fairly well established. However, competencies are generally associated with highly formalized professional activities and not applied to ill-defined tasks. Ill-defined tasks certainly include many forms of teaching. This narrow view of competence runs counter to common sense and professional practice, but brings into attention the mainstream approach to elaboration of teacher competencies where it is essential to clearly identify the conditions of teaching. The delivery environment is a particularly relevant condition to identify competencies for online teaching.

ONLINE CLASSROOM TEACHING

Information technology can be integrated into both online and classroom settings, but the interaction between these technologies and new approaches to learning and instruction may vary. The range of activities available in online settings and the multiple conditions of time in which they take place are evidence that the technology demands placed on online teachers are somewhat more significant than those associated with classroom teachers.

Much of what has already been published with regard to online teaching has focused on technical skills and requirements of successfully moderating and facilitating online discussions and chat sessions. This body of literature suggests that becoming an effective online moderator requires training and that there are competencies unique to online environments. In online asynchronous discussions, the moderator's competencies involve (1) allowing learners time for reflection, (2) keeping discussions alive and on a productive path, and (3) archiving and organizing discussions to be used in subsequent lessons.

In online synchronous discussions (e.g., chat), the moderator must (1) establish ground rules for discussion. (2) animate interactions with minimal instructor intervention. (3) sense how online text messages may appear to distant learners, and (4) be aware of cultural differences. How are these competencies unique to online teaching? At the applied level, animating discussions, displaying cultural sensitivity and so on, apply to all teachers. At the environment level, however, the ways in which a teacher demonstrates such competence is quite different, which suggests that there are competencies unique to online settings.

Teaching competencies and online teaching competencies have generally been considered separately. However, efforts to interrelate the two are being undertaken by IBSTPI in association with the research center for Tele-universite, Universite de Quebec (LICEF).

Implications of competencies for online teaching

The current interest in competencies for online teaching is coming from business and industry, primarily with regard to technical training and professional development courses offered in online settings. It is quite likely that some of the interest in competencies for online teaching is a result of hastily crafted online courses and inadequate preparation of online facilitators.

Clearly technology offers the potential to create and implement highly engaging and effective online environments to support a wide variety of learning goals. It is also quite clear that our capacity to make effective use of information technology in educational settings is impaired by inadequate preparation of teachers (as well as learners) and by a shortage of properly trained instructional designers and educational support personnel.

The development of competencies for online teaching should lead to the associated development of training for online teachers and (in some cases) to the certification of online teachers. To develop competencies for online teachers is not without challenge. Competencies are dynamic in nature, and they largely depend on the relevant social context. The constant transformation of IT makes the development of competencies for online teachers a continuous process and demands continuing professional preparation and training for online teachers. Such endeavors will improve our ability to make effective use of technology in learning and instruction.

TELECOMMUNICATIONS AND DISTANCE EDUCATION

Recently a growing number of distance education institutions throughout the world have been utilizing telephone tutorials and audio conferences to supplement print-based interactions. A characteristic of this means of distance education by telephone is that communication is synchronous in nature. That is, the participants in the discussion or the tutorial are online at the same time, although they may be separated by distance.

Recent developments in telecommunications technologies such as fax machines and electronic mail through computer networks have introduced a new element in the form of rapid Asynchronous communication. This has the characteristic of the participants being separated in time, even if not necessarily by distance. This form of communication is destined to play an increasingly significant role in future distance educational systems.

Another aspect of progress in telecommunications is increasing capacity and greater standardization of electronic communication media. Increasing capacity is a result of the widespread availability of satellites for long distance communication and the gradual replacement of copper wires by fiber optic cables of greater capacity. Standardization is being promoted by the gradual implementation of a worldwide Integrated Systems Digital Network (ISDN).

The ISDN network will be capable of carrying all types of messages, whether they are in the form of audio, video, text, or computer data, through the same channels in the same digital format. This will enable the messages to be integrated at end user terminals into multimedia presentations. This is the impetus for most of the developments in distance education.

Developments in distane education

The print-based model of correspondence education supported by distance instruction through written messages has survived the test of time and continues to be utilized intensively. However, as distance education has become more institutionalized, other media have been applied.

A "second generation" of distance education through the 60s and 70s was characterized by heavy reliance on open broadcast by either radio or television, supported by correspondence instruction and print materials. The "third generation" of distance education has been characterized by teleconferencing systems. These began with audio conferencing but progressed to more sophisticated audiographic conferencing systems that supported the telephone audio conference with visual and text material.

Another parallel development has been video conferencing. Until recently this was a somewhat expensive alternative to the audio conference, but due to developments in digital computer-based desktop video, it is now becoming economically accessible to an ever larger section of the educational community.

We are now entering a fourth phase of development of distance education based on the integrated use of new developments in telecommunications and computing and characterized by the integrated use of remote study materials supported by computer-based multimedia teleconferencing. Integrated multimedia computer technology will provide the platform which will most resemble real-time, interactive instruction.

The various technologies available for telecommunications-based distance education can be schematized as in the figure below. In the synchronous communication mode, we are witnessing a development from predominantly audio communication by telephone, or amplified telephone in the case of audio conferences, to multimedia interactive real-time communication, either between individuals or groups.

The result is that virtually all of the activities that can be undertaken in a conventional classroom situation can also be undertaken over distance, in a form of "virtual reality". In the asynchronous communication mode, the predominant medium of the past (print) is being supplemented by voice messaging facilities and other graphic communication potential so that once more we are working towards an integrated multimedia environment for educational communication.

Costs

The telecommunications option for education is often perceived as being expensive compared to either face-to-face education or the more conventional distance education methods based on print and correspondence by mail. However, this is not a completely accurate perception. Cost calculations that include the communication costs as well as the costs of tutor time in generating feedback messages to students show that telecommunications-based instruction can be more cost efficient than print-based instruction. The experience of AT&T in utilizing audiographic teleconferencing has demonstrated cost reductions of over 50% in the real costs of training if these are calculated to include the cost of transport and accommodations of participants from remote sites. Furthermore, the costs of telecommunication are falling whereas the costs of educational space, staffing and transport are rising, so that over time the economical equation will favor the increased use of telecommunications-based education. One should also remember that over the long view it will not be necessary for educational systems to invest in the basic infrastructure for telecommunications as this is a requirement for society and business in general.

Potential benefits

Given the technological scenario for the future that has just been painted, it is fair to ask whether such future systems are capable of delivering an appropriate level of quality of education. Research on distance education by and large has shown that, when appropriately planned, distance education can be as effective as conventional classroom based education. While there are some exceptions in terms of certain types of content or certain groups of students, the move towards integrated multimedia networking may be expected to extend the range of effective distance education applications.

One potential benefit of such integrated networks in distance education is that they may be "user driven." Groups of students may form naturally because of common interests at a given point in time, largely independent of decisions made by any single educational institution. A program of study might be composed of modules of materials pulled in from various institutions as required by the particular individual or group. Potentially, such a development offers the promise of overcoming a major weakness of conventional educational provision, namely the long reaction time required by institutions to adapt curricula and content to the changing needs of society. To extend the currently popular hypertext/hypermedia jargon, we might look forward to the hyper-school or hyper-university, a network of the world's educational institutions that may be browsed at will by a student interested in planning and following through an individual program of study.

WEB-BASED TRAINING

Education and training via the World Wide Web are growing rapidly. Reduced training costs, world-wide accessibility, and improved technological capabilities have made electronic instructional delivery to adult learners a viable alternative to classroom instruction.

Market demand

It is estimated that technology-assisted training will represent half of all training methods by the year 2002 (McGee 1999). Particularly appealing to industry are the cost savings such training affords. PNC Bank Corp in Pittsburgh, for example, recently installed a system for self-paced online training through which it expects to save as much as 40 percent per user in training expenses. MCI WorldCom slashed approximately $3 million in travel, facility, and labor costs over a year by offering 20 percent of its classes over the Web. The company expected to increase this to 50 percent in 1999. By switching from classroom to Web-based training, some companies have realized up to 75 percent savings in their training budgets, making this mode of training especially appealing to companies that have large numbers of employees to train.

Travel expenses, instructor fees, facility costs, materials, and office equipment costs, in addition to the cost of lost time on the job when employees are in training represents some of the savings that are realized through Web-based training. Efficiency of operation is another advantage Web-based training offers to companies that must now compete in a global marketplace. Intranets help to eliminate delays in introducing new products by offering companies the capability of training their entire sales staff simultaneously, even when they are located at different sites across the globe. Additionally, as organizations become increasing flat through restructuring, Web-based training delivery is a welcome alternative to managers who have little time to devote to the training of new employees and to administrators who no longer need to find, schedule, and staff classes that will meet the varied training and educational needs of diversely skilled employees.

Learner participation

The flexibility of time, place, and programs offered via Web training is appealing to learners who are trying to balance school with work and home responsibilities. They can mix modes of instruction, even accumulating college credits and meeting residency requirements for degrees. Employees who seek flexible work hours and telecommuting work arrangements are being drawn to companies that offer similar opportunities for them to upgrade their skills. Given the choice, increasing numbers of learners are taking distance education courses, often congruently with their on-campus coursework. Community residents who wish to engage in lifelong learning are finding many options available to them via the Internet.

Online learning communities such as Senior Net make it possible for learners of any age to connect with people in a variety of geographic locations who have the same interests and needs, thus eliminating many of the barriers imposed by physical limitations and age. Most successful in using computer-based, online programs are people who are focused in their study habits, engaged in learning tasks that require creative thinking and analysis, and task and detail oriented. Grill describes the typical American distance learner as one who is 25-50 years of age, taking courses to learn new subjects and skills or to update old ones, and experienced in participating in education.

Virtual classrooms are of two types-asynchronous and synchronous. "Asynchronous classrooms allow students and instructors to engage in collaborative learning activities without being online at the same time. They are well suited to develop skills that require analysis, synthesis, and evaluation". Synchronous classrooms are more reflective of the traditional classroom as they allow the instructor and student to be online at the same time—brainstorming, questioning, discussing, and debating.

E-mail, online forums, bulletin boards, chat rooms, and listservs are a few of the tools available to students in these classrooms. In spite of its utility for a variety of purposes, the Internet is not always the best training option. Tasks that require use of interpersonal skills are better facilitated through classroom role playing and one-on-one interactions. Heckler contends that "WBT courses tend not to be as interactive as instructor-led ones, and the absence of an instructor means that most students will not push themselves as hard". However, some notes that the type of training offered on the Web is the determining factor in whether or not learning occurs. For example, when multimedia instruction that includes sound, animation, and/or video is used, the learner can become actively involved in learning processes through online animation. When interactivity is added to the mix, the program's capabilities are similar to those of CD-ROM programs and "can be used to construct 'guided discovery' environments, e.g., courses that teach physicians to diagnose patients by taking a medical history, conducting an examination, and running lab tests".

Programme design

Because "most WBT programs are little more than self-paced learning, success in these programs hinges on the learner's ability to engage in self-directed learning and to develop metacognitive skills for the Web". However, a focus on the development of problem-solving and critical-thinking skills requires that Web-based training programs be designed to accommodate the needs of the learner, giving him/her the freedom to follow a unique path to learning in his/her own cognitive style. For example, to learn about ways to relieve the symptoms of arthritis, one learner may search the ABI Inform database to find information on a drug to relieve arthritis pain by using the drug's name, e.g., Celebrex; another learner may search the Medline database to find information about the disease by using the name of the disease itself, e.g., arthritis; yet another learner may use a search engine to find information about companies that manufacture arthritis drugs, e.g., Pfizer. In each of these searches, the learner accesses information in sequences that are appropriate to his/her unique style of learning. Web-based learning tasks should require students to construct meaning rather than repeat information they have read or heard.

The instructor must assume the role of facilitator or coach and develop activities with advanced organizers, hyperlinks, and appropriate scaffolding to help students in their knowledge construction. This constructivist approach to teaching and learning, when applied in Web-based learning environments connects "content (knowledge), form (documents and activities), and thought processes".

With more advanced program designs, the networking power of the Web must be well integrated with the design elements. "Designers make use of learning communities, foster communication between teacher and student, and use the computational power of the Web to provide rich media that enhance the learning process". Recommendations for designers of Web-based instruction that are consistent with current research in Web design include the following:

— Give a detailed timeline, but provide external cues and imposed deadlines to help students stay on track.

— Obtain data and evaluate student reactions to the course throughout the semester to gain insight into the workload a student must handle at any given time.

— Provide adequate technical support.

— Offer a variety of presentation forms to gain and maintain student attention and continuing motivation.

Ball State University conducted a study to compare students' impressions of classroom training and Web-based training when the same instructional method was used in each program. One group of students engaged in learning in the traditional classroom, and another group used Web-based electronic modules developed by nursing faculty. Comparison of the traditional classroom methods (seminars) and electronic modules revealed the following: In the classroom setting, students perceived that the content was covered more adequately, there was more interaction and participation, and faculty preparation and expertise were more important to -learning. Students expressed the need for better communication skills, self-discipline, and knowledge of computer technology.

In general, however, the WBT students felt that electronic instruction facilitated greater depth of learning and afforded greater ability for them to participate in discussions as no one student was able to monopolize the conversation. In discussing the difficulties with electronic instruction, students mentioned that they felt disconnected from their class members, frustrated by a poor flow of communication and technical problems, and confused by feedback that was not always clear.

They missed having face-to-face contact with their instructor where they could experience verbal as well as nonverbal communication. A significant outcome of the study was that teachers came to recognize their need for better preparation, time, and effort in delivering electronic instruction.

Clark and Lyons emphasize the importance of good instructional methods that are based on the needs of the learner and on the job they are being trained to perform. The effects of learning cannot be determined until the principles of learning and instruction that have been successfully used in the classroom can be replicated in another form for computer-based instruction. Some tips for doing this include the following:

— Offer short classes.

— Make graphics simple and easy to read.

— Foster collegiality by asking students to contribute information about themselves and their interests.

— Vary the way you interact with learners.

— Avoid superfluous media; e.g., it might be important for a nurse to hear the sound of a pulse beating, but unnecessary to hear the package ripping when extracting a disposable needle.

— Use a combination of synchronous and asvnchronous instruction to reinforce new material, make assignments, and improve learner retention.

Web-based education and training are here to stay. Companies can train thousands of employees in interactive sessions that allow for consistency of messages and facilitate the exchange of different insights and perspectives as well as sharing knowledge and asking questions. Teachers can use technological capabilities built into the Web to advance their teaching and learning goals and foster construction of meaning. All learners—business, college, and community—can engage in collaboration with many people or groups as a means of enhancing their learning. These advantages, however, can be realized only when Web-based training is of the same quality as the best classroom instruction.

INTERNET TECHNOLOGIES FOR AUTHENTIC LANGUAGE LEARNING EXPERIENCES

With the focus on language, communication, and culture in the national standards for foreign language learning, foreign language teachers are continually searching for better ways of accessing authentic materials and providing experiences that will improve their students' knowledge and skills in these target areas. As the Internet transforms communication around the world, it is natural that it should play a major role in the foreign language classroom. The Internet enables computers throughout the world to communicate. To do this, each computer must have its own Internet address, be connected to the net, and be able to talk the same language, TCP/IP.

Any kind of computer can be networked in this way. Internet applications are computer programs that know how to use the Internet to interact. Many Internet applications use a client/server relationship where a client computer requests information from a server computer that sends the requested files. Other applications use a peer-to-peer relationship in which the computers exchange information in both directions.

These packets of information are sent from computer to computer, sometimes passing through many intermediaries before arriving at their destination; nevertheless, this process is usually extremely rapid. What matters to the typical foreign language professional are not these technical details but the software that enables communication over the Internet and how it can enhance the classroom experience. The wide range of these programs (text, image, sound, video, multimedia) makes them powerful additions to the foreign language teacher's repertoire.

Electronic mail

Email was in use before the Internet as we know it today even existed and is probably the most commonly used Internet application. With a single email account, foreign language teachers can integrate email-based activities into their curriculum. For example, international keypal projects that enable students to correspond with native speakers of the target language are easily implemented where participants have the necessary access, equipment, and foreign contacts. Distance learning is another curricular area where email is being used.

Electronic discussion groups or "lists" use email to provide a forum where people of similar interests can participate in a professional dialog and share resources. Hundreds of lists of interest to language teachers are available on the Internet. Some are service lists such as the Language Learning and Technology International (LLTI) list, which distributes information about all aspects of the technology used in language teaching; the Intercultural E-Mail Classroom Connections, K-12 (IECC) list, which provides a service for teachers seeking partner classrooms for international and cross-cultural electronic mail exchanges.

Others are language specific and address topics as specific and diverse as their membership warrants. FLTEACH, the Foreign Language Teaching Forum, is a good example of a list that cuts across language lines to discuss methodology, instructional innovation, professional articulation, and enhanced student learning, among other topics. Participation in electronic discussion lists can be a useful tool for professional development, particularly for educators who are isolated geographically or within their districts from other teachers of the same language.

When participating in discussions, certain rules and protocols (netiquette) should be observed. Following list guidelines and learning how to accurately express and gauge the tenor of a post or response (often by using smiley faces) are very important skills in this faceless communications environment. In addition, some lists are very active, and keeping up with the messages may be a daunting job.

ELECTRONIC JOURNALS

Several electronic journals target foreign language professionals. Generally, these journals are free, are published quarterly, and do not exist in paper form. There are a number of reasons for publishing a journal electronically. First, by using electronic communications technologies, electronic journals can reach a large and diverse audience in a timely manner. Second, the hypermedia nature of Web-based journals enables articles to include links to related background information located elsewhere on the Web. Third, many of these journals have a technology focus, and electronic dissemination illustrates many of the technologies treated in a given issue. Of particular interest is "Language Learning & Technology (LL&T)," which disseminates research on issues related to technology and language education. Another journal that deals with timely topics in language education is "Teaching English as a Second or Foreign Language: An Electronic Journal (TESL-EJ)".

World Wide Web

Although it is only one of the various Internet applications, the Web browser may be the only one that many people know. Thanks to its flexibility and integration of other services, the Web represents the broadest and most powerful Internet application. Its defining element is the hypertext link, which allows anything on one page to link to something on any other page in the world. The multimedia nature of the Web and the use of the Web page as an interface to other services have greatly expanded the power of the Internet by making it possible to display information using a combination of formats.

This is essential for the delivery of authentic materials in the form of texts, images, sound recordings, video clips, and even virtual reality worlds. For some media formats, additional helper applications or plug-ins must be downloaded and installed to enhance the Web browser. In addition, sophisticated programming functions, such as CGI and JavaScript, can turn a Web page into an interactive computer program. This can allow the student to work in interesting ways with the authentic materials found on the page.

One way of connecting students with native speakers and authentic materials is by using the technologies of streaming audio and video, which virtually transport the target language environment to the second language classroom without wasting time downloading huge files. Students can hear live or pre-recorded broadcasts of music, news, sports, and weather from countries around the world or watch the nightly news from France or live TV from Chile transmitted to their computer in real-time. This technology is in its infancy but is being developed and improved at a rapid rate. An Internet search will keep the foreign language teacher up to date on the latest free streaming media software that will place target language audio and video files a click away.

Search engines

A search engine is an on-line "private eye" that does detective work for the user. Search engines use keywords to find any site (documents, files, Web pages) that contains those words. Some even calculate a probability of the degree of relationship so the listing of hits is presented in order from most to least likely to be what is sought. The Web is a vast place, and trying to navigate it and locate desired information without search engines would be a formidable task at best. The Web has numerous search engines; many are language specific (e.g., Ole, Encuentrelo, Crawler.de Suche, FOCUS Suche, Il ragno italiano, LOKACE, ECILA, SAPO). Each one performs a little differently, so experimentation aids in the decision of which to employ for a given search. It takes frequent practice to become adept at structuring queries that generate optimal search results. Many library catalogs, bibliographic resources, and other types of databases are available on the Internet. Gopher, telnet, and the Web are all applications that enable users to access these databases on their own computers.

File transfer

File transfer protocol (FTP) enables users to move files between accounts on different computers wherever they might be, at home and at the office or even in different cities, as long as both computers have Internet addresses. The requirements are an FTP server running on a remote machine and an FTP client running on the local machine. Requests are sent via client software located on the desktop to a remote server located somewhere on the Internet, which performs the service of returning the requested information.

The two major ways of using FTP are by moving files between computers on which the user has accounts, or retrieving files from an anonymous FTP server that is open to the public. This latter use is transparent in many instances; users are often unaware that numerous files are downloaded from the Web via FTP.

Real-time communication takes place via several different types of chat, audio, and video communication programs. One such application is Internet Relay Chat (IRC), which enables synchronous "conversation" among participants anywhere in the world. Users enter a channel and "talk" by typing messages to all of the other people on that channel; everything that is typed is seen instantly by everyone. Hundreds of channels exist, with names usually reflecting the topics and language discussed (e.g., francais).

Private closed channels can also be created for use in the classroom. Audio and video communication programs, such as CUSeeMe and MS NetMeeting, are other options for engaging foreign language students in synchronous conversation. Users can talk directly to their interlocutor and, using the proper software, even see and be seen by the person they are addressing. These applications take a large amount of bandwidth and depend on a clear and direct Internet connection; network traffic will also affect the results. Though only in the initial phases of development, these new technologies are already powerful and have the potential of making a tremendous impact on the ability of students to communicate directly with native speakers in target language environments.

In the end it is incumbent upon the foreign language teacher to integrate these tools into the curriculum in a meaningful way. Clearly, target language communication and cultures are well within reach through current and emerging technologies, and information about using these resources is readily available on-line. The intrepid and creative teacher will venture into this virtual realm, find authentic resources, and use them to make the second language classroom a marvelous place to learn.

THE VIRTUAL CAMPUS: TECHNOLOGY AND REFORM IN HIGHER EDUCATION

The virtual campus is a metaphor for the electronic teaching, learning, and research environment created by the convergence of powerful new information and instructional technologies. Today there is a pressing call for technology to provide expanded higher education opportunities to a very wide spectrum of present and potential clientele.

A paradigmatic shift, from a professor-centered to a student-centered system of learning, has particular implications for the profession of teaching. One implication is a recommitment to creating an ideal learning environment for students, employing new technologies to address variances from the ideal. A second major implication for faculty is a shift from traditional to new roles and classroom responsibilities. The transition from lecturer to facilitator will not happen overnight and must be accompanied by institutional and professional commitment to incorporate research findings into professional development activities. Beyond merely providing technical training in the latest technology, professional development activities will need to focus on crucial classroom variables that will ultimately determine the level of productive interaction and intellectual engagement apropos to the individual and group.

Systemic reform has brought about a number of changes to postsecondary education, none more significant than what students learn and how they learn it. With time and distance effectively removed as constraints, colleges and universities are serving a more heterogeneous clientele with diverse educational backgrounds and needs. Some suggests that these new century students confront us with the possibility that a postsecondary educational system designed to manage enrollment growth by weeding out unprepared or uncommitted students may no longer be appropriate or economically defensible.

Perhaps the most telling difference between learning in the traditional and virtual modes is the kind and extent of interaction. In the traditional classroom, the potential for learner-instructor and learner-learner is very high, but instructors have largely ignored this mandate for change and continue to employ the lecture mode as the predominant method of instruction. In the virtual classroom, on the other hand, technology supports collaborative learning, heterogeneous groupings, problem-solving and higher order thinking skills—educational processes that a lecture format cannot facilitate.

Today's American higher education establishment is an aggregate of three functions=teaching, service, and research. Critics of American higher education today contend that especially since the Second World War faculty have placed emphasis on the research function to the detriment of teaching and service at a time when our culture demands the preparation of workers for a competitive and volatile economy.

Voices from within the academy have proposed a reconceptualization of scholarship, one that expands the practice of present-day research to include integration, application, and teaching. New forms of scholarship may necessitate a new epistemology. The scholarships of integration, application, and teaching entail "action" research that may fall outside the boundaries of prevailing institutional epistemology. College and universities must become learning organizations that foster originality and innovation.

Calls from external constituencies for academic institutions to demonstrate greater accountability and systemic improvement have prompted many colleges and universities to adopt the principles of Total Quality Management (TQM). Less a set of specific tools than an underlying philosophy, TQM has been distilled by Chaffee and Sherr into three simple ideas: defining quality in terms of customer needs, bettering work performance, and improving administration. If TQM is the underlying philosophy, Information Resource Management is the facilitator of broad access to information. In the academic sphere, TQM faces stiff faculty resistance. Many faculty see TQM as "another management fad from the evil empire of business". If academic TQM is to emerge as an agent of organizational reform, it is likely to come about more through faculty initiative than external pressure.

As large sums of money are contemplated and eventually allocated for educational technology development, college and university boards face a number of daunting tasks. First, boards must closely monitor regulatory legislation and actively participate in public policy debate. Distance education providers must stay abreast of federal and state regulations which often adversely affect the inter-state delivery of programs and services. Second, boards must establish a telecommunications policy and a strategic plan for its implementation. Third, boards must shepherd resources by defining genuine instructional needs and identifying appropriate technological solutions to fulfill them.

Colleges and universities are just now crossing the threshold between modest experimentation with and mainstream adoption of information technologies. Because of the serious repercussions reform efforts are already having on the academy, a number of conclusions and recommendations are warranted. Following are seven conclusions:

(1) a paradigm shift can occur only in institutions committed to comprehensive reform;

(2) attempts to change the classroom focus from "the sage on the stage" to collaborative learning are likely to fail without a substantial commitment to professional development;

(3) higher education will continue to be market driven, requiring redoubled efforts to define academic productivity;

(4) new constituencies appear to be well served by a variety of distance learning venues;

(5) the TQM movement has made impressive inroads in higher education administration; however, very little penetration has occurred where it most matters on the academic side of the institution; (6) even as instructional use of technology rises, institutional support for applications development has been dilatory; and (7) the historic commitment to core values in traditional undergraduate education has wavered; the same vacillation threatens to undermine general education requirements in electronically delivered certificate and degree programs.

In the absence of conclusive data with respect to wise technology choices and successful teaching/learning models, institutions must carefully prepare today for what is anticipated as a widespread integration of information into teaching, learning, and research. Following are seven recommendations for beginning this process of integration:

(1) create a venue where key stakeholders can analyze major technology issues and purchases;

(2) assert the value of technology-based learning from a variety of research perspectives;

(3) establish quality standards for certificate and degree programs;

(4) avoid pitting traditionalists against technology enthusiasts;

(5) make collaboration and cooperation, not reengineering and restructuring, the new institutional buzzwords;

(6) retain a strong commitment to adequate library staffing and funding; and

(7) prepare for success by creating the necessary support structures.

COMPUTERS IN THE EARLY CHILDHOOD CURRICULUM

Despite the promises and predictions made by educational researchers in the early 1980s, computers have not revolutionized education overnight, and few schools have invested wholeheartedly in instructional technology. Instead, in an effort to provide computer access to all students at an affordable cost despite the low ratio of computers to students, and because some critics feel there is a lack of quality software or that technology is too complex, schools have often put computers in a single room where children use them once a week under a specialty teacher's supervision.

Unfortunately, this practice has undermined the most valuable aspect of the computer—its ability to cut across traditional subject boundaries as a practical and useful tool. Papert compares the isolation of computers in labs to the body's immune response to a foreign intruder; by removing computers from the classroom and relegating them to an isolated lab, schools have effectively minimized the potential impact computers can have on children's learning by turning the technology into a separate, unrelated subject area called "computer literacy." In this lab approach, Papert further argues, students have access to about 1/50th of a computer in school, far from the critical level needed for this technology to have a major impact on educational practices or learning experiences of children.

The fatal flaw in taking computers out of the classroom is that any information learned about the computers today will be obsolete by tomorrow. Only when computers are integrated into the curriculum as a vital element for instruction and are applied to real problems for a real purpose, will children gain the most valuable computer skill—the ability to use computers as natural tools for learning.

The term "integrated learning" has gained popularity over the past half-decade, evidenced by the appearance of numerous prepackaged reading, math, and science curricula on the pages of educational software catalogs. Unfortunately, these well-marketed packets are often no more than unrelated activities clustered around a single topic and give little consideration to the development of larger concepts or goals.

These misnamed integrated learning systems view a topic, such as dinosaurs or planets or fish, as only a series of superficially related activities and isolated skills linked casually together in sequence, much as a worm appears to be no more than a chain of loosely attached segments that can be severed and still function independently. Real knowledge is much more than a group of unrelated segments; each section supports a particular function, and all are related to one another. If the severed pieces are thrown into a box (brain) and shaken up without the support of their natural connections, neither the worm nor deep understanding will grow.

True integration respects the interrelationships of the disciplines—language, mathematics, science—as natural and necessary to achieving the goal of becoming educated about a particular topic. As in the "project" approach, children exercise all the developmental or curricular domains as they complete self-initiated projects individually or in small groups. For example, if the teacher selected the topic "Fish" for integrated study, the first step in planning might be to define several central concepts about fish that are meaningful and relevant to the students' lives. Next, activities might be chosen based on the desire to further explore these concepts. The teacher would then determine the most effective medium for supporting the activities selected. Sometimes computers will be the most appropriate material for concept exploration; at other times, they will not. Computers, like any learning material, are neither panacea nor pernicious.

Computer use in Integrated Curricula

When exploration of a concept encourages students to write letters, stories, poems, or reports, using a word processor allows children to compose, revise, add, and remove text without being distracted by the fine motor aspects and tedium of forming letters. Research demonstrates that children who write on word processors compose longer and more complex stories, are less worried about mistakes, and are more willing to revise.

The teacher implementing the unit on "Fish," for example, might use the KID PIX program with very young children to construct a story through pictures and labels that can be narrated in the child's own voice by recording through the computer's microphone. With KID WORKS2, students might write and draw what they have learned about fish and hear their composition read back. Slightly older students could use CD-ROM encyclopedias to gather data and STORYBOOK WEAVER to compose and illustrate original stories and reports about their topic. MY WORDS, a simple program, can be used to write letters to local experts asking for information or extending an invitation for a classroom visit. Any one of these programs provides an excellent medium for teachers to record a group report or story.

One of the most powerful uses teachers can make of computers is to provide students with a MICROWORLD (a microworld is software with which children play and discover concepts and cause-effect relationships included by the software developer for this purpose), a bridge between hands-on experiences and abstract learning, in which children can learn about a topic through exploration and experimentation. An example is EZ LOGO, which is often used to introduce young children to geometric concepts in a playful way that is intuitive to them, just as one might use blocks to teach size and shape relations. Microworlds are developmentally appropriate software programs that are harder to find than are drill-and-practice programs, but that are much more valuable.

For example, ODELL DOWN UNDER allows children to explore the ocean's ecological interactions by becoming a fish, with all the abilities and vulnerabilities of the particular species selected. ZOOKEEPER and SAN DIEGO ZOO PRESENTS THE ANIMALS! give students the chance to examine the habitats of several aquatic creatures. Graphics programs, such as COLORFORMS FUN SET provide students with the tools and props to construct their own underwater environment.

Teacher Roles in Computer-enriched Classrooms

1. *Instructor* : When the computer is introduced into the classroom, an initial learning period occurs during which the children need time to become familiar and comfortable with the technology. It is during this period that the teacher needs to assume the most active role in instructing children, guiding them through new software and encouraging their exploration of the material.

2. *Coach* : As students gain experience with computers, the focal role held by the teacher gradually diminishes; children are able to perform tasks independently, and peers begin to take over the role of instructor. The teacher then moves into the role of facilitator, providing guidance and support when needed and ensuring appropriate behaviors, while control of the situation remains in the hands of the child.

3. *Model* : Children will be much more likely to use the computer as a practical, integrated tool for learning if they see the teacher doing the same. Using the computer during whole and small group instruction and for recording stories and producing classroom signs and charts are ways in which the teacher can be a highly visible user of technology.

4. *Critic* : Responsibilities of the teacher in the computer-enriched classroom begin before the computer is introduced to the students. In providing a rich, challenging, and appropriate learning environment, teachers must take an

active role in selecting the software that will truly enhance children's learning and development.

Despite revolutionary advances in the field of educational computing, technology remains simply a tool. Potentially powerful and stimulating, the computer is only an inert object that can never be a substitute for the personal touch of the classroom teacher. How teachers implement computer use in their schools is critical. Without proper integration of computers into the curriculum, the benefits of technology to foster children's learning cannot be fully achieved, regardless of the creative potential of any software used.

NETWORKING: K-12

At-risk high school students in the states of Washington, Texas, Massachusetts, and California "meet" online to discuss teenage pregnancy, drug prevention, Middle East foreign policy, and other topics of current interest. Students of all ages collaboratively produce a newspaper, Global Village News, using input from dozens of worldwide student "news bureaus" linked through more than 15,000 free computer bulletin boards in over 50 countries.

Students from the United States and other countries go on a simulated space shuttle journey, assuming various roles including secondary mission control, selecting alternative landing sites and docking other shuttles. What makes these common educational experiences exciting and unique? They all involve students and teachers from around the world interacting through computer networks.

Long-distance, or wide-area, computer networking can change teaching and learning dramatically. Teachers and students with access to a computer, a modem, and phone lines are freed from the physical limits of a school building and the time limits of an 8 a.m. to 3 p.m. school day. They can communicate with peers and gain access to electronic resources as they wish, making individualized instruction and personal inquiry the norm, not the exception.

Interaction through networks helps break down communication barriers and inhibitions that often stifle the open exchange of ideas in traditional classrooms. There is also a strong motivational aspect to network use: kids bring an energy and enthusiasm to it that's often missing in traditional classrooms, and teachers are thrilled to be able to share ideas, problems, and solutions with colleagues across the country as easily as if they were next door.

The excitement and enthusiasm for networking is not wistful speculation based on theoretical possibilities—it's happening right now. Thousands of students and teachers are tapping into networks, sharing experiences, and engaging in a wide range of learning activities. As the pace of networking accelerates, so too will the creative uses and the overall impact of the movement.

Whether connected to a state, regional, or private network, or to the Internet, network users can undertake three primary activities: electronic mail, computer conferencing, and accessing information from remote sources. Each of these offers opportunities to expand the learning environment, foster better communication, and excite learners and educators. Electronic Mail (or E-Mail). Using e-mail, learners can exchange information with teachers or other learners, and teachers can communicate with students or colleagues, locally and worldwide. E-mail messages offer immediate access to others on the same network.

— Teachers, administrators, librarians, and other educators can consult with colleagues in the district and across the country on curriculum, policies, technology, and other concerns.

— Students can "talk" to others across time zones and continents and get responses much more quickly than by mail.

— Texts, or files, can be transferred through e-mail, facilitating the exchange of papers, reports, and resource materials for teachers, administrators, and students.

Group communication: Network communication also makes it easy for groups of people to work cooperatively and share information without having to be in close physical proximity. It is possible to create "global classrooms" where students work with others as if they were in the same location. Educators and students can join organized discussion groups on specific topics. The networks are filled with hundreds of such groups (sometimes called "listservs"), many having international membership. LM[underscore]NET, for example, is an Internet discussion group for the library media field; EDTECH-L is dedicated to educational technology.

Remote information access: Through computer networking, information from around the world becomes available in the local school and even in the individual classroom or library media center. A few examples of the wealth of information available to students include:

— Research data, discussions, libraries, and additional services related to drug and alcohol abuse from California's Drug and Alcohol Abuse Prevention Net.

— Text and commentaries of Supreme Court decisions, information on space flights and space science, and data from the U.S. Commerce Department through the Cleveland Free-Net.

— The full text of the Federalist Papers, the U.S. Constitution, the Koran, and a host of other books through Project Gutenberg, a non-profit organization seeking to prepare electronic editions of more than 10,000 books by the year 2001.

Getting started

To get into wide area networking, you need to know: (1) how to operate your own computer, modem, and telecommunications software; (2) how to connect to and communicate with a computer already linked to the network; and (3) how to use the network to communicate with others. User manuals, classes, and general reference books can help you master these basics. Finding a connection to a computer on a network is not always an easy task. Options include:

— *Local bulletin board systems (bbs):* Telephone dial-up to a local bulletin board is a readily available and generally free connection to a computer network. Computer stores, the public library, education agencies, or computing centers at local colleges should be able to provide information about bulletin boards in your area.

— *College and university computer systems:* Most colleges and universities provide free or low-cost accounts on their computer systems to all students. These systems usually connect to BITNET or some other network that in turn provides access to the Internet. Educators who are enrolled in college or university courses should inquire about network access.

— *State-wide and regional systems:* A growing number of states, including Texas, Virginia, Florida, and North Dakota, provide low-cost or free connections to schools and/or teachers, administrators, and students within the state. These networks generally provide some statewide services (e.g., bulletin boards, conferencing, curriculum resources sharing, administrative data transfer) as well as a gateway to the Internet and other networks. In addition, some of the National Science Foundation mid-level and regional networks are providing fee-based access to the Internet. Contact state education agencies to learn about services and costs.

— *School computing facilities:* Local schools and districts are just beginning to develop wide area network capabilities. Check with your building or district computer support personnel to see what is available to you.

— *Commercial vendors:* Commercial vendors provide a wide range of fee-based information resources and services, including electronic mail and messaging. Many of the commercial systems offer, or intend to offer, connections to the Internet.

K-12 Network resources

Academy One: Affiliated with the National Public Telecomputing Network (NPTN) and the Cleveland Free-Net, this program aims to create a "national online information cooperative for K-12 telecomputing activities." Schools throughout the world access the resources of Academy One's community computer systems and participate in a variety of online projects and events.

@AppleLink: This official online information resource of the Apple Computer community offers a K-12 Education Area with discussion forums, software reviews, conference listings, lesson plans, and research results.

FrEdMail: The "Free Educational Mail Network," the oldest and largest educational network in the U.S., uses the Internet to link more than 150 electronic bulletin boards operated by individuals and institutions. FrEdMail offers collaborative activities designed to help students become better writers and learners. It also promotes the sharing of resources and experiences among teachers. For information on finding a local node or setting up your own electronic mail center.

K12Net: This bulletin board-based system works through "echo" forums around major curriculum areas for teachers and students interested in particular topics. These forums facilitate cooperative projects such as Global Village News. Access to K12Net is through FidoNet, a free general-interest computer network that joins more than 15,000 computer bulletin boards in more than 50 countries. Participation is free to anyone with local bulletin board access. To find active bulletin boards in your region, call a local computer store or your public library.

KIDSNET: Accessible through the Internet, KIDSNET is a global discussion group for teachers and others interested in networking for children and education. Participants discuss general questions regarding computer networking and user interfaces, and specific projects that link teachers and students using the Internet. KIDS is an associated list just for children.

INDEX